MSTiepedia

MSTiepedia:
One Man's Journey Through 30+ Years Of The Best Tv Show Ever

Volume 1

BearManor Media
2023

MSTiepedia:
One Man's Journey Through 30+ Years Of The Best Tv Show Ever
Copyright ©2023, All Rights Reserved.

No part of this book may be reproduced in any form or by any means, electronic, mechanical, digital, photocopying or recording, except for the inclusion in a review, without permission in writing from the publisher.

This book is an independent work of research and commentary and is not sponsored, authorized or endorsed by, or otherwise affiliated with, any motion picture studio or production company affiliated with the films discussed herein. All uses of the name, image, and likeness of any individuals, and all copyrights and trademarks referenced in this book, are for editorial purposes and are pursuant of the Fair Use Doctrine.

The views and opinions of individuals quoted in this book do not necessarily reflect those of the author.

The promotional photographs and publicity materials reproduced herein are in the author's private collection (unless noted otherwise). These images date from the original release of the films and were released to media outlets for publicity purposes.

Published in the USA by
BearManor Media
1317 Edgewater Dr. #110
Orlando, FL 32804
www.BearManorMedia.com

Softcover Edition
ISBN: 979-8-88771-278-9

Printed in the United States of America

CHAPTER 1

<u>Joel</u>

By the fall of 1984, Joel Hodgson had had it.

He'd spent the last two years in Los Angeles, and it was more than enough. Perhaps it was because success had come so quickly. Perhaps it was because that success, once gained, seemed so empty. Whatever the reason, Joel's blooming career had lost its luster for the one person to whom it ought to have been most important: Joel himself.

By any measure of the time, he was a hot property. Billing himself as a "comic, magician and spy," his comedy act combined his off-beat persona, witty wordplay, magic and clever props. There was the "chiro-gyro" (a device that fit over his head and appeared to twist his head around several times) and a stick of cotton candy that appeared to scream when he bit it. There was no act quite like it.

Since grade school, he'd had a fascination with puppets, convincing his parents to buy him a ventriloquist dummy, on which he diligently practiced and with which he posed on school photo day. He was scarcely into his teens when he was named Green Bay's Junior Magician of the Year. During his junior and senior years at Ashwaubenon High School near Green Bay, he had stunned and delighted his classmates and neighbors with a 45-minute show he called the Folderol Magic Review.

After high school, he attended Bethel College in St. Paul, Minnesota, first as a drama major, then as a speech communications major, but the lure of performing made concentrating on his studies impossible. He dropped out and began performing full time.

In 1981, he won a campus comedy contest. That got him noticed by local impresario Scott Hansen, who selected him to be the headliner for the grand opening of his new Minneapolis comedy club, the Comedy Gallery.

He was supporting himself with his comedy, but very quickly it became clear that the Midwest could only offer so much. After winning the Twin Cities Comedy Invitational in 1982, he was starting to attract attention on the West Coast. Joel moved to Los Angeles, hit the club circuit and was an almost immediate hit. He quickly attracted the attention of TV producers, and appeared in several HBO comedy specials.

Within only a few weeks of his arrival, he met a producer on the hit talk/variety/comedy series "Late Night With David Letterman." Joel gave the producer a tape of his act, and only weeks later Joel found himself on a plane headed to New York to appear on "Late Night." Joel became a favorite of Letterman's, in part because Joel's offbeat persona proved a perfect foil for Letterman.

While in the NBC building, Letterman introduced him to Lorne Michaels and the staff of "Saturday Night Live." The "SNL" cast took to him at once and Michaels signed him for an appearance. In all, he would make five appearances with Letterman, and four on "SNL." Among those who enjoyed the performances, and saw Joel's potential, was NBC programming chief Brandon Tartikoff.

Back in Los Angeles, Joel was now in constant demand, working at several different comedy clubs. In the process, he would meet and become friends -- or enemies -- with some of the biggest names in the standup comedy world. Jerry Seinfeld would become one of the former. The two remain friends to this day and Seinfeld has called Joel "a pop-culture visionary." Gallagher became one of the latter after an unpleasant backstage incident. Joel came offstage one night and found the mustachioed prop comic digging through Joel's props without permission, a definite no-no in the world of prop comics. Joel says Gallagher stole some of his bits as well.

But even as he was becoming a hot commodity, he found himself becoming disenchanted with success. Being occasionally recognized in public made him uncomfortable, and he was turned off by the Hollywood "system." Fearing that he was turning into a "showbiz person," he contemplated quitting but couldn't bring himself to do it. It took an incident with NBC and Tartikoff in 1984 to send him packing.

Tartikoff's office contacted Joel, and offered a major role in a new sitcom they were developing. They sent him the script for the pilot, and after reading it, Joel turned the part down, telling Tartikoff's people it just wasn't funny. Perhaps predictably, the executives assumed this was just a bargaining ploy. Their response was to offer the role to Joel again, at triple the amount of money they'd first offered.

For Joel, this was the proverbial last straw. Joel was appalled that the executives could not grasp the notion that he would turn a project down purely on its merit and that no amount of money was going to get him to change that stance. He refused again, and in a few months he was back in Minneapolis, declaring he was quitting comedy. (Incidentally, the series, called "High School USA," which Joel astutely pegged as "a 'Fast Times at Ridgemont High' rip-off," was one of Tartikoff's most notable failures. Three episodes aired before it was yanked from NBC's fall schedule.)

With performing seemingly behind him, Joel made a living with a series of jobs, including working at a T-shirt factory and building toys and robot sculptures. He was drawn back to the comedy scene in 1986 by his friend Seinfeld, with whom he co-wrote an HBO special (Joel also appeared in it briefly). Eventually, Joel began having second thoughts about his retirement. He later told the Minneapolis Star-Tribune that "not doing comedy for me was like living my life with my arm and my leg tied behind my back," Joel made his official comeback at the Ha-Ha Club in Minneapolis that same year. More than ever, what he called "gizmonic" gadgetry was now the centerpiece of his act, and he referred to the place where he created the gizmos as the Mystery Science Lab.

In reality, he was creating his props in a Minneapolis-area warehouse that happened to be next door to a film production studio where a guy named Jim Mallon worked.

Jim

Jim was something of a wunderkind himself. He grew up in Rochester, Minn., where his dad was an engineer for IBM. "I started making comedy movies in the fifth grade," he recalled. "I was inspired by "Laugh-In," and my friend had a regular 8mm camera. When I was in seventh grade, Sony came out with the first inexpensive b/w reel to reel video gear. Our junior high bought one, and I was hooked. Later, in high school, I made a parody of Mutual of Omaha's Wild Kingdom and put it on public access."

At the University of Wisconsin, he was elected student body president twice. He ran on a somewhat comedic platform, his "Pail & Shovel Party" handing out "tuition rebates"--pennies taped to pieces of cardboard.

His fame grew after he executed two elaborate pranks at the school. Making good on a campaign promise to "bring the Statue of Liberty" to the University, one brisk winter morning students awoke to find what appeared to be the statue, submerged up to its nose in a local lake. (In reality, only the upper portion of the statue's head, as well as a portion of its arm and torch, were built. Those pieces, sitting on top of the lake ice, made it appear that the entire statue had been dropped through the ice.)

The next year, to celebrate his re-election as president, students awoke one morning to find hundreds of plastic pink flamingo lawn ornaments on the school's common. The group also threw what he claimed was "the world's largest Toga party."

After college, Jim worked at a number of jobs, and even got a chance to make a movie. He directed a low-budget "slasher" flick he eventually sold to Troma Studios. Called "Blood Hook," it's a tale of a small Wisconsin fishing village and the crazed murderer who is doing in the townsfolk, one-by-one, using a giant hook. Jim and Joel met, hit it off, and discussed the possibility of someday working together.
Not long after that, Jim became the production manager for the independent Minneapolis UHF station KTMA-TV, channel 23, the last-rated station in the Twin Cities TV market.

Trace
About that time, Joel began attending an improvisation workshop. There he met a struggling actor/standup comic named Trace Beaulieu. Trace grew up in the Minneapolis suburbs, and after a short stint at the University of Minnesota, began a rather eclectic entertainment career: In addition to stand-up comedy, he worked as a performer at trade shows, and even spent some time in Europe touring with an ice show.

When he returned to Minneapolis, he began "hanging around The Comedy Cabaret in Minneapolis, and hooked up with a group, joined their improv classes and we would perform on the weekends."

Kevin

While working at WHA-TV in Madison, Jim met a multi-talented jack-of-all-trades named Kevin Murphy.

"He was working on the remote truck crew," Jim remembered. When Jim was signed to direct "Blood Hook," Jim tapped him to be on the movie crew. Then, when Jim got hired at KTMA, he quickly got Kevin hired as a videographer.

For Jim, Kevin was a dependable known quantity. Like Jim, the gregarious Illinois native was married, with roots in the Twin Cities area. His energy and organizational skills were a great help, both at KTMA and on the set of "Blood Hook."

The best part: when their regular duties at the station (including presenting a pro wrestling show) were completed, Jim and Kevin were permitted to use the station's equipment to produce home-grown comedy specials, which met with a modest amount of viewer success.

Josh

In the spring of 1987, Joel started teaching a class for aspiring comics called "Creative Standup and Smartology." Among his students was a young but promising teenager named Josh Weinstein.

"I started standup when I was 15 at a place called the Ha- Ha Club," he remembered. "I don't think most people knew my age at first. I made no effort to hide it but I was a big kid and my act didn't make reference to my age so most people assumed I was in my early 20s.

By the time everyone found out, they saw that I was serious about stand-up and working hard, so what could they say? Sure there were some bitter, older guys that resented me occasionally but for the most part it was a non-issue."

When, in the summer of 1988, Jim's boss at KTMA asked him to find a way to fill a two-hour time slot on Sunday evenings, Jim thought of Joel. He met with Joel over lunch at a nearby deli to pick his brain for ideas. Two weeks later, Joel returned with a rough outline of a show which involved a lone human on an orbiting satellite watching movies with robot companions.

The germ of the idea that was to become Mystery Science Theater 3000 was born.

CHAPTER 2

Joel has said the idea for MST3K had many inspirations.

The "shadowrama" element at the bottom of the screen was inspired by an image on the jacket of Elton John's "Goodbye Yellow-Brick Road" album. He has also cited Warner Brothers Looney Tunes cartoons, which occasionally included theater seats in silhouette. The idea of a satellite dweller watching movies came from the Charlton Heston movie "Omega Man." The idea that he would have only robots as companions was loosely based on the Bruce Dern movie "Silent Running."

"As time went on, I noticed some connections to other shows -- particularly 'Beanie and Cecil,'" Joel said in an interview. "'Beanie and Cecil' was the first cartoon I remember watching and I think there are analogies. The SOL is sort of like Leakin Lena. Joel is like Beanie. Servo is like Captain Huff-n-Puff. Gypsy is sorta like Cecil, and Dishonest John is like Dr. Forrester-- there's even a Crow that shows up occasionally in the Crows nest! On a bigger level, I was in love with a show called, 'The Children's Film Festival with Kukla, Fran and Ollie. I just think it's very close structurally -- a human host with puppets watching a movie."

Joel mashed up all of these concepts and the seed began to grow.

Joel enlisted a wary but game Trace and an enthusiastic Josh to help him make a demo tape of the concept. Jim tapped Kevin for help. As work began, Kevin ended up doing a little of everything, from writing to lighting to camera work. He also created the theater setup, including the "seats" that were cut from foam core board. Kevin also created a primitive "movie sign" door sequence, and the group shot a theater segment (where Joel sat alone, commenting only occasionally) featuring about a half-hour of the 1969 movie "The Green Slime," (which was in the KTMA vaults, but was used without legal permission) and a crude introductory host segment in which Joel explains that he himself built the Satellite of Love and intentionally blasted it into space.

As Joel tells it, he created rough versions of the bots in a single night from bits and pieces that he had on hand. (Joel once noted that the "sleepiness" of his character grew out of the fact that he was indeed very sleepy when the pilot episode was shot and "it just stuck.")

When Trace and Josh arrived to shoot the pilot, there was a pile of bots before them. Trace and Josh each picked one up. Trace picked up Crow.

"I guess I liked the look of Crow," he said years later. "I'm attracted to shiny things."

Joel has given several explanations of where that name came from, but he told me that the puppet was named for a childhood friend of a guy he knew in college, about whom many tall tales were spun. In addition, the name was an homage to a song by the punk rock group The Jim Carroll Band, in which the band sings, "Crooooow."

Josh selected a proto-Tom Servo character called Beeper. Joel initially thought Beeper would speak only in incomprehensible noises which only Crow could understand (somewhat like "Star Wars" robots R2D2 and C3PO).

Also in the pile was a rough version of Gypsy, named, Joel said, in remembrance of a pet turtle his brother had as a child. "I knew

Gypsy was going to be big and slow, so Gypsy was the logical choice," Joel said.

The pilot, as originally shot had no theme song … yet.

One detail remained: What to call the show? The way it happened depends on whom you ask. In the version Jim told for many years, "I said to Joel, 'What do you think?' And, without blinking, he said 'Mystery Science Theater 2000.' But since we were so close to the year 2000 we decided to shift it up one thousand years."

That story was included in the official internet FAQ, and had been approved by BBI and it stayed there for years. But, later, Joel insisted to us that the number had nothing to do with a date at all.

"I thought of it more as a series number, like the Hal 9000 computer or the Galaxy 500," he explained. "I guess the difference is Arthur C. Clark and the Ford Motor Company had the vision to pick a number that couldn't be confused with a year."

The Pilot

Episode K00- THE GREEN SLIME (the unaired pilot)
A half-hour "proof of concept" video, and very rough pilot.
Segment 1: Joel tries to make contact with anyone, then introduces the movie
Segment 2: Joel, with Crow and Beeper looking on, demonstrates the chiro-gyro
Segment 3: Joel introduces Gypsy and reveals that he has taught the bots to laugh at his jokes
Segment 4: Joel discovers that his vacu-flowers are sick, and the illness spreads to Gypsy

Segment 5: As Joel works on Gypsy, he discovers that the illness has spread to Beeper and … himself!

Segment 6: Everybody has recovered from the foam sickness, but Crow has a parting shot

Comments:

- Joel has shown an edited version of this episode at conventions, which focuses on the host segments and leaves out most of the theater sequences, due to rights issues. Videos of those appearances are on YouTube.
- This video's target audience was one guy, KTMA station manager Don O'Connor. Its purpose was to convince Don to let them go forward with the concept. And I gotta say: as interesting as this is to look at more than three decades later, I am AMAZED that it accomplished that purpose. Maybe ol' Don had an eye for talent and potential (though from the stories I've heard, that doesn't sound likely) or maybe Jim just talked him into it. However they managed it, they got the green light.
- You can definitely see Joel's "'Silent Running' meets 'Omega Man'" concept but, as Joel himself has said, it's a little dour.
- The primitive door sequence always gets a laugh from fans the first time they see it.
- Riffing doesn't really seem to have been a big part of the concept at this point. Instead, Joel is just sort of watching along with us. It's much more like a standard "Svengoolie"-style movie show. The fact that Joel (and then the bots) is there at all, and supposedly in a theater, is the breakout concept here.
- The second segment is one fans have seen as part of "The MST3K Scrapbook," a video tape containing bits and pieces of rare footage that was sold by Best Brains.
- The "chiropractic helmet," a prop from Joel's standup act, would reappear in episode K03- STAR FORCE: FUGITIVE ALIEN 2

12 • MSTIEPEDIA

as the "Chiro-helmet" and in episode 105- THE CORPSE VAN-ISHES as the "chiro gyro."
- Gypsy is male here. We fully support this.
- Joel also says there are "25 other robots doing various complicated operations around the ship." That's very "Silent Running."
- One element is already in place: the ubiquitous background noise — that non-stop engine hum and occasional "plink." It is present even in this, the very first iteration of the show.
- Joel comes into the theater by himself in the first theater sequence; Crow joins him the second time; the third time it's Joel, Crow and Beeper (who seems to be sitting on Joel's lap); then Joel, Crow and Gypsy; and finally Joel by himself again.
- Another surprising element: Joel mentions the "spiral-on-down," a hatch that brings him to and from the theater, which he would mention a few times in the regular series. It's amazing (to me, any-way) that so little of the premise has been thought up at this point, but the "spiral-on-down" is already a thing.
- Fave riff: "...Speaking of the number 2 position..." At the screen-ing, Joel declares it "The birth of movie riffing.

O'Connor gave them the okay to give it a try and Joel and crew immediately set about refining the product.

The group threw together the sets, designed the first model of the Satellite of Love (to allow for external shots of the ship) and refined the robots. The first bot to be changed was Beeper. Both Joel and Josh were unhappy with the character and Josh wanted to have a larger speaking role.

"It wasn't all that fun sitting there going "BEEP BEEP- BEEP" and I'm sure I made some wise-ass remarks about it, but I don't remember having to convince Joel [to make the change]. We all just thought a character that didn't talk was a waste. Beeper quickly gained a voice and was renamed Servo (after a vending machine they'd spotted in a mall named "Servotron"); which Josh later expanded to Tom Servo, adding a new, imposing voice.

"Josh told me he thought of it sort of like those deejays on local radio shows who always had an on-air nickname," Joel recalled. (When actor Howard Hesseman died, Josh posted on Twitter that Hesseman's smarmy character Rip Tide on the TV show "WKRP in Cincinnati" was just the sort of guy he was thinking of when he developed Tom Servo.)

The premise was also re-thought. Joel's character, now named Joel Robinson, had been a janitor at a top-secret research lab, and was on board the SOL as it was launched. Now marooned in orbit, the Institute (no mention, yet, of mad scientists) was forcing him to watch bad movies.

Acknowledging that the premise "was probably hard to under-stand," Joel decided a theme song was called for, and he wanted it to be like one of those 1960s-era theme songs that explained the premise, a la "The Brady Bunch" Or "Gilligan's Island." Not being a musician himself, he turned to a friend, Charlie Erickson (also known by his stage name, Chuck Love), a local musician and deejay. Erickson soon had a tune, and Joel provided the lyrics.

The next question: what movie should be the first to be riffed? They dug around in the KTMA vaults and found "Invaders from the Deep," which was actually four episodes from the British Super-marionation series "Stingray" mashed together.

"I was thrilled to be working with 'Invaders from the Deep' because, like many people my age, I grew up loving the work of Gerry and Sylvia Anderson," Joel said in an interview.

K01- INVADERS FROM THE DEEP
First shown: 11/24/88

Theme lyrics by Joel and Josh. Sung by: Joel and the Joels Joel:
In the not-too-distant future -- Next Sunday, A.D. -- There was a guy named Joel, Not too different than you or me. He worked in a satellite loading bay, Just polishing switches to pay his way; He did his job well with a cheerful face, But his bosses didn't like him So they shot him into space. We'll send him cheesy movies, The worst ever made. Joel says when you got lemons, You make lemonade. Now keep in mind he can't control When the movies begin or end, Because he used the extra parts To make his robot friends. Robot roll-call: Cambot! Servo! Gypsy! Crow! If you're wondering how he eats and breathes And other science facts, Just repeat to yourself "It's just a show, I should really just relax
For Mystery Science Theater 3000."
Movie: (episodes originally aired 1967; compilation released 1981) A submarine pilot and his cohorts battle an evil aquatic civilization. Opening: Joel introduces the movie briefly and then it's movie sign Host segment 1: Joel shows off his airbag helmet Host segment 2: Joel shows off his vacuum-flowers and discovers they are sick Host segment 3: Gypsy has caught the mysterious illness End: The flowers and bots are recovering; Joel shows off his electric bagpipes

Comments:

- On Nov. 25, 2016, 28 years and one day after this episode aired on KTMA-TV in the Twin Cities, Joel announced that the master tapes for this episode, and episode K02- REVENGE OF THE MYSTERONS FROM MARS, which had been thought lost forever, had been found, and he made them available to backers of the relaunch kickstarter. There was much rejoicing -— well, some.

- It's interesting (to me, anyway) that this, the first episode broadcast, is also the first of many "movies" the show would feature that is actually an edited-together compilation of episodes from a TV series, including "Master Ninja" "Time of the Apes," "Mighty Jack" and "Riding With Death."
- For the record, the episodes cobbled together here are all from season one of "Stingray": episode 4, "Hostages of the Deep;" episode 27, "Deep Heat;" episode 6, "The Big Gun" and episode 11, "Emergency Marineville."
- The opening host segment contains none of the dour "people of Earth" stuff that was in the pilot. Instead, Joel is all business. He speaks directly to the camera, refers to "the station," introduces the movie and gets out.
- Joel calls Gerry and Sylvia Anderson "Gene" and Sylvia. Oops.
- Joel arrives in the theater after the movie's opening credits have rolled. He seems to be climbing over the little monitor on the floor and the wires that are in the space where the "seats" are. It apparently takes some effort to climb past it all. Ever the polite Midwesterner, he says "Excuse me" to the row of empty seats.
- Joel's first real televised riff: "Lettuce man!"
- Listen carefully as the first missile battle begins: Joel slurps up the last of some beverage through a straw. Things were very casual.
- The riffers come and go several times in the theater, other than when it's time for a host segment. The first time Joel leaves there is quite a bit mic noise. They were still figuring it out.
- I do like the frame that says: PLACE COMMERCIAL HERE. Good idea. Do that!
- Joel again seems to be stepping gingerly over things as he re-enters the theater.
- We get the first use of "pull my finger," and it then becomes a running gag.

16 • MSTiepedia

- There's a point where the mic picks up the sound paper shuffling, They didn't have scripts yet, so I'm not sure what that is.
- The airbag helmet, a prop from Joel's standup act, would be reused in episode 102- THE ROBOT VS. THE AZTEC MUMMY.
- Listen carefully to Crow in the theater. That is clearly Josh. Most folks were aware that Trace and Josh (and even Joel once) were occasionally absent when the show was taped. But now we know that, in addition to his other absences, Trace wasn't there for this, the FIRST SHOW. Wow.
- Joel wanders out of the theater and leaves a confused Crow behind. We're used to expecting a host segment to come next when the riffers leave, so it's disorienting to have them leave and nothing comes of it. Joel just wanders back in. Was he takin' a leak?
- Then-current reference: a character said to look like a "governor of Massachusetts." Took me a minute to realize he was talking about Michael Dukakis.
- At one point, Joel irritatedly says "cut it out!" It's unclear what's happening, but it's presumably Josh causing trouble.
- Crow then wanders out a couple of times (to get "some WD-40" and to "check on Gypsy," respectively).
- Segment 2 is essentially a redo of segment 4 in the pilot, even to the extent that Joel mentions an unseen Beeper.
- Not to be overly binary, but Gypsy, again, is a he.
- At one point Joel asks at what point a puppet stops being a puppet and becomes a costume. This issue was further addressed in a host segment in episode 318 – STAR FORCE: FUGITIVE ALIEN II.
- The electric bagpipes, a prop from Joel's standup act, would be used again in episode 101- THE CRAWLING EYE.
- Nobody has thought of calling the main SOL set the "bridge" yet. Joel calls it "the main part of the show." Okay…
- Slightly disorienting is the credit sequence at the end of the movie, which features a brass band version of the Beatles' "Yellow Submarine." How did Lew Grade manage THAT?, you may be wonder-

ing. Seems Lord Lew's company purchased Northern Songs (the Beatles' music publishing outfit) in 1969.

- Fave riff (though there's not much to pick from here): "Are they sweating or is that sap?" Honorable mention: "I'd be tired too if I had a diving board on my head."

The next episode, like the last one, premiered on the evening of Thanksgiving, Nov. 24, 1988, making the debut a double feature. It was watched by only a few thousand people (the ratings were dismal), even fewer of whom, apparently "got" it. Still, it's no wonder some found the concept hard to understand. The KTMA episodes are barely recognizable as the forerunner of what was to be. Little or no writing was done ahead of time, and most of the riffs in the theater were ad-libbed (although, as time went on, cast members began to preview the movies and jot down a few riffs). This meant that sometimes the comments were brilliant, sometimes not. It also meant long stretches of silence.

Of the three performers in that season, many fans now credit Josh as the one who was most adept at popping off one witty ad-libbed comment after another. While the others did their best, it was often Servo who stole the show in the theater.

But there were also problems. The station paid the group about $250 per show (the performers got $35 each), and it looked it. The bots were very crudely made, the sets were minimal. In the theater, the "theater seat" silhouettes were quite small and were placed on the far right hand side of the screen. This was done at the behest of worried station manager O'Connor, who feared viewer complaints that the movie was being obscured.

Still, they slogged on.

Episode K02- REVENGE OF THE MYSTERONS FROM MARS
First shown: 11/24/88 (directly after episode K01)

Movie: (four episodes from the Supermarionation series "Captain Scarlet" mashed together; episodes originally aired 1967; the compilation "movie" was released 1981.) The commanders of anti-terrorist submarine force Spectrum battle a subversive alien force.

Opening: Joel and Crow discuss the Thanksgiving parade Host segment 1: Joel uses Gypsy to demonstrate a horn of plenty Host segment 2: Joel is explaining Thanksgiving to Crow until Tom arrives and turns it into a game of "Pyramid." Host segment 3: Joel leads the "puppet bots" in an arts and crafts project. End: Dinner, such as it is, is served.

Comments:

- This episode was also re-released in 2016 (see above).
- The four episodes of "Captain Scarlet" are: episode 12, "Shadow Of Fear;" episode 15, "Lunarville 7;" episode 21, Crater 101" and episode 22, "Dangerous Rendezvous."
- The title of this episode has been incorrectly identified since BBI released its list of KTMA episodes in the 1990s. I am adding the words "From Mars" to every mention because that's what the title card says.
- After a bit of a slow start, the riffing picks up to a more typical KTMA-like frequency.
- Trace is doing Crow, unlike in episode K01. This makes this Trace's first broadcast episode.
- A Geraldo joke starts things off. Shows you how long he has been in the public eye.

- Joel enters the theater alone, then Crow joins him. Both seem to have less trouble getting in and out than in the previous episode. A path must have been made among all the stuff at their feet.
- The voice of Captain Scarlet is basically an impression of the legendary actor Cary Grant, attempted by voice actor Francis Matthews.
- After the first break. Servo pops up with a "What's going on here?" He sounds a little like Gomer Pyle. Tom later asks Joel why he gave him such a silly voice. I was wondering that too.
- We get the very first "...at first" riff, which makes Servo laugh.
- Servo extends his neck at one point, making this the first time that happened.
- Movie stuff: What exactly is the rolling countdown thingy measuring?
- Servo reacts with terror at the first gunfire.
- Servo: "I personally don't think that puppets should be on TV."
- Col. White kinda looks like James Brolin, no? Guess it's just a co-incidence.
- The characters in the movie keep saying "S-I-G" and I kept going "huh?" Turns out it means "spectrum is green," more or less equivalent to "A-okay."
- Tom had chores. Before the second segment, Tom just sort of ducks down, saying "I have to go do some radiator maintenance." I assume they thought this up because Tom can't leave with the others.
- When they come back into the theater, Tom pops up again. I think they hadn't worked out the details of Tom coming and going.
- Joel seems to have popcorn in the theater at one point. There is much crunching into the mics. Then he pours it into Tom's bubble. Tom seems to approve.
- Crow calls Joel "Hoel Jodgson." On purpose, I think.
- Again Tom leaves by ducking down, saying "Time for me to drain my radiator."

- They still don't have a word for what would later be called The Bridge. Tom refers to it as "the front thing."
- Gypsy is Gypsy sometimes and Gypsum other times. Joel has acknowledged that this was just a thoughtless mistake. Nobody seems to notice or care.
- Fave riff: "You know there was an off switch, dumb-o." Honorable mention: "Be careful! It's the worst special effect yet!"

Episode K03- STAR FORCE: FUGITIVE ALIEN 2
First shown: 11/27/88.

Comments:

- No fan copy is known to exist of this episode, and if a master still exists in Joel's (or Jim's) vaults, he has not released it, making this the show's only true "lost episode." However, back when Jim controlled the MST3K.com URL, he released some clips from this episode, giving fans some hope that a full episode may still be released.
- As of 2008, Jim said publicly that he had half-inch tapes of the first three episodes. Then the tapes could not be found.
- The clips released by Jim include a host segment in which Joel tries to explain drugs to Crow by whacking him repeatedly. Joel does the same thing to Crow in episode 212- GODZILLA VS. MEGALON, attempting to show him what pain feels like. I think Joel just liked doing it.
- In another clip (where Gypsy is Gypsum), Joel seems to have come up with a good rationalization for reusing all his props from his standup act: "Outer space is really an excellent place to develop new projects and new ideas." The nun-clucks he demonstrates here were re-used in episode 321- MASTER NINJA I. (By the way, Joel's comment about programming the robots to laugh at

every joke sounds a bit of programming he did in episode 424-'MANOS' THE HANDS OF FATE.)

- The head-spinning prop from Joel's standup act would appear here as the "Chiro-helmet," in episode 105- THE CORPSE VANISHES as the "chiro gyro" and, of course, in the pilot it was the "chiropractic helmet."
- The movie was re-riffed in episode 318.

Episode K04- GAMERA VS. BARUGON
First shown: 12/4/88

Movie: (1966) In the second outing of the movie series, a group of conspirators travels to a remote jungle island to retrieve what they believe is a giant opal. In reality it is the egg of lizard-dog creature Barugon ... and it's hatching.

Opening: Joel introduces the movie and plays a message from a happy caller
Host segment 1: Joel plays two more messages: one negative, one positive
Host segment 2: Joel plays another call, which upsets Gypsy
Host segment 3: Crow discusses his favorite body orifices
End: Servo and Crow make prank phone calls and Crow explains doggie-doo.

Comments:

- When this episode aired, two or three Minneapolis-area TV viewers had the presence of mind to lunge for the VCR, pop in a tape and hit "record." Some of these people spent many lucrative years selling VHS, and later DVD, copies of those tapes, UHF artifacts and all, to collectors and the curious.

- All in all, this episode is quite a slog, unless you are a hardcore kaiju fan. I was able to get through it in one sitting (but I admit I dozed off for about 10 minutes). The movie is dark and chaotic and violent, but I will give it this: at least it's a story aimed at adults, rather than the kiddie fare several other Gamera movies were.
- Joel has explained that the monster is repeatedly referred to as "Gammer-on" because they mistakenly thought that was the giant turtle's name. Just another silly mistake by people on a UHF puppet show, the people who gave you "Gypsum." Oops.
- The caller in the opening segment had clearly just watched episode K03. She mentions it was on "the 27th," which was the date that episode aired. Her three-year-old liked it. That kid must now be fully grown.
- Servo again just kind of pops up behind the seats at the beginning of the first theater segment, and he seems capable of getting in and out of the theater on his own power, though Joel does carry him a couple of times.
- The scarcity of riffs in the theater takes some getting used to. Did you, almost by force of habit, start thinking of jokes for the quiet spaces? I sure did.
- Even back then they were playing with the screen. At one point, a character points directly at Servo and he panics.
- If the cast members are to be believed, the station began receiving some complaints from people who did not catch on to the concept and were irritated by the "immature junior high kids" (as one caller dubbed them) talking over the movie. But (again, if you believe that the calls that were played on the show are genuine) they also got supportive calls, including a call from one guy, perhaps the first MSTie ever, who simply panted "MORE!! MORE!! MORE!!" into the phone. If genuine, it's a sentiment to which we all can relate. By the way, this segment appears on the MST3K Scrapbook tape, which is further evidence that this episode existed and was accessible well into the 1990s.

MSTIEPEDIA • 23

- Among the many things that are different about this show from shows in later seasons: Joel and the bots get up and leave, and the movie continues for several minutes, playing to an empty theater, before the show goes to commercial. I have to admit that I fast-forwarded through these sections.
- Something else that's different: Crow's arms work.
- The "Chapstick" segment is very funny. But, I'm sorry, there is no way that the caller actually said "slapstick." He clearly said "Chapstick." Why, I have no idea, but this is more evidence that some of the calls they played were staged. However, I've asked several cast members about it, and nobody remembers doing that.
- Sometime between the pilot and this episode, Gypsy has become a girl. We fully support this.
- The phone number is thrown up on the screen during a theater sequence, and Joel thanks Cambot. He's so polite.
- Kevin is already listed in the credits as one of the show's writers.
- Fave riff: "Way to go, mister Freudian slip!" Honorable mention: "This monster does not know the concept of 'around.'"
- This movie was re-riffed in episode 304.

Episode K05- GAMERA
First shown: 12/11/88

Movie: (1965) In the first of a long-running Japanese movie series, a giant mutated turtle with super powers is accidentally revived from hibernation and, of course, attacks Japan. Meanwhile, young Kenny is fascinated by the beast.

Opening: It's Christmas time, and Crow has "volunteered" to be the SOL's Christmas tree
Host segment 1: Servo is thankful he wasn't frozen. A caller wants to know who does Joel's hair

Host segment 2: Inspired by a caller, Gypsy does her Godzilla impression. Viewers are invited to take a Ted Turner quiz

Host segment 3: Callers offer opposing views on a Gamera fight, so Joel and Servo go to the video tape

End: Joel explains some Christmas traditions, then its time for carols.

Comments:

- Joel watches the film by himself; as such, this episode contains what is surely the sparsest riffing in MST3K's history. It's common for Joel to go more than two minutes without making a single comment. Servo appears in the host segments, but there's no explanation why he does not join Joel in the theater. Trace was out of town during the shooting of this episode, and Josh is pretty sure he had a standup gig at the time the scenes were being shot. This illustrates the incredibly casual gig the show was. Trace just couldn't make it, so they wrote him out of the sketches, end of problem. You can hardly blame Trace. $35 is nothing to sneeze at, but it's not worth changing your holiday travel plans, either.
- That does not sound like Trace in the bit where he is frozen. It sounds like Josh. Which makes sense, since Trace wasn't there.
- There's a little teaser of Gamera mayhem at the beginning of the movie. They edited that out of the season 3 version.
- Without the support of Josh and Trace, Joel resorts to what he enjoys most, interacting with the screen. He does it a lot in this episode.
- Some may not remember, and kids may not be aware of, the whole kerfuffle in the late '80s about Ted Turner colorizing classic black-and-white movies. Many movie buffs – and Joel seems to have been one of them – were horrified at the prospect and Turner came in for much derision. He converted a few public domain movies, but quietly backed off the project after a while.

- Joel resorts to talking to himself (or us). At one point he asks, to nobody in particular, "Would you consider that a plot device?"
- In these early episodes, some riffs are what Mary Jo later called "state park" jokes (i.e.: "That looks like a state park.") Not so much a joke as a simple observation; and something they later tried to avoid.
- Joel laughs heartily at the movie when a scientist suggests that Gamera has "special organs that operate like a hydro-electric plant."
- It's pretty clear the two calls in segment 3 where made by the same person. That's all I'm sayin'.
- Fave riff: "That could take years!"
- This movie was re-riffed in episode 302.

Movie stuff:

1) So, the old eskimo is the latest in a long line of keepers of the ancient Gamera stone that's been handed down in his tribe for thousands of years, right? Then these complete strangers show up in the village and eskimo guy happily hands the stone over to them?

2) What's with the scientist pretty much lying through his teeth when he vouches for the reporter? Is he just doing him and the lady researcher a favor so they can continue their tepid romance? He says the reporter guy has extensive knowledge of Gamera. What does he know that scientist guy and lady researcher don't know? He never demonstrates any real knowledge of the situation, that I noticed.

3) Kenny thinks he has some sort of psychic connection with Gamera. But the movie never presents any evidence that this is the case. Yes, Gamera doesn't kill Kenny when he has the chance, but that could just be luck. (And I'll admit this may be a lost-in-translation thing.)

26 • MSTiepedia

Episode K06- GAMERA VS. GAOS
First shown: 12/18/88

Movie: (1967) In the third outing of the long-running Japanese movie series, the giant flying turtle monster takes refuge in a volcano. His arrival releases Gaos, a shovel-headed bat-monster with the ability to shoot laser beams. Caught between the two monsters are some nearby villagers, who want to stop the construction of a highway through their land (or at least get a good price when they sell it). The grandson of their leader is young Itchy who, after Gamera saves him from Gaos, becomes an instant expert on both creatures.

Opening: After a complaint about the movies, Joel explains that he doesn't control what movies are shown
Host segment 1: Joel changes Tom Servo's voice. Tom is very pleased
Host segment 2: Gypsy wants a new voice too. Joel explains again that Crow has been frozen. Gypsy has been snacking on decorations
Host segment 3: Joel and Tom offer birthday wishes to a young viewer
End: Joel and Tom preview the KTMA's New Year's Eve programming

Comments:

• The MST3K premise was evolving further. The team decided that audiences needed to be able to put faces on Joel's anonymous tormentors, so, in this episode, viewers were introduced to two scientists, Dr. Clayton Forrester (Trace; the character name was swiped from George Pal's "War of the Worlds") and Dr. Laurence Erhardt (Josh).
• If you don't count the theme song, this show contains the first mention of the Mads. There's a kind of historic moment during

the opening, as Cambot puts up a still from the opening theme, and the names of the Mads are spoken for the first time. Joel seems to be laying the groundwork for the arrival of the Mads as actual characters.

- Joel's comment in this episode about the Mads contradicts what he said in the opening segment of the previous episode. In that episode, Joel said that he "raided the movie library," giving the impression that he, Joel, decided what movies they watch. More recently, Joel admitted to me that, yes, they were "sloppy with the concept" in those early days.
- Trace is still away, so Crow is still frozen.
- Joel says "Your eyes won't believe what your hands have done." That was the commercial tagline for a toy called a Spirograph. Ask your grandparents, kids.
- Servo is back in the theater for this episode. Servo sits in Crow's seat rather than his own, probably because it's easier to exit.
- We seem to come in with the movie already under way. Just like last week, it's a teaser. Again, this portion was cut from the season three version.
- With this episode we get our first Sandy Frank comment.
- Let me just say: I hate Tom Servo's new voice! Kidding. I'm sure it helped Josh that the new voice was much closer to his natural voice.
- Portions of segment 1 appear on the MST3K Scrapbook tape.
- The clip of Crow being frozen is shown again.
- In the theater, there are several instances when Joel is in mid-riff when Tom just blurts out a riff and interrupts or talks over him, a phenomenon the riffers called "runover." For the first few times, Joel, ever the Midwestern nice guy, stops talking and gives way to Josh. Then Joel seems to have had enough and shushes Josh. It doesn't seem to have any effect. After Josh does this about four more times, Joel covers his mic and says something to Josh. Josh stops interrupting after that. Joel confirmed to me that, yes, he

asked Josh not to interrupt. I think Josh was a little excited about his new voice.

- Joel calls Servo "Josh" at one point. Servo replies by calling Joel "Hodgie."
- The whole "Grandpa mooing" running joke is great.
- Fave riff: "Grandpa thinks he's a saxophone now!"
- This movie was re-riffed in episode 308.

Movie stuff:

1) Sometimes Gamera doesn't have to spin to fly, though sometimes he does. Weird.
2) Unlike Kenny in the previous episode, Itchy does seem to have a genuine relationship with Gamera.
3) The whole "blood turntable" thing ranks right up there on the list of dumbest schemes in MSTed movies.

Episode K07- GAMERA VS. ZIGRA
First shown: 1/1/89.

Movie: (1971) In the (sigh) seventh outing of the long-running Japanese monster movie series, aliens from a distant planet, called Zigra, send a spaceship, called Zigra, commanded by a strange creature, called Zigra, to Earth with a plan of world domination. Opposing him is a pair of concerned marine biologists, pesky kids Kenny and Helen, and of course giant turtle monster Gamera.

Opening: Crow gets unfrozen.
Host segment 1: Joel gets a call from The Mads. Joel asks when they will bring him back to Earth. Rather than answer, they taunt him.
Host segment 2: Joel is depressed so Cambot plays some messages from callers to cheer him up.

MSTiepedia • 29

Host segment 3: J&tB make their New Year's wishes, then try to count down to the new year. Movie Sign interrupts.
End: J&tB review the movie.

Comments:

- This episode contains the first appearance of the Mads as speaking characters.
- The footage of Josh performing stand-up comedy in host segment 1 came from the "KTMA Melon Drop," a KTMA-produced New Year's Eve special, starring Kevin as news reporter Bob Bagadonuts. It aired just after midnight on New Year's Eve, 1988-89.
- Trace is back, Crow is back and all's right with the premise.
- We get to see the footage of Crow being frozen for the FOURTH time in three episodes.
- Trace is a little quiet during the first hour or so. He must be out of practice. He gets into the swing of riffing a bit the more as the movie goes on.
- Tom's head is more transparent in the theater.
- Segment 1 is included on the MST3K Scrapbook tape.
- It's the first transmission from the Mads and they are still being developed. Trace uses a sort of Gregory Peck-ish voice. Josh uses a sinister growl.
- First use of the word "dickweed."
- Crow's silent reaction to Zigra's spandex-clad henchwoman cracks Joel up.
- A couple of times in the theater, Tom Servo extends his neck, something he did a several more times in season two.
- At some point they started previewing the movies. Proof: Crow warns the henchwoman about the stuff on the arm of the chair just before she knocks it off. Later, Joel and Tom foresee the whole fish-fin xylophone thing.

30 • MSTiepedia

- Also, it would seem they have they been watching the other Gamera movies in the library. Twice, Tom Servo sings o/` "We believe in Gamera," o/` even though that song with those English lyrics will not be heard until the next movie.
- In addition, the first germ of the "Gamera is really neat, he is filled with turtle meat" lyrics, which would be fully fleshed out in Season 3, can be heard here.
- It was actually about 1:30 a.m. on New Year's Day when segment 3 – featuring a New Year's Eve countdown – happens. Joel covers by saying there's a "time delay."
- Fave riff: "Nice jammies, babe." Honorable mention: "Perhaps they should start looking for Allen Funt."
- This movie was re-riffed in episode 316.

Movie stuff:

1) This is one weird mamajama of a movie, though I'm guessing most of the weirdness can be blamed on a really bad translation. That said....
2) Once again the little kid is named Kenny.
3) I don't really understand the anti-science message that floats through the movie. Kenny and Helen's father and his pal are biologists. Doesn't that make them scientists? And are scientists actively polluting the sea? So, why are scientists the problem?
4) After discovering that Kenny and Helen have come along on their fishing trip, the biologist guys see Zigra land and express a desire to investigate. One says: "What about the kids?" The kids then express a desire to go along. This seems to settle the issue. The adults are, like: "Fine, let's go." So no concerns at all for the kids' safety?
5) I have seen this movie a dozen times now and I still cannot make heads or tails out of the weird Zigra monster up on the shelf in

the alien spaceship. It looks a little like a skeksis from "The Dark Crystal," but what's with the billowing cobwebs?

6) In a similar anti-science thing, how did "your Earth science" pollute a planet 400 light years away? I ran that back and listened to it again and that's definitely what he says. Doesn't make any sense.

7) Similarly, what was the point of the whole "who gets to buy the fish" subplot?

8) Apparently thinking her spandex attire is too outlandish, the henchwoman hypnotizes some bathing beauties and steals a bikini from one of them to wear instead. And this makes her less outlandish as she walks through the busy streets of Tokyo?

9) Uh, general guy? You MIGHT want to check with somebody before surrendering the entire planet.

10) So, they plan to revive the biologists and the kids with electric shock. But later we just see them shaking Helen awake. Did they have second thoughts on the electric shock thing?

11) Gamera now flies straight all the time, no more spinning.

12) The appearance of the Japanese version of the Monty Python "It's!" guy also goes nowhere.

13) I love the way Gamera delivers the bath-o-scope like Lynn Swann scoring a touchdown.

Episode K08- GAMERA VS. GUIRON
First shown: 01/08/89

Movie: (1969) In the fifth movie of the long-running Japanese monster series, two boys accidentally hijack an alien spaceship and fly it to a dying planet, where they encounter two evil ladies and knife-headed monster Guiron. Can Gamera save them?

Opening: The Mads think they're out of Gamera movies, but at the last minute they find one more.

Host segment 1: Crow gets conked on the head and dreams that he controls the experiment while the Mads are trapped in space
Host segment 2: Crow is still thinking about his dream in the last segment, and discusses it with Joel and Servo
Host segment 3: More dream talk with Joel, Crow and Gypsy
End: J&tB sing "Satellite of Love"

Comments:

- This show featured the last Gamera film of the KTMA series.
- For the first time in a while, J&tB did not listen to any viewer calls.
- There's also a tiny continuity error: at the end of the last episode, Joel announced the name of this week's film. And Joel starts this week's episode by saying they're going to do another Gamera movie. But then, everyone seems shocked when the Mads say that they're doing another Gamera movie.
- The opening feels very much like a season one segment.
- It's becoming increasingly clear that the idea that they completely ad-libbed the riffing in KTMA eps is a myth. For example: it's clear that they had prepared the lyrics they sang to the Gamera song.
- Servo's head extends again.
- The carnage we witness once the boys get to the planet is pretty intense. It appears to upset Joel, even though they're just models.
- Crow calls Gypsy Gypsum again.
- Crow's dream is strangely prophetic! What he dreamed will come true in episode 613- LAST OF THE WILD HORSES.
- I like the "Batman" (the '60s TV show)-esque slanty camera angle when they show the Mads.
- After the second segment, Josh has a little problem getting Tom Servo set up in the theater.
- In segment 3, we get a rare political joke. Dan Quayle was set to be sworn in as vice president in a few weeks, so I guess he was on their minds.

MSTiEPEDIA • 33

- Crow's riff "Ya gotta shave 'em!" cracks Joel up.
- In the final segment, J&tB sing Lou Reed's "Satellite of Love." It would become a traditional closing number at their live shows.
- Fave riff: Bad haircut! Help! Bad haircut!
- This movie was reriffed in episode 312.

Movie stuff:

1) Terrible, terrible dubbing. The pauses are ridiculous.
2) So Gamera was just passing by in outer space when the kids needed rescuing?
3) The long stretch of clips from other Gamera movies is a bit hard to sit through.

Just as the show began to find its feet, a new problem arose. KTMA station manager O'Connor, in an effort to save money -- and ominously foreshadowing future events -- decided to cancel MST3K in favor of showing movies unriffed. Not taking the cancellation lying down, the next edition of "Satellite News" included an article asking fans to contact KTMA and voice their displeasure at the cancellation. The ploy worked. Fans sent cards and letters to the station. O'Connor relented and announced that MST3K would continue.

Episode K09- PHASE IV
First shown: 1/15/89

Movie: (1974) An astronomical event endows an ant colony in the Arizona desert with sentience. Two scientists are sent to investigate, but who's testing whom?

Opening: The Mads are running low on funding
Host segment 1: Joel discusses Isaac Asimov's Laws of Robotics

Host segment 2: J&tB discuss the first thing they plan to do when they get to Earth

Host segment 3: A game of "I spy" becomes a performance of "Wipeout."

End: Joel programs Crow and Gypsy to recite a new robotic law

Comments:

- There's lots going on in the opening. It's the first time the show has started with The Mads instead of Joel. It's also the first time we get a sense that there is somebody with authority over The Mads (by the way, the nickname "Old Leadbottom" is taken from a '60s TV show called "McHale's Navy." Look it up, kids!). We also get the first mention of "the madscientist-mobile," which would come up again.
- Also this is the first time, as far as we know, that Joel did the "getting run down by Cambot" routine, which both he and Mike would do again.
- I saw this movie when it first came out. I thought it was a pretty good little sci-fi thriller and I still do. The ant photography, as well-done as it is, goes on a little long and slows the pace down too much, and the acting by the humans is pretty low-key. But it's not really a "cheesy" movie, to my mind.
- The Brains must have thought so too. They seem to get into it. Several times they say something like "uh-oh" when a plot development unfolds, a sure sign they are caught up.
- That said, Josh never seems to quite get the premise of the movie. "Yes, because most ants have the power of reasoning…" he says, sarcastically, when the movie suggests that these particular ants do. Later he yells: "They're ants!!" when a character suggests that there is an intelligence behind their actions. That's the premise of the movie, Josh.

- A segment of riffing in the theater, starting at about 7 minutes into the episode (not counting commercials), was included on the pitch tape that was used to sell the show to the Comedy Channel. That tape was included on the MST3K Scrapbook tape. My question: Was that really the most sparkling few minutes of riffing from the whole 21-episode KTMA season? I would say no. But, hey, you can't argue with success. (Or, as MSTies might say, "But he bought the car!")
- Servo extends his head again in the theater.
- Another first in segment 2: This ep is the first time anybody mentions that the bots have something called a "load pan."
- Now-dated reference: When a high-pitched sound makes some glass break, Crow says "Ella!" That's a reference to a then-popular Memorex commercial featuring jazz singer Ella Fitzgerald.
- Uh, could segment 3 get any more random? It's completely stream-of-consciousness. Were they just killing time?
- At one point in the theater somebody drops something and it makes a rather large noise, so loud the performers feel they can't ignore it, so they acknowledge that it happened. Then there is a strange scraping noise, which they don't acknowledge. Was someone dragging whatever it was away?
- Joel calls Gypsy Gypsum again.
- Fave riff: Meanwhile Grandma and Grandpa are patty melts out on the lawn. Honorable mention: Hope nobody's eating rice at this point...

Movie stuff:

1) For a science lab that was just built, it sure has a lot of shelves full of spare parts laying around, like a warehouse that has been sitting there for years.

Episode K10- COSMIC PRINCESS

First shown: 1/22/89

Movie: (compilation 1982; original episodes 1976) The inhabitants of a space station encounter a hostile alien and his shapeshifting daughter. Later, her shapeshifting ability goes out of control and endangers the ship.

Opening: It's Superbowl Sunday. The Mads show off their "no-d" glasses
Host segment 1: Crow gives Joel a haircut
Host segment 2: Crow suggests Servo can learn to fly. It doesn't go well
Host segment 3: The Bots help Joel with his taxes, and find out more than they wanted to know
End: Joel, Crow and Gypsy play football, and Gypsy and Joel sing "We Are the Champions"

Comments:

- This episode aired on Superbowl Sunday 1989, which explains all the football stuff. Servo's head comes off for the first time (that we know of) in this episode.
- Segment 1 was re-done in episode 105- THE CORPSE VANISHES; some of the football game during the end segment was featured in the MST3K Scrapbook Tape.
- Servo's head extends again during the riffing. Josh just liked doing it, I think.
- Joel says something silly and Crow turns to him and calmly asks: "What color is the sky in your world, Joel?" That one would come back later.
- During the transition period between episodes, Joel keeps saying "series" when he means "episode."
- Servo just gets up and leaves at one point.

- The riff "there go the music lessons" is an early version of "There go the piano lessons" from "MST3K the Movie."
- About Servo's head falling off: I think the first time it happens, after Crow has talked Tom Servo into base jumping off the desk, was on purpose. But when it falls off again later, I think that was an accident. They just kept going.
- Servo's head is still off when they return to the theater. Joel reconnects it.
- Servo is still steamin' mad at Crow after segment 2. The two almost come to blows!
- This is a re-edit of two episodes of the TV series "Space: 1999." The episodes that were combined were "The Metamorph" and "Space Warp." The former was the debut episode of the show's second season. The latter came 13 episodes later. Yet when the second half of the "movie" begins, alien Maya is again in sick bay, giving the incorrect impression that she's been in sick bay for 14 episodes.
- Can I just note that this movie is mostly really really boring? It is occasionally punctuated by some actual action, but still, it nearly put me to sleep.
- Fave riff: The reference to the "Dennis Hopper segment of the film." Honorable mention: Joel sings a few bars of the Banana Splits theme song as characters from the movie climb into the ridiculous moon buggy.

Episode K11- HUMANOID WOMAN
First shown: 1/29/89

Movie: (1981) In the future, a clone is rescued from space, lives on Earth for a while, then leads her friends to her polluted and desperate home world.

Opening: The Mads are furious to learn that last week's ratings were higher, despite being opposite the Super Bowl

Host segment 1: J&tB enjoy a game of tag
Host segment 2: Servo hits on a blender
Host segment 3: J&tB demonstrate surrealism
End: Servo and Joel discuss the Village People and end with a "Dating Game"-style goodbye kiss

Comments:

- Three of the host segments from this episode were later re-used in season one shows, making this one of the most heavily-plundered KTMA episodes. Segment 1 was later re-shot and used in episode 105- THE CORPSE VANISHES. Segment 2 was later recycled, almost word-for-word, for a segment in episode 103- MAD MONSTER. A sketch somewhat similar to segment 3 appeared in episode 107- ROBOT MONSTER.
- It's unclear why the Brains think the movie is Czech (maybe it said so in the Leonard Maltin movie guide?). It's Russian. But that doesn't stop Servo from making a "corn Czechs" joke.
- In the opening segment, after movie sign is announced, the Bots chase Joel down the corridor leading into the movie theater. Both Joel and Mike have run down the corridor, but Crow, Tom and Gypsy following is unique.
- I've been noticing something in these episodes: Joel hasn't really embraced the whole "the right people will get it" mentality yet. This comes from a comment Joel made in a 1992 documentary about the show. He said: We never say, 'Who's going to get this? We always say: 'The right people will get this.'" In other words, they don't like to explain jokes. A lot of times Josh or Trace will make a reference and not explain it, and then Joel will, almost reflexively, explain the joke. A good example in this episode is the "Kiki Dee" reference which Servo makes and Joel then explains.
- Not sure if this is my DVD or the way it actually happened, but there is no "movie sign" transition between segment 3 and the theater.

- During the ending segment, Crow discusses what he plans to do in the upcoming week. This segment feels improvised, and it's one of the few times in MST3K's history in which Trace can't think of anything funny to say. It's almost painful to hear him bluff his way through.
- Fave riff: "Why did she crawl inside the espresso machine?" Honorable mention: "You better close your little ticket window, there."

Movie stuff:

1) The movie was originally titled "Cherez Ternii K Zvedam" (in Russian) and was shown in two parts: "Iskusstvennyl Chelovek" and "Angely Kosmosa." When exported to the west, it was initially titled with the Latin phrase "Per Aspera Ad Astra" then retitled with the rough English translation of that phrase: "To the Stars by Hard Ways." Sheesh. (Adding to the potential confusion, there was a 2019 film called "Ad Astra.")

2) According to the IMDB, the director's son has reedited/restored the original, which purists insist is far more interesting than the Sandy Frank version (which, according to Wikipedia, is missing more than an hour of footage). This sounds a lot like the "purists" who swear by the restored version of the movie "Solaris" (which I found impenetrable, but others, whose opinions I respect, really enjoyed).

3) It's definitely another case, like all the other Russian films that were riffed over the years, that, whatever its flaws, this movie clearly had a huge budget and it's fascinating to look at, even if you don't know what the Sam Hill is goin' on.

Meanwhile, instead of waiting for fans to create a fan club for the show, the creators founded one themselves. In the early days they encouraged viewers to call in and leave messages on an answering machine they'd set up. But as the series went on, they changed course and instead encouraged fans to write in with letters of support. The addresses of those who wrote in were saved and placed in a database. (The staff were early PC adopters.) To cultivate that audience, the team created "Satellite News," a free newsletter sent to all those addresses a couple of times a year, containing bits of comedy and promotional material.

Episode K12- FUGITIVE ALIEN
First shown: 2/5/89

Movie: (1978 original TV show episodes; 1986 compilation movie) Alien marauder Ken becomes a fugitive from his home planet, then joins the Earth spaceship Bacchus 3 to fight against his former masters. Meanwhile, his girlfriend Rita is sent with a deadly mission.

Opening: Dr. E. calls Dr. F., who is attending a mad scientists' convention in Las Vegas
Host segment 1: Servo and Gypsy have disassembled Crow
Host segment 2: Ever notice how you never see certain celebrities in the same room together? Joel and Servo discuss
Host segment 3: Joel hosts a robot dance competition
End: Joel announces the formation of the fan club

Comments:

- The third-season riffing of this movie is one of the most seminal episodes in the series, so I guessed this version was going to really pale in comparison ... and it does. Plus, Trace is AWOL again, making it an even weaker incarnation. But if you take it on its own merits and don't compare it, you can definitely see them getting stronger and more comfortable in the format.
- The Mad Scientist Convention would come up again.

MSTiepedia • 41

- As happens every time Trace is away, Servo sits in Crow's seat. Probably looked better. Although he does not appear in the episode, Trace is still listed as a writer, puppeteer and "mad scientist" in the credits.
- The second half of this two-part "movie," "Star Force: Fugitive Alien 2," was riffed in episode K03, of which no fan copy exists that we know of.
- The opening is really pretty funny; Josh is channeling Bob Newhart, while Joel is disturbingly distraught. "I MISS MY FRIENDS AND FAMILY! GET ME DOWN!" Acting!
- Servo cracks Joel up with his "Strawberry Fields" parody.
- With Crow gone, Tom Servo really takes up the slack in the theater. It feels like he has many more riffs than Joel, but the two of them seem very in sync.
- One thing about this version: We get to see a lot of footage that was cut from the season three version. If you're into that sort of thing.
- I wonder if that's Kevin running Gypsy in the segments where Servo is there.
- It was a fairly typical February night in Minneapolis the night this show aired: a balmy 1 degrees at 7 p.m.
- So many riffs from the third-season version are ingrained in me. Every time Ken says "Rita!" I reflexively say: "Meter maid!"; every time anybody says "Rocky!" I reflexively say "Again?" But it's especially true of the score, and the lyrics that the Brains wrote for that music. I defy you to sit through this version and NOT burst out with o/` "He tried to kill me with a forklift..." o/`
- Josh appears to genuinely amuse Joel with his dance competition comments during segment 3.
- I've been meaning to mention this for several episodes: "Heavy on the 30-weight," which Joel says to Cambot in several episodes, is a Firesign Theatre reference.
- Joel seems a little distracted during the closing.

42 • MSTIEPEDIA

- Fave riff: "Don't you have, like, a Highlights Magazine I could wait with?" Honorable mention: o/` …and no refrigerator to stick on to. o/`

Episode K13- SST-DEATH FLIGHT
First shown: 2/19/89

Movie: (1977) Aboard the maiden transatlantic flight of a super-sonic plane, mechanical problems and a killer virus cause a crisis for an all-star cast.

Opening: Dr. F. is back from Vegas, bringing money, gifts and this week's movie. They send it to Joel, catching him off-guard
Host segment 1: Joel shows Servo what it's like to feel pain
Host segment 2: Gypsy has a sexy new voice … or does she?
Host segment 3: Joel, Crow and Gypsy have a limbo contest; Servo provides the music.
End: Viewer mail.

Comments:
- This is a movie I'd have loved to see them tackle again. It's got everything: stupid plot, a huge "Fantasy Island"/"Love Boat" cast, hackneyed story lines, the works. And it sure is a breath of fresh air after so much Sandy Frank.
- The opening is very similar to a segment in episode 105- THE CORPSE VANISHES.
- Portions of the theater segments were included on the MST3K Scrapbook tape.
- Local jokes: "We can bail out Midwest Federal." "They look like they got their suits at Foreman & Clark."
- At one point Crow mispronounces a word and Tom immediately mocks him for it. It's the kind of thing they seldom did later on.

- Pre-riff: I said, "You sank my battleship!" a few seconds before Servo did.
- In between segments one and two, in a jump cut between two scenes in the movie, it looks like they stopped tape and then restarted it. Servo is suddenly off his chair and Joel says "Whoa! Turbulence!"
- That's make-up lady Faye Burkholder doing the sexy Gypsy voice and some puppetry in segment 2.
- Firsts: Crow mentions ram chips, the Mads say "push the button," we get the very first reading of letters to the show and we get the first mention of Cambot's "stillstore" function (which appears to be a piece of cardboard and some masking tape).
- My DVD contains a commercial for the show, in which J&tB perform the "SST Death Flight Theme Song."
- CreditsWatch: We now begin an ongoing feature in which we note changes in the closing credits. In all the previous episodes (as far as we know) Vince Rodriguez is listed as director and Todd Ziegler is credited with handling the audio. For some reason, in this episode and the next one, both their credits have vanished.
- Fave riff: "If I could do that, I wouldn't leave the house!" Honorable mention: "Put the masks on the important stars first!"

Episode K14- MIGHTY JACK
First shown: 2/26/89

Movie: (1968 TV series; 1987 compilation movie) A top secret organization, called Mighty Jack, makes use of a giant submarine, called Mighty Jack, to battle terrorist organization Q.

Opening: Dr. E thinks he and Dr. F need a change; Joel listens in
Host segment 1: As a joke, Servo, Crow and Gypsy weld themselves together

Host segment 2: Crow and Servo admit they have no idea what humans think is funny

Host segment 3: Crow bowls, but Crow and Servo don't want to play games with Joel anymore

End: Viewer mail

Comments:

- In the theater, as the opening credits roll, Joel addresses the viewers and promises a fan club newsletter in two weeks. He does so again about half-way through the movie.
- I have been pleasantly surprised at the viewability of these KTMA episodes: they ARE, after all, several-generation copies of VHS tapes of an over-the-air TV feed. But I should mention that there are some pretty rough spots in this one, and I can't tell if it's just VHS tape artifacts or if whoever was originally taping this just had their rabbit ears adjusted badly.
- During segment 1, Joel "accidentally" drops a pencil, then bends down behind the desk, out of shot, to pick it up. For a moment, no one is in the frame ... then Joel pops back up. That way the editors could cleanly cut the action.
- Host segment 2 is a little dark, what with the bots contemplating Joel's death.
- One of the fan letters refers to the part of "SST Death Flight" in which Servo says "His eye needs some air." This line was actually said by Crow, but no one corrects the viewer's error.
- Also in Segment 2, as an example of what is clearly NOT funny, we see a little snippet of the TV series "Punky Brewster." If you're too young to remember it, don't worry, you didn't miss anything.
- Two odd comments in the theater: At one point, Servo says: "That's the kind of entertainment Josh — this guy I know — really likes." Weird. Even weirder, Crow says that one character "looks like Frank Conniff."

- Watch Servo as J&tB leave the theater right before segment 3. As he exits, Josh lifts the puppet too high and it completely clears the theater seats. We can see the control rod, a little of Josh's hand and we can also see that Servo doesn't have the lower half of Servo's body. Wow.
- Segment 3 was redone in episode 106- THE CRAWLING HAND.
- Toward the end of the movie, one of the characters yells "Launch!" and Joel riffs "I said lunch, not launch!" A rare example of a riff that appears in both versions.
- Crow waves goodbye at the end of the episode. Ah, the days when Crow's arms worked.
- CreditsWatch: Additional writing: Faye Burkholder. Additional puppet operation and voices: Alexandra Carr, Faye Burkholder. Alex, taking on even more work, is now also listed as fan club coordinator.
- Fave riff: "Ew. Get a mop." Honorable mention: ""Hmmm… how to drive a boat."

Movie stuff:

1) As with some of the other Sandy Frank movies, we get to see lots of footage we didn't get to see in the season 3 version, including a long segment before the credits. And I have to say that it helps. The season 3 "Mighty Jack" is a thick, almost impenetrable, plot stew. It took many repeat viewings of it before I could figure out what the heck was going on. I was able to follow the plot, such as it was, much more easily watching this version.

2) In this more complete version you can really see the dividing line between the two episodes, which happens when Atari is introduced as the team's new commander and all the old grudges are smoothed over.

46 • MSTiepedia

Episode K15- SUPERDOME
First shown: 3/12/89

Movie: (1978) A star-studded cast, each with their own subplot, descends on New Orleans for the Super Bowl, but a killer is on the loose.

Opening: In a letter to his uncle, Servo recalls how he almost talked the Mads into bringing Joel back to Earth
Host segment 1: Still writing his letter, Servo recalls when Joel showed Servo what it's like to feel pain
Host segment 2: Still writing his letter, Servo reveals that Joel isn't really like his lovable on-air persona. His crabbiness seems to trigger recreations of memorable movie moments in the bots
Host segment 3: Still writing his letter, Servo experiences a sentimental montage
End: Joel and Crow show off some artwork sent in by viewers; then present the stuff you'll get if you join the fan club.

Comments:

- The host segments in this episode appear to be a spoof of sitcom clip shows, although only one segment, the one in segment 1, features an actual clip from a previous episode (it's from episode K13- SST DEATH FLIGHT), but the others were made to look like they were.
- For years, the only known existing copy of this episode was missing the final host segment. That changed on October 2004, when the missing final segment came to light in the possession of a Minnesota woman named Teresa Dietzinger. She sent some artwork in to the show (it's the first one shown in the final segment, she says she included her name on the drawing, nonetheless Joel says he can't remember it and mistakenly assumes a guy did it). She taped the episode and held on to the tape for 16 years. Although

her father long ago taped over the rest of the episode with family footage and such, the final host segment remained intact and was included in DVDs sold by some fans.

- For you young folks, that object Servo is using is called a "typewriter." (Looks like an old IBM Selectric; probably some KTMA office equipment.) You couldn't get Facebook on it, but it was useful sometimes.
- Servo has feet? (He claims to be typing with them.)
- "Is that your head or did your neck blow a bubble?" is a joke already used in an earlier episode. Sounds like it might have been a standard heckler putdown from somebody's standup act.
- Callback: "Did these guys fly in on SST Death Flight?"
- Servo coughs and kind of chokes in the theater.
- Servo seems to be malfunctioning in the theater. At one point he falls over into Joel's lap. Joel casually shovels him back the other way. Tom recovers, mumbling something about "narcolepsy." Later he again sags to one side and suggests Joel needs to adjust his "equilibrium functions." For a lot of the episode he bobs up and down in the seat as if Josh is having trouble holding him steady.
- Joel is smoking in segment 2, in order to telegraph that he's a being a jerk. That segment reminds me of the host segment in episode 608- CODE NAME: DIAMOND HEAD in which Mike is mean to the bots.
- Some of the clips in the montage in segment 3 are from episodes K01 and K02. Others appear to be from K03, of which no fan copy is known to exist.
- What do you bet they didn't clear the rights to that Louis Armstrong song they used in the montage in segment 3?
- As they enter the theater after segment 3, Crow gets into his seat and then adjusts his position with a lovely mechanical noise that would please the guy in the "Police Academy" movies.
- As the fan club address appears on the screen, Crow says, apparently to the audience, "Don't call. Write." This would appear to

48 • MSTIEPEDIA

be the official shift away from taking voicemail calls and in the direction of letters.

- At one point toward the end, Joel admits to being completely unable to think of anything funny to say. This prompts Servo to recall the flashback in the opening segment, in which Crow ruins Servo's attempt to get the Mads to bring them down to Earth. The two bots begin bickering. It's a strange moment.
- Minneapolis joke: An overhead shot of the seats in the Superdome prompts Crow to identify it as "The Guthrie," which is a theater in Minneapolis.
- J&tB stand up in the theater for the national anthem.
- It's interesting (to me, at least) that the fan club membership cards appear to be the same ones that were handed out years later. Maybe they bought a whole bunch in the initial order?
- Although the final host segment was saved from oblivion, the closing credits of that show were not. If you have the copy of this that includes the final host segment, that DVD includes the closing credits from episode K20 "just for consistency," as Ms. Dietzinger told us.
- Fave riff: "And a gun FOR the doberman!" Honorable mention: "Women cause weak knees. It's a fact!"

Movie stuff:

1) This movie's just chock full of late-'70s casual hooking up. The Pill, and cures for many known STDs, had arrived and HIV had not arrived, yet. The result was an era in which everybody was pretty much having as much consequence-free sex as they wanted, as depicted in this little time capsule of a movie.
2) There are a lot of extras in this thing. Were they all actors, or did they just shoot this on game day?
3) I wonder what marching band that is that gets so much screen time. It's not named in the end credits.

4) Remember when NFL games had marching bands during half-time? Neither do I.
5) The announcer keeps hyping the madness that has descended on New Orleans with the arrival of the Super Bowl. He's really over-selling it. It's not like New Orleans has never had large numbers of tourists visit it before.

Episode K16- CITY ON FIRE
First shown: 3/19/89

Movie: (1979) A disgruntled former refinery worker starts a city-wide conflagration and a star-studded cast, each with his or her own subplot, must cope with the disaster.

Opening: The Mad Scientist League threatens to revoke Dr. F. and Dr. E.'s licenses. Seems they're merely "mildly peeved researchers."
Host segment 1: Servo and Crow pull the old "telescope black eye" prank on Joel
Host segment 2: Joel demonstrates his new anti-theft device, "hell in a handbag"
Host segment 3: J&tB perform a military cadence
End: Joel again shows the stuff you get when you join the MST3K Fan Club

- The "hell in a handbag" invention in segment 2 would be re-used in episode 103- MAD MONSTER. It's from Joel's standup act.
- The Brains apparently thought they had done some of their best work in this episode. Portions of segments 1 and 3 and a couple of segments of theater riffing (the "good morning!" sequence and the childbirth scene) were included on the compilation pitch tape that sold the show to The Comedy Channel. That compilation tape was also included on the "MST3K Scrapbook" tape that was sold to fans by the Info Club.

- A portion of segment 3 also appeared in the Comedy Central special "This is MST3K."
- A commercial advertising Joel's stand-up comedy act (with an unmistakable voiceover by Kevin) aired during this episode, and is included in some fan copies.
- This is the first reference to the "Mad Scientists League" that is forever checking up on Dr. F and, later, Pearl.
- There's no "movie sign" sequence at the beginning of the movie. It goes right from the Mads, into the movie.
- In the theater, Joel and Servo start talking at the same moment, but this time Joel doesn't give way and finishes his joke. Instead, it's Servo who gives way. Joel asks him what he was going to say. Servo tells him what it was (it isn't very funny). Joel says: "I'm glad I interrupted you." Crow adds: "Hey, we're beginning to annoy ourselves! Cool!"
- It's almost spring in Minneapolis and it was a balmy 34 degrees when the show started, moving up to 35 later on.
- Coming back from Segment 1, the Barry Newman character mentions "unintelligible symbols" and Joel says "sounds like viewer mail." Wow, he's only started getting mail for a few weeks and he's already jaded?
- The sound mixing is a little rough in this one: during some of the louder movie scenes it's hard to hear the riffers.
- After segment 3, Joel again runs down the hallway and is run over by Cambot.
- Servo uses the term "kindler gentler"–a popular, if ungrammatical, phrase in 1989.
- Crow sneezes. They keep going.
- CreditsWatch: Todd Ziegler gets the director credit back. Brian Funk (who?) is listed as an "additional" writer. Alex Carr gets the audio credit. Clayton James would do makeup for this episode and the rest of the season.

- Fave riff: "Boil some newspapers! " Honorable mention: "It's the creature from the gross lagoon."

Movie stuff:

1) Crow mistakenly identifies the kid who starts the fire as Brandon Cruz of "The Courtship of Eddie's Father." He does look a little like Cruz, but it's actually another child actor named Steven Chaikelson. He had a very short career, and with his terrible acting in this movie, you can see why. By the way, the little girl playing his sister Debbie is his real-life sister Janice. Her career was a little longer – but not by much.
2) You can see that Henry Fonda and Ava Gardner pretty much phoned their parts in. Probably were on the set for a day or two at most.

"I haven't been in research since I was at the U doing kitchen cabinet analysis for Ken Keller's house." Keller was president of the University of Minnesota – known in the Twin Cities as, simply, "the U" – in the '80s. He was nice enough to reply to an email I sent him and explain this joke.

"In 1988, renovations to the university president's house (Eastcliff) were the hot scandal of the day with lots of talk about a $600,000 kitchen. Aside from the fact that there was no such kitchen (that was the price of the whole renovation, but that's a longer story), it made great headlines for a couple of months. Since I was the president at the time, the headlines were about me and "my house." So Twin Citians at the time would have known the reference.

Never thought of hiring researchers to do the kitchen cabinet analysis. We did it the old-fashioned way: you buy the cabinets and you hang them."

52 • MSTiepedia

Episode K17- TIME OF THE APES
First shown: 4/2/89

Movie: (1974 TV series; 1987 compilation movie) A trio of young people take refuge in cryogenic capsules during an earthquake, and awaken in a world populated by intelligent apes.

Opening: The Mads try to reach Joel, but Crow and Servo give them the ol' runaround
Host segment 1: The bots look for Joel and find his empty uniform in a pod bay. They guess he's floating in space
Host segment 2: Crow and Servo ponder mutiny as Joel pounds on the door to get back in
Host segment 3: Cambot uses a tape of Joel to fool Crow, but Servo isn't fooled
End: Joel floats outside the Satellite of Love, as Crow and Servo discuss their new Joel-less life together

- This is the only MST3K episode that does not feature a human character aboard the Satellite of Love. Joel had to go out of town, so the episode was shot without him; therefore, Servo and Crow watch the movie alone, together. (Crow sits in Joel's seat; Tom in Crow's.)
- For me, this one gets dragged down by the film, which is just a big giant carbuncle of a movie. Though it's much funnier, of course, I'm not a big fan of the season 3 version either.
- This is one of very few episodes that has a continuing plot line running through the host segments.
- As with the previous Sandy Frank movies, we get to see a bit more of the movie that was cut in the season 3 version.
- Springtime has definitely come to the Twin Cities. It's a lovely 57 degrees as the show begins later dropping to 56 and to 54 by the end of the show.

MSTiepedia • 53

- Callbacks: Servo recalls the episodes when Crow was frozen and served as the SOL's Christmas tree. Crow is not amused. Also: "That flame is leftover from 'City On Fire.'"
- Both Crow and Servo sneeze. They keep going.
- This movie reminds us of a goof they would make about a decade later. In the introduction to "Deep Ape," Bobo lists his noble lineage, including Godo, a name used in this movie. Except, as we know from watching this episode, Godo wasn't an ape. They could have said "Pepe," (which is who I think they were thinking of) but I guess that sounds less ape-ey.
- The imdb says the main ape's name is Gaba, but it is variously pronounced by the voice actors Gaybor or Gaybar. Not that there's anything wrong with it.
- The guy we see behind the doors in segment 3 is longtime Twin Cities weatherman Barry ZeVan.
- That ending segment is the first time we've gotten a look outside the ship, other than in the opening.
- CreditWatch: Vince Rodriguez is back as director. Todd Ziegler is back on Audio.
- Fave riff: "More gorilla warfare." Honorable mention: "A guy with a flea collar concession could clean up around here."

Episode K18- THE MILLION EYES OF SUMURU
First shown: 5/7/89

Movie: (1967) A pair of CIA agents are assigned to stop a female supervillain's plans to take over the world.

Opening: Joel gets back inside the ship, only to be mocked by the Mads
Host segment 1: After Joel disciplines Crow and Servo, he finds out where Gypsy has been

Host segment 2: Joel tries to do a courtroom sketch, but Crow and Servo are too busy doing stream-of-consciousness game show riffs

Host segment 3: In answer to Servo's question, Joel does an acoustic version of the last lines of the theme song, with Servo harmonizing

End: Even though his mouth is broken, Servo gives fan club information

- Servo only watches the first half of the movie with Joel and Crow, opting instead to "bake muffins." Presumably Josh had to be somewhere else that day.
- Apart from the show's opening credits, host segment 2 is the last time we see Gypsy in the KTMA era.
- This is, I think, the first time in the series that a plot from a previous set of host segments is picked up immediately in the following show (something they would do again in the season eight story arcs). This prompts them to use the old "Previously...!" bit (which they would parody many years later). Note the use of the "Fugitive Alien" music in the background.
- Joel suggests the show could be around for another "three to 12 weeks." Turns out it was the former.
- It's early May and it's getting nice out in the Twin Cites. It's 67 degrees after the first host segment and some of the snow may be starting to melt in Minneapolis.
- They always shot the host segments before the movie theater scenes, as is referenced in this episode. Servo announces he won't be staying for the second half of the show and Joel asks him to just be present for the host segments. He replies, "I wouldn't miss it. I feel like they're already done." Droll.
- As many fans have observed. Josh seemed to thrive most in the ad-lib atmosphere of the KTMA era, and Servo's absence is definitely felt in the second half of this episode.
- Then-current event reference: "Cold fusion experiments."

- The characters in the movie break the fourth wall a few times. The worst one is when Frankie says, "I wonder if this is where I'm supposed to sing … nah." Joel calls him on it and Crow keeps bringing it up.
- Late breaking news — In late 2021, Joel announced the titles that will be riffed in season 13 and perhaps the most surprising addition to the list was this film.
- Fave riff: "Where do I get socks like yours?" Honorable mention: "Oh, they brought their autoharp with them."

Movie stuff:

1) Wow, this is a terrible, washed-out, pan-and-scan print, which Crow comments on several times.
2) As soon as I saw the name "Sax Romer" in the credits, I immediately detected the stench of o/` Harry Alan Towerrrrrs!!! o/` Yep, it's the madman who would later give us the nightmare that was "Castle of Fu Manchu." And it has very much the same feel – Sumuru is pretty much a female Fu Manchu. It also feels like they're using some of the same locations, but I could be imagining things.
3) Yes, our star is none other than George Nader of "Robot Monster" and "Human Duplicators." If your gaydar went off while watching him, it is well-tuned. Nader was a very popular actor in the late 1950s and his star was on the rise when a tabloid threatened to expose his gay relationship. With no chance for roles in Hollywood, Nader acted in grade-B films produced in Europe (like this one). And since he's the romantic lead, we get several scenes in which we see Nader "REALLY acting," as Crow would say. Not that there's anything wrong with it!

Episode K19- HANGAR 18
First shown: 5/14/89

56 • MSTiepedia

Movie: (1980) Government officials try to cover up the crash of an alien spaceship, but two astronauts know the truth.

Opening: Joel gives the name of the film, and immediately it's movie sign!

Host segment 1: Crow, in 2-year-old mode, responds to every comment with "why?" and "so?" Joel is not amused

Host segment 2: Joel and Servo purge Crow's memory. It's mostly informercials

Host segment 3: Joel shows Crow his first memory, and explains how Crow got his name (but it's just a practical joke)

End: Joel says the 1,000th fan club member will get a special prize

- Spring has definitely sprung. It was a balmy 76 degrees, then 75, then 73 as the sun set.
- In the first half hour, Servo derisively mocks one of Joel's riffs. The comment is followed by an uncomfortable silence. It feels a little like the kind of thing that probably would be okay in the writing room, but it was a little awkward when he did it on TV.
- The opening is one the shortest host segments ever, right up there with "Pancakes!"
- Segments 1 and 3 appear on the MST3K Scrapbook tape.
- Local references: River Place. Also, weatherman Barry ZeVan is mentioned again.
- In segment 1, after driving Joel crazy with childish questions, Crow asks: "Daddy, what's Vietnam?" This is a reference to a Time-Life Books commercial that ran in the '80s, promoting its "History of the Vietnam War" book series. In the commercial, a man and his son stand before the Vietnam Veterans Memorial in Washington, DC. The son looks up and asks, "Daddy, what's Vietnam?" At which point, a voiceover somberly intones "A question a child might ask – but not a childish question."
- Callback: "City on Fire!"

- Segment 2 seems to be a case of biting the hand that feeds you: a subversive little dig at TV23's apparent penchant for showing informercials. But to be fair, in the late spring of 1989, KTMA was already in pretty deep financial trouble. The official bankruptcy filing happened in July, only a couple of months after this show aired. So the station probably needed all the informercial revenue it could get.
- Does it feel to anybody else like a movie with this title should have been used in episode K18? Or am I just being OCD?
- It's interesting (to me, anyway) that a demon dog pops up in the end segment, with no explanation of what a demon dog is or why it's there. It appears in the opening theme, but you could be forgiven for never noticing it. Demon dogs would become a plot element in an episode in season one.
- CreditsWatch: As with K16, sound guy Todd Ziegler moved up to director and Alex Carr filled in at the audio board. The "camera: Kevin Murphy" credit is removed and "Cambot: Kevin Murphy" is added to the cast list.
- Fave riff: "Mine are more pouty." Honorable mention: "I feel like I know more than I already do."

Movie stuff:

1) The movie feels very "Capricorn One"-ish (and that's not a good thing). The IMDB notes that the studio fiddled with it a bit. When it was shown on TV (the same year it came out in theaters!) it was retitled "Invasion Force," and had a different ending from the theatrical version. That new ending is the one we see in this episode. In the original ending, the news report says that everybody was killed when the plane crashes at the end of the movie. In our ending, the report indicates that the people inside the spacecraft were somehow shielded from the explosion and survived.

Episode K20- THE LAST CHASE
First shown: 5/21/89

Movie: (1981) In a carless, gasless, oppressive future depopulated by a plague, a disgruntled former racecar driver attempts to escape to California with a nerdy kid in tow.

Opening: Dr. F. tries to create cold fusion … in Dr. Erhardt's mouth!
Host segment 1: Crow and Servo don't respond well to their humanity lesson
Host segment 2: Joel announces the 1,000th fan club member
Host segment 3: Servo reads a fan letter
End: Joel reads another very complimentary fan letter

Comments:
- Trace is trying desperately hard not to laugh during the opening host segment. Watching him struggle is at least as entertaining as the sketch itself.
- After the opening, we see the doorway sequence and the start of the film, without having first seen J&tB.
- Trace would reuse the phrase "Here comes the steam shovel, chug-chug-chug" when feeding Tim "the miracle growth baby" Scott in season three. Maybe somebody remembers it from his/her childhood?
- In the theater, Servo says "bitch." Joel is aghast, sort of.
- Does the pairing of Chris and Lee remind anybody else of Troy and Rowsdower?
- Josh does a silly voice as Burgess Meredith's plane. Joel likes it.
- Trace seems to have heard the National Lampoon Radio Hour's "Immigrants" sketch. He makes two references to it.
- Is Gidget Howell out there somewhere?
- Summer is on the way in the Twin Cities. It's still 80 degrees at 7 in the evening.

- "Daddy, what's Vietnam?" is trotted out again.
- A character mentions "gypsies" and Joel asks "Where IS Gypsy." Servo shushes him. Hmm.
- A few moments later, the Servo puppet seems to develop problems. Josh covers by telling Joel he's "lost the equilibrium cycle." Joel seems to pull the puppet back together.
- CreditsWatch: Vince Rodriguez is back as director for the two remaining episodes, and Todd Ziegler is back at audio.
- Fave riff: "Hope nobody pushes that guy's flush button." Honorable mention: "I just never imagined the future being lit so poorly."

Movie stuff:

1) Is the plague everybody died from related to there being no gas or cars? Or was no cars or gas just inevitable and the plague was a whole separate thing? The movie, or at least this edit of it, never makes it clear.
2) What?? They don't have McDonald's in this dystopian future??? NOOOO!!!!
3) Why doesn't that car have a windshield? Chris and Lee must have been picking bugs out of their teeth f0r days.
4) Wow, that lady fell into bed with Lee awful quick! Ah, the sexy early '80s.

Episode K21- THE 'LEGEND OF DINOSAURS'
First shown: 5/28/89

Movie: (1977) A plesiosaur is discovered living in a lake near Mount Fuji, then volcanic activity awakens still more prehistoric creatures.

Opening: The Mads come up with clues to support the "Joel is Dead" rumor they want to start. Joel is dubious

Host segment 1: Joel demonstrates the way special effects can be used to make a person look really small

Host segment 2: J&tB put on a sitcom, complete with laugh track, canned applause and pointless catchphrases

Host segment 3: Joel uses his model lizard, which breathes real fire, to demonstrate monster special effects

End: What are you going to do on hiatus?

Comments:

- This was the final KTMA episode, though the last host segment makes it clear that the Brains expected to return to KTMA after a summer break. Fortunately for them (and us), they had a larger destiny in store for them.
- Host segments 1 and 3 were apparently aired in the wrong order: in host segment 1, Joel refers to their "earlier" segment ... it's pretty obvious he's referring to host segment 3. Oops.
- The model in segment 3 would be re-used as an invention exchange in episode 103- MAD MONSTER.
- Segment 2 appears on the MST3K Scrapbook tape.
- It has been fascinating to watch these and to watch the concept of MST3K grow and coalesce. But, as many have said, I doubt that I will come back to watch any of these episodes for pleasure.
- That said, the riffing in this one is pretty solid and pretty much as good as anything we're about to get in season one coming up.
- For one thing, by this time they were routinely previewing the movie and pre-writing jokes, even though they weren't willing to admit it yet. Example: At one point in this episode, Joel repeats a line of dialog along with a character in the movie. Tom (Josh apparently tweaking Joel for doing so) asks: "Have you seen this before, Joel?" Joel replies: "It's something I learned in camp."
- Callback: "The Two Eyes of Su-Maru."
- It's both depressing and somehow fitting that the final movie is yet another confusing Sandy Frank outing (and maybe the most

disjointed one yet). It makes you wonder why they came back and did a lot of these movies again. That's a lot of pain to take.

- This is one of the rougher tapes from the KTMA era, making the viewing experience even more exasperating.
- Not once, not a SINGLE TIME, in any of these episodes, did anybody EVER use the word "Gizmonic." Joel once told me that, in the KTMA episodes, The Mads are transmitting from their lab in Gizmonic Institute. And that makes sense. After all, in the next episode, (the first of season one) we learn that The Mads have fled Gizmonic Institute to Deep 13. But now it's pretty clear that that's a notion that developed after the KTMA era was over.
- All this time, we have listed this movie as "Legend of the Dinosaur," when the title card actually reads "The 'Legend of Dinosaurs'" (including those quotation marks). My DVD also calls it by the wrong name. The IMDB, on the other hand, gives its full title in English as "The Legend of Dinosaurs and Monster Birds" ("Kyôryuu: Kaichô No Densetsu" in Japanese).
- I wonder where that retouched "Abbey Road" album cover is. That would be a great collector's item.
- The kid in segment 1 is listed in the credits as Ralph Smith. Wonder where he is now.
- The giant hand in that segment would be used again.
- In segment 3, Joel handles a tiny replica of a Kentucky Fried Chicken store. That little model would later be incorporated into the "Big G Burger" scene seen during commercial bumpers for several seasons.
- It was a comfortable evening in the Twin Cities on Memorial Day weekend: 74 degrees, 73 an hour later.
- At one point somebody says: "Watch out for overly sensitive producers!" Huh? Is that a jab at somebody at the station or are they referring to Sandy Frank?
- There's a very strange moment in the riffing, when Joel says, "Finish the job, man! Open the tank!" Then he seems to realize that

he's said something wrong. He tries to correct it. He gets as far as "I meant to say 'Open the...'" before all three riffers collapse into laughter. Servo declares that Joel has "snapped a twig," but I have no idea why.

- In this episode we get our first set of renaissance fair jokes, including a "huzzah!" They would return in season three's "Pod People" and then become a running gag throughout the series.
- CreditsWatch: Special Guests: Ralph Smith & Ralph's Mom.
- Fave riff: Servo: "YBS?" Joel: "People seem to accept it!" Honorable mention: "We haven't heard from her."

CHAPTER 3

In the late spring of 1989, Joel called in some favors and managed to get meetings in New York with executives at The Comedy Channel and Ha!, the two competing 24-hour comedy basic cable channels that had just started up, or were about to. Jim and Joel were armed with a nine-minute "Best Of" tape featuring snippets culled from the 21 shows they'd done on KTMA.

The Ha! executives took a pass (the show really didn't fit in with their lineup of mostly sitcom reruns) but the Comedy Channel executives liked what they saw – especially the fact that the show would be two hours long, really helping to fill their programming grid. Stu Smiley, a well-regarded TV producer who was then working at HBO (The Comedy Channel's parent company) once told me that the other reason they went with the show is that the executives knew and trusted Joel; he had worked previously on successful HBO comedy specials). They offered a 13-show deal and Jim and Joel signed.

Within weeks of their triumphant return to Minneapolis, Jim and Kevin quit their jobs at KTMA (the station was circling drain anyway) and, with Joel, Trace and Josh, founded a company called Best Brains Inc. (hereafter called BBI). A friend had some empty office/warehouse space in the Minneapolis suburb of Eden Prairie. It was just what they needed. They moved in and set about building new sets, new bots and generally rebooting the whole show.

In the KTMA episodes, the Mads (as the Mad Scientists, Dr. Forrester and Dr. Erhardt, were known) had spoken to Joel from a nondescript lab. But never, at any point in those episodes, was Gizmonic Institute mentioned. And it was never suggested that the movie-watching experiment was a secret, or that anyone might disapprove of such activities.

All that changed. Now, the movie-watching experiment was presented as a rogue activity and, fearing it would be discovered by the management of Gizmonic Institute, the Mads had fled from Gizmonic in order to continue their work.

"They had grabbed Joel and pushed him into the Gizmocrats satellite, then launched it into space," Joel explained in an interview with Satellite News in 1999.

"Then, through a diabolical cover up, made the authorities think Joel had stolen the ship on his own, had a mishap and had destroyed himself and the Satellite of Love. They were banished from Gizmonics, but they just moved down into Deep 13 to tap into the Gizmocrats hardware to track Joel and the Bots."

In episode 101- THE CRAWLING EYE, the Mads tell Joel they have "moved" to a place called Deep 13, so named because it was 13 floors below ground level, deep in the sub-basement of Gizmonic Institute. One of the first lines of the episode is Forrester telling Erhardt, "No one can know we're down here doing this!" and in the first few episodes, it is implied that the two are living a double life, spending some time in Gizmonic and some in Deep 13. But over time, Gizmonic Institute would fade from the premise, and by the third season, it was almost completely forgotten.

Another new addition to the cast of characters was Magic Voice. What exactly she was has never been explained, but she appears to have been the voice of the SOL's computer (inspired by the female voice of the Starship Enterprise's computer on "Star Trek"). In season 1, she was a feature of nearly every episode and her voice was mostly provided by Alexandra Carr. Later, Jann Johnson, Mary Jo Pehl and Beth "Beez" McKeever would take the role.

As they had done at KTMA, a self-created fan club, soon modestly renamed the MST3K Information Club was formed, archiving the mailing addresses of fans who wrote in. BBI put the Info Club's mailing address on the screen during every episode, and encouraged fans to write them letters. Each fan was assigned an Info Club member number. (Numbers had been assigned to fans who'd written in during the KTMA days, but apparently the KTMA fan database was not carried over to Best Brains, and the numbering process began anew in 1989.) And, as before, Info Club members began receiving twice-irregular editions of a newsletter called The Satellite News.

MIKE

As BBI was setting up shop, a promising comic caught Josh's eye. After Mike's set one evening, Josh approached him about doing "some typing. That was how the job was described to me," he later recalled. His name was Mike

Mike grew up in Illinois and Wisconsin, and was trying to make a career as a stand-up comic (but also working as a waiter at a local TGI Friday's restaurant to make ends meet). In addition to occasional gigs in the Twin Cities, he spent some time touring the informal circuit of comedy clubs that had sprung up in the upper Midwest during the comedy club boom of the late 1980s. While on the road, he met and became friends with two other comics working the same circuit. One was a refugee from the East Coast named Frank Conniff. The other a quick-witted charmer from Sauk Rapids, Minn., named Bridget Jones. Nelson and Frank found that they shared a similar comedic sensibility, and became fast friends. Mike and Bridgett, meanwhile, fell madly in love. The two married in 1989.

Shortly after returning from his honeymoon, Mike started work at BBI. He quickly moved from typist to writer, and Joel and the rest of the team were increasingly impressed by his wit, his outstanding organizational and leadership abilities and -- a bonus they had not expected -- his musical skills.

"Mike was always killer funny," Jim said in an interview. "As what was funniest tended to carry the day at Best Brains, Mike very quickly earned the respect of everyone there."

The first season on the Comedy Channel is often described by cast members as "a work in progress" and that's a fair, if perhaps overly modest, assessment. The first four or five episodes did lack many of the elements that fans would later come to expect from the series. It would not be until the fifth episode (episode 105), for example, that somebody would think to add a series of buttons to the desk on the Satellite of Love's "bridge" set. Before that, when "movie sign" arrived, Joel baffled audiences by simply slapping the empty table top where buttons would eventually be placed.

A feature of many of the season 1 episodes was a turgid Republic Pictures adventure called RADAR MEN FROM THE MOON. In all, eight full episodes were shown before BBI finally wearied of trying to wring comedy out the repetitive serial.

There was a lot of experimenting going on in the first season. Comedy Channel executives, worried viewers would not see the shadowrama silhouettes in dark scenes, suggested colorizing the theater seats slightly to make them more visible. It looked, as Mike would later write, "stupid."

The bots were also still in the formative stages. Crow often sported a thick, very distracting stick connected to his jaw. Servo sported shoulders that made him look like a fullback. And Gypsy was presented as so dimwitted that she could barely be understood when she spoke. But Jim's biggest problem was not his dialog.

"The hardest part was figuring out how to deal with Gypsy's huge size," Jim recalled. Eventually he fashioned something out of a harness designed for tuba players. "That solved that problem."

Episode 101- THE CRAWLING EYE
First shown: approx. 11/25/89? (See below.)

Movie: (1958) After some mysterious deaths in the Swiss Alps, a U.N. troubleshooter is sent to assist a scientist who is investigating the situation. But a pretty young psychic may be the most help.

New theme song:
Lyrics: Joeland Josh Sung by: Joel and the Joels [Joel] Joel: In the not-too-distant future -- Next Sunday A.D. -- There was a guy named Joel, Not too different from you or me. He worked at Gizmonic Institute, Just another face in a red jumpsuit. He did a good job cleaning up the place, But his bosses didn't like him So they shot him into space. We'll send him cheesy movies, The worst we can find (la-la-la). He'll have to sit and watch them all, And we'll monitor his mind (la-la-la). Now keep in mind Joel can't control Where the movies begin or end (la-la-la) Because he used those special parts To make his robot friends. Robot Roll Call: (All right, let's go!) Cambot! (Pan left!) Gypsy! (Hi, girl!) Tom Servo! (What a cool guy!) Crooooow! (He's a wisecracker.) If you're wondering how he eats and breathes and other science facts (la la la), Then repeat to yourself, "It's just a show, I should really just relax... ...For Mystery Science Theater 3000!"

Opening: None
Invention exchange: Electric bagpipes, canine anti-perspirant, welcome to Deep 13
Host segment 1: Crow and Tom fail to understand why losing your head is a big deal
Host segment 2: Gypsy uncoils
Host segment 3: J&tB discuss the whole "giant eye" premise
End: Good thing/bad thing, the Mads are happy

Comments:

- The Comedy Channel went live on Nov. 15, 1989, and we now believe, thanks to the diligent work by uber MSTie Tom Noel, that the first episode that actually aired was 102- ROBOT VS. THE AZTEC MUMMY, on Nov. 18, and that this episode appeared the following weekend, on Nov. 25.

Cast members have said, somewhat casually, that the show first ran on Thanksgiving day, 1989. That year Thanksgiving fell on the 23rd, but we do not believe an episode actually aired on that date. That was a Thursday, of course, and the show aired on Saturdays.

But, let's face it, back then, nobody was keeping track of this stuff. If somebody has TV Guides (where's George Costanza's dad when you need him?) or some other TV schedule from the second half of November, 1989, that lists The Comedy Channel, that would be a huge find.
- The stretch between the end of the KTMA season and the beginning of season one (if we assume the first episode aired on Nov. 18) was 173 days.
- Do I like it? This episode has become such an icon that, like the Taj Mahal, it almost seems above my likes and dislikes. Yes, the riffing is funny and steady, but the whole thing is still pretty rough.

Really, it's not much more than a polished KTMA episode, not even close to the level of entertainment we'd get, even later this season. And it certainly wouldn't stack up against some of the episodes in season two and forward. But there are definitely some fun spots, and it's where it all began for real.

- This episode is included in Shout! Factory's "Mystery Science Theater 3000 Collection: Vol. XVII."
- Firsts (assuming this was the first national show produced): The first episode to be fully scripted, first mention of Gizmonic Institute, first invention exchange, first episode to be filmed at Best Brains studios, first episode to feature a film used with permission, first episode with Jim doing the voice and puppeteering for Gypsy and the first episode with scenes set in Deep 13. Also this was the first episode to end its credits with the words: "Keep circulating the tapes."
- Changes from KTMA: A completely redesigned dog-bone shaped satellite, a new door sequence, new sets and new theme lyrics.
- A little about The Comedy Channel (since there is VERY little video of it on YouTube that I could find): The premise was that it was going to be a comedy version of MTV — MTV the way it was back when it first started and they actually showed music videos, that is. When MTV started, they had hosts (veejays, as they were called) who introduced the videos and generally chatted between videos, the way a radio deejay would chat between playing songs. The Comedy Channel wanted to emulate that setup: It called its hosts "ceejays" and they generally showed clips of comedy shows (they had all all those HBO comedy specials in their vault) and movie clips.
- But, one by one, most of the ceejays evolved their shows into something else. Alan Havey turned his into a talk show. The Higgins Boys and Gruber turned theirs into a sketch comedy show, and so forth. But not all the programming was like that. Rich Hall had a terrific series called "Onion World." And then, of course, there was MST3K.

- Initially the channel ran it on Saturday mornings, playing off the idea that it was a parody of a kids' show, but it also played in the wee hours, when people were up partying. Many early fans would recall that their fist encounter with the show was at some friend's house, during a party.
- The Comedy Channel was not available in many areas of the Twin Cities when the show debuted. But eventually cast members found a bar that carried it and went there to celebrate and watch when it debuted.
- Quibble: During the theme song, we see Joel (as the lyrics say) "working" and "cleaning up" but in these shots we can see that he's in Deep 13 and on the SOL. We never actually see him working at Gizmonic Institute, as the lyrics promise. You'd think they could have just had him go out into the hallway at the BBI offices and shot some footage. Maybe that footage in Deep 13 is from when he cleaned up that Flubber spill? I know, it's just a show...
- During the opening theme, you can spot Jim's head sticking up – it's during the section where Joel sings "...to make his robot friends..." You can also spot the PVC pipe that was used to work Crow.
- There is no opening host segment between the theme song and the first commercial, something that became institutionalized later.
- In Deep 13, Dr. F. appears to be controlling the camera with some sort of remote control device that looks like a little satellite antenna. In season two, they would introduce the Mole People and have them assisting on camera and such. Later, they just stopped worrying about explaining who was behind the camera in Deep 13.
- We get as much information as we're ever going to get about Deep 13 in that first host segment.
- Joel wore a tan jumpsuit in the KTMA episodes. With this episode he switches to bright red and the red jumpsuit continues through the entire season. In season two, he switches up the colors a bit, but we'll deal with that when we get there.

- The "electric bagpipes" used in the invention exchange were the first of many props from Joel's old standup act that would re-appear as inventions.
- During the KTMA shows, Joel and the bots (usually Servo) used to note the approach of a commercial during the theater riffing. It's a habit they continue in this episode and for many to come before it fades away.
- Both Tom Servo and Crow have been rebuilt. Tom is built slightly different from later eps – larger shoulder thingies and a larger white beak.
- Trace has pretty much abandoned the "baby" voice he used for Crow during KTMA, though we get occasional, er, traces of it.
- As noted earlier, there are no buttons on the table. At Movie Sign, Joel just sort of slaps the table. Movie Sign is a somewhat lifeless affair all the way around ... no flashing lights, just a little camera-shaking.
- In this episode, the colorized theater seats are just sort of a dark gray.
- BBI was using a "thinner" bluescreen level than they would use later – the result is that Crow's "net" seems to vanish, and you can see some odd gaps between Servo and the theater seats.
- Even taking the bluescreen level into account, you may notice that Crow's silhouette in the theater looks a little strange. BBI used the KTMA Crow for the theater segments here – all they did was add an extra floralier tray and clean him up a little.
- Tom walks into the theater by himself in the first movie segment, just as he often did during the KTMA episodes. Joel carries him in after the first and second host segments, and Tom seems to like it.
- Of course, this is the movie that Mike and the Bots were watching at the end of the final episode of Season 10. As we will discuss then, it was a cute "full-circle" kind of thing, but the writers forgot (or decided not to care) that this movie doesn't start with the credits. It has a "cold" opening right into a mountain climbing scene. Maybe Mike and the bots tuned in late?

72 • MSTIEPEDIA

- Fans of the terrific cartoon series "Freakazoid" may recall an episode that did an almost scene-for-scene (in spots) takeoff of this movie.
- I was still pretty new to the show when I saw this, and when they said "directed by us!" during the credits, I thought that was some sort of catchphrase that they were going to say every week. I later figured out that they were just referring to the fact that an arrow was pointing at them during the "directed by" credit.
- A couple of times Joel does a funny bit where he provides the the voice of the other person on the telephone when somebody is talking on the phone. Cracks me up.
- You can see the shadows of the puppeteers on the wall during the second host segment. Cambot should not have pulled back quite so far.
- We meet a whole new Gypsy in segment two. She's completely redesigned and has a new person running her and doing her voice, but her mouth mechanism squeaks so much you can barely make out what she's saying. And that whole comment from Tom about discovering something that "narrows down" what Gypsy's sex is – that's just odd. Also, her light isn't on. And this is the one and only time Joel removes her "eye" – something that seems to upset her quite a bit.
- Joel blows a line in the the theater: "Pick up some ice and some cubes." They keep going.
- I like the radio conversations between the pilot and the guys on the ground, clearly written by somebody with no aviation experience. The guys on the ground address the pilot as "plane." The pilot addresses the guys on the ground as "party."
- We get the origin of the "Richard Basehart" running gag in the final host segment. If you ever wondered what the whole Richard Basehart thing was about, it was just a weird non-sequitur.
- CreditsWatch: The basic credits for season 1 are: Writers: Trace, Joel, Jim, Kevin, Mike, Josh. Featuring: Joel Hodgson's Puppet

Bots. Associate Producer: Kevin. Production Manager: Alexandra B. Carr. Editor: Randy Davis. Art Direction: Trace, Joel. Set Design: Trace Joel. Lighting: Kevin. Make-up: Faye Burkholder, Clayton James. Costumes: Bow Tie. Gizmonic Devices: Joel. Production Assistants: Jann L. Johnson, Steve Rosenberer, Sara J. Sandborn. Production/Post Production: Fuller Productions, Minneapolis, Minnesota. Production Staff: Ken Fournelle, Jim Fuller. Production Assistant: Jim Erickson. Special thanks: Randy Herget, Skyline Inc., Bryan Beaulieu, KTMA TV23, The Teachers of America, David Campbell, Rick Leed. Keep circulating the tapes.

- Over the years, I have heard from people who were interns and whose names appeared in the credits, telling me that the credits are sometimes wrong. As with the IMDB, which is the final and absolute source for the movie into, these credits are likewise my only source and will remain so. I simply have no way of fact checking these credits list and I must therefore submit to their authority.
- Since these episodes didn't have stingers, I will offer my own suggestions for moments that would have been perfect, in my opinion. In this one, it's: On the train, Miss Pilgrim lands in Forest Tucker's lap.
- Favorite riff: "o/` I'm Popeye the sailor man. I've got a guy's head in my hand." o/` (Great Popeye voice.) Honorable mention: "Fannie Flag and Groucho and Carl Sagan….."

Episode 102- THE ROBOT VS. THE AZTEC MUMMY (with short: RADAR MEN FROM THE MOON, Chapter 1: 'Moon Rocket')
First shown: approx. 11/18/89? (See below.)

Short: (1951) A jet-pack-equipped scientist and his team investigate reports of sabotage by spies from the moon and their hired thugs. Movie: (1957) A mad scientist builds a robot to battle the mummy guarding an Aztec treasure.

74 • MSTiepedia

Opening: None.

Invention exchange: Joel demonstrates the airbag helmet; The Mads unveil The Chalkman, and then show off Deep 13's new security system.

Host segment 1: Demon dogs attack; Tom takes them on, and fares poorly.

Host segment 2: Talks with Enoch, the demon dog king, don't go well.

Host segment 3: Crow's attempt to impersonate Enoch also fails.

End: Joel's trick fools the demon dogs ... or does it? D'oh!

Comments:

- As discussed in the previous entry, it appears that this episode was actually the first one The Comedy Channel showed, just days after going on the air.
- This episode is included in Shout's "Mystery Science Theater 3000 Collection: Vol. XVII."
- Again, no opening segment.
- Again, the early Tom Servo design
- Again, no buttons on table, so Joel just slaps it.
- No Bots are present during invention exchange.
- The "airbag helmet" was another bit from Joel's standup act.
- The Mads' invention, a riff on the old Close and Play phonograph, has one small problem. The dialog has the Mads' saying that you are to "close it" and "open it," echoing the old Close and Play TV commercial (which you can find on YouTube), but they're not actually closing and opening it. They're just lifting the tone arm up and putting it down (the whole point of the Close and Play was that kids wouldn't have to fiddle with a tone arm). Kinda ruins the joke but, hey, they were just getting the prop shop up and running, so I will let them slide on this one.

MSTiepedia • 75

- This is the first time we get the classic unison line "THANK YOU!" from the Mads.
- Josh was really "inside" Tom Servo; Kevin never used a phrase like "You can look me in the bubble and say that??" as Josh does here.
- The thinner bluescreen level makes Tom Servo look very odd in the theater – kind of elongated. Tom is also VERY animated in the theater – a stark contrast to his wooden behavior in the host segments.
- After the little tiny KTMA theater seats, the standard-size seats take a little getting used to.
- In some scenes, the seats are fully black this week, not tinted at all, that I can see. But in very dark scenes the seats are tinted dark gray, like last week.
- The demon dogs were made out of a "Masters of the Universe" toy called "Battle Bones," painted red and black, with some contruction-paper ears added.
- That is clearly Jim doing the voice of Enoch, the king and charismatic leader of the dog people. Unfortunately, it's really hard to make out what he is saying thanks to the incessant clacking of the puppet's mouth. They would get better at making puppets.
- Josh makes an odd comment during host segment 2, calling the SOL "the 2525" and telling Cambot that the SOL's schematics are under "2525" in his files. I did not see a Zager and Evans reference coming.
- Watch carefully early in the feature during the flashback of the Aztec ceremony scene, as Joel covers the irritating singing lady's mouth: Joel clearly has something in his hand, between two fingers, as one would hold a cigarette. Was Joel smoking in the theater? (Answer from Joel: Yes, he was.)
- In addition to smoking, reportedly this was the only episode in which the riffers were drinking alcohol while shooting the theater scenes.

- There are also two spots where the Brains experimented by playing with the sound. In one spot — as the men stand in a row with their backs to the camera in a way that suggested that they were relieving themselves — the show added the sound of liquid streaming. And in the aforementioned musical ceremony, when Joel covers the lady's mouth, the sound cuts back as if he is muffling her. They seldom did something like that again.
- At one point, Joel comments that the cemetery was another place that would make a great miniature golf course. "Like that other movie," he says. That one had me scratchin' my head.

'• The demon dog in the theater at the end is the first of many unexpected guests who would invade the theater over the years.
- CreditsWatch: Special Guest Puppet: Enoch (Jim)
- My pick for stinger: A snippet of the silly Aztec ceremony and the singing lady.
- Favorite riff from short: "Oh, I hate to shoot a butt like that." Honorable mention: "Eat lead, space pansy!"
- Favorite riff from the movie: "We're hitting people!" Honorable mention: "Maybe she should choke up on it a little."

Episode 103- THE MAD MONSTER (with short: RADAR MEN FROM THE MOON, Chapter 2: 'Molten Terror')
First shown: 12/2/89 (unconfirmed)

Short: (1951) Cody and Ted manage to steal the Moon Men's gun, but are soon cornered.
Movie: (1942) A discredited scientist succeeds in turning his servant into a werewolf, and begins to plot revenge.

Opening: None
Invention exchange: Hell-in-a-handbag, acetylene-powered thunder lizard

Host segment 1: Tom hits on a blender
Host segment 2: Crow and Tom have questions about the werewolf in the movie
Host segment 3: Joel switches Crow and Tom's heads (it's Servo-Crow-ation!)
End: Good thing/bad thing. The Mads are not happy

Comments:

- This one, eh. I used to think this felt like a KTMA, but that was before I saw the KTMAs. It's better than that, at least. The riffing rate is, of course, much higher than most of the KTMAs and the pre-written jokes are more consistently funny. But there are plenty of klunkers and state park jokes. The segments DO feel very KTMA-like — perhaps because one of them IS a re-do of a KTMA sketch — but at least these all have a beginning, middle and end. And I'm not sure whether it's the cheapness of the movie or the horribleness of the print, or a little of both, but the movie is just barely watchable.
- This episode is included in Shout's "Mystery Science Theater 3000 Collection: Vol XIV."
- Again, no opening segment.
- Again, no buttons: table slapping.
- Again, no Bots during invention exchange.
- Both inventions were previously shown on KTMA and "hell in a handbag" is from Joel's standup act.
- Great line from the opening segment: "No, that's when I became a SCIENTIST." That gag has a very "Far Side" feel to it.
- As Joel enters the theater, he is grumbling about having to carry Servo, and mutters "I gotta get wheels for you…"
- During the short, when the opening text appears, Joel and Crow duck out of the way so people can read it. Tom doesn't care.

- The blue screen is still somewhat "thin" making Tom look a bit strange.
- The seats are again dark gray.
- Somebody on the staff was the big NASA fan. The mention of Alan Shepard and his golf cart is incredibly space-program-nerdy.
- Host segment 1 is a first-season classic, as Tom Servo deploys his best game on an unsuspecting blender. It's also an almost word-for-word do-over of a segment from episode K11- HUMANOID WOMAN. Great line: "Nobody drinks from my gal!"
- Joel's hair is never in good order on the show but, in segment 2, it's particularly weird.
- Joel calls Servo "Crow" at one point ... both bots react with irritation. They keep going.
- Joel turns the bots off at the end of segment three, something he did not do much 'cause it's kinda mean.
- There's a comment about keeping one's computer plugged in. This is at least a couple of years before people began to buy home computers in any real numbers. These guys were ahead of their time.
- In segment 3, they again reference the idea that Tom Servo looks like a fire hydrant. I don't really see it.
- Naughty line: "You're very well equipped." "Thank you, I didn't think you could tell through the trousers."
- In a very KTMAesque moment, J&tB leave the movie before it is over and we get about 20 seconds of empty theater.
- Gypsy is still barely understood over her squeaking jaw joint, and her light is still off.
- My pick for stinger: Petro, sitting in the chair, "gettin' a whiff of his own overalls." Or Zucco, laughing maniacally as he holds up a vial of his serum.
- Fave short riff: How come they got Groucho Marx mustaches on their helmets?
- Fave movie riff: "Now, Bingo is his name-o." Honorable mention: "Now I'm going to go turn my daughter into a woodchuck."

Movie stuff:

1) This movie has a plot we will see again and again on MST3K: The mad scientist determined to prove his detractors wrong ... even if that means KILLING them (preferably by way of the very invention at which his detractors scoffed). But there's an interesting twist to the plot this time: This guy may be mad, but he's a patriot! He says he plans to give the war department his invention to help them build an army of werewolf soldiers to win World War II! What a guy!
2) It's amazing that this movie came out in 1942. It feels like 1932, especially the audio, which sounds like an early talkie.
3) The plot is somewhat similar to the "Phantom Creeps" serial of season 2 and I swear some of the same sets were used. If not they're pretty similar.
4) Does the title refer to the doctor? It can't refer to poor Petro. And is the monster angry mad or insane mad? Wolf Petro is pretty surly but I don't think you can call him angry or insane.

Episode 104- WOMEN OF THE PREHISTORIC PLANET
First shown: 02/10/90 (unconfirmed)

Movie: (1966) A spaceship crashes on a prehistoric world, and its companion ship heads back, at light speed, to search for survivors.

Opening: Joel has redecorated and seems to be the host of a talk show; Crow made brownies
Invention exchange: Clay & Lar's Flesh Barn, toilet paper in a bottle
Host segment 1: During "This is Joel's Life," a strange machine appears outside the ship, so Joel brings it inside
Host segment 2: J&tB try to disarm the Isaac Asimov's Literary Doomsday Device, but the instructions are no help
Host segment 3: The device explodes, with horrific consequences

End: The effects wear off, letters, the winners of the "name the plant guy" contest.

Comments:

- I'm out of order?? This episode's out of order! The whole show's out of order!! Sorry. Yes, this is the episode with the weird production number. In the ACEG, the Brains confirmed what many fans had long suspected: despite its number, this was the final episode BBI shot for season one.
- It was pretty clear to fans that something was up long before the Brains admitted it: this episode features a number of elements indicative of a late-season show, including an opening segment before the commercial, buttons on the desk in the SOL and a Movie Sign that looks much more like the Movie Sign we know. There were more clues in the references to several "later" episodes, most notably in the closing segment when Joel announces the winners of a contest that was announced in episode 110- ROBOT HOLOCAUST. Also in that segment, a letter refers to episode 105- THE CORPSE VANISHES and episode 109- PROJECT MOONBASE.
- Why was the number changed? We sweated Jim until he finally divulged.

"There was a sense on the network level that we got better as the show went on," he said. "So I vaguely remember them re-ordering the shows to put the "better" shows first." So it was the suits.

- So why aren't I waiting to do this one at the end of season? It's about consistency. I have no idea what other episodes were produced out of order from their production numbers (and I think there are some). If I had a complete, definitive list of every episode in the order it was produced (and I don't), I might do them in that order. But if I can't do them ALL like that, I'm not going to do any like that, and I will stick with the only ordering system I'm sure about.

- This episode is included in Rhino's "The Mystery Science Theater 3000 Collection, Vol. 9."
- For the record, they encounter only one woman, and she is not "of" the prehistoric planet.
- The shadowrama seats are just straight black with no colorization that I can see.
- I've told the story before, but this was the first episode I stumbled on to. I'd actually seen this movie on TV many years before and had been looking to catch it again, so my first delight was in recognizing the movie I'd been looking for for so long – then that delight was compounded by the commentary. I was hooked.
- So, all that said, this is definitely one of the best of season 1. The riffing is full-on and fierce, at full season 2 level. It's got a big, bright, wacky movie with a typically smug John Agar, a clearly soused Wendell Corey, a young Angel from "The Rockford Files," the stupid "hi-keeba!" racist comic relief guy and on and on. It also has a nice story arc in the host segments that is, admittedly, more clever than funny (a problem we'll encounter often in season 2, but we'll get to that), but they're fun all the same. You can really see greatness in their future.
- In the opening bit, Joel says he has "redecorated." That appears to mean only that they've lowered the desk and added a somewhat ratty-looking couch. Nothing else appears to be different.
- This episode contains the first original song on the national series: the "Clay and Lar's Flesh Barn" jingle (and I would love to know who that is playing the kazoo in the background; Mike maybe?).
- The catchphrase "Wonder what SHE wanted?" arrives.
- When Joel wants to see the alien spacecraft that's approaching, he shouts: "Give me an exterior of the ship." No Rocket No. 9 just yet.
- Joel's line "...and he's nobody sweetheart" is a Firesign Theatre reference.
- This show features the first speaking role for Mike (he's the voice of the killer satellite).

- Tom twice refers to one of the leading men as "Johnny Longtorso," a name that would later be used in an invention exchange in episode 421- MONSTER A-GO-GO.
- Of course, this episode is where the oft-repeated phrase "Hi-keeba!" came from, shouted by actor Paul Gilbert (NOT Wendell Corey, as the ACEG incorrectly states).
- Great line from segment three: "Ah, the Samuel Becket method!"
- After being turned into Asimovs. when J&tB return to the theater they are still wearing their Asimov facial makeup.
- Tom's head comes off in the closing segment. They keep going.
- This movie contains several needle-drops of some very familiar incidental music. I tend to think of it as the musical sting from "This Island Earth" (o/` Da-da-daaaaaaa! o/`) but maybe that was a needle-drop too.
- CreditsWatch: Alexandra Carr and Jann Johnson both got "additional writers" credits. Melanie Hartley was an "additional production assistant" starting with this episode and continuing through the end of this season, except for episode 107. Neil Brede was an "additional production assistant" in this episode and from episode 109 through the end of the season.
- The obvious stinger: "HI-KEEBA! HUT!" (THUD).
- Favorite riff: "Oh, I'm gonna go spank myself!" Honorable mention: "Let's make some friction with these pelts."

Episode 105- THE CORPSE VANISHES (with short: RADAR MEN FROM THE MOON, Chapter 3: 'Bridge of Death')
First shown: 12/9/89 (unconfirmed)

Short: (1951) After Cody and his team escape, Retik sends his hired thugs on Earth to set up an ambush.

Movie: (1942) A series of brides die on their wedding days, then their bodies are stolen. A feisty lady reporter investigates.

Opening: None
Invention exchange: Dr. F has a gift for Larry, Joel demonstrates the chiro-gyro, the Mads show off the flame-throwing flower
Host segment 1: Crow and Tom are reading "Tiger Bot" magazine
Host segment 2: J&tB play tag0
Host segment 3: Joel gets a haircut
End: Good thing/bad thing (Tom's head explodes).

Comments:

- The best way to describe this one is: They're getting better. The presence of Bela saves this otherwise dopey movie, the riffing is getting stronger each episode and the host segments are really coming along. Nowhere near where it's going to be, but showing improvement.
- And we're back to the early days, after last week's flash-forward to the end of the season: There's no opening segment after the theme song, no Bots are present during the invention exchange and possibly no buttons on the table (the table is not visible during movie sign, so we can't be sure, but Joel slaps the right side [his left] of the table top, which is not the spot where the buttons eventually would be).
- Both this movie and "Mad Monster" were released in 1942, but this movie opened in theaters a week before "Mad Monster." But, in any case, "Undersea Kingdom," made in 1936, beats them all for the oldest film riffed.
- Shadowrama is green this time.
- This episode is included in Shout! Factory's "Mystery Science Theater 3000 Collection: Vol. XVI."
- More Asimov references in the sketches, although technically the two shows where he's mentioned were made seven episodes apart, so it's not like they were intentionally piling on.

84 • MSTIEPEDIA

- The "chiro-gyro" and the "flame-throwing flower" were props from Joel's standup act.
- Joel refers to the Mads as "The professors" at one point. Huh?
- Servo and Crow are in place in the theater when Joel arrives.
- Servo's has had some alterations and is slowly evolving into the Servo we know: his weird fat white beak has changed to the familiar silver one. Also: Servo's arms are working in segment 1.
- There are two mentions of driver's ed jargon ("hands at 10 and 2 on the wheel," "signal your intentions"...). That's what happens when you have a 17-year-old writer.
- Gypsy's light is still off during segment 2 (which is a do-over of a segment from K11- HUMANOID WOMAN).
- At the end of segment 2, Joel runs down the doorway sequence and is run over by Cambot. This is the first time he's done it in the national series. He did it twice in KTMA episodes.
- The third host segment is another classic moment from season one, a re-think of a sketch originally done for episode K10- COSMIC PRINCESS. Great line: "They're STILL pickin' up clown noses!"
- In the theater, Joel produces a broom and proceeds to "clean up" the screen.
- Tom Servo's head blows up for the first time in the final segment. It won't be the last.
- CreditsWatch: Jim Erickson was "additional production staff" beginning with this episode and through the end of the season. Post production audio was handled by "Rich Cook, TeleEdit, Minneapolis" for this episode and the next two.
- My pick for stinger: "The moment where the reporter is suddenly slapped in the face by Bela's wife."
- Fave riff from the short: "Nipple, nipple, tweak, tweak, fly! fly! fly!" Honorable mention: "Nice shot of me!"
- Fave riff from the movie: "Hey, lady, art exhibit in my nose!" Honorable mention: "Audience baffled by free-floating headlines."

Episode 106- THE CRAWLING HAND
First shown: 12/16/89 (unconfirmed)

Movie: (1963) An astronaut's space capsule crashes in the ocean and his severed hand (controlled by an unknown force that is never adequately explained) washes up on a beach, where it is found by a moody teen. Soon both the teen and the hand are on respective rampages.

Opening: Joel explains the premise
Invention exchange: Joel demonstrates his scary safety saw; the Mads demonstrate the limb lengthener
Host segment 1: J&tB bowl, then Crow and Tom don't want to play any more games with Joel
Host segment 2: J&tB do Shatner with their own crawling hand
Host segment 3: The bots ask: Why is a dismembered hand scary?
End: Good thing/bad thing, letter, Larry's limbs are still lengthy

Comments:

- Not too much to say about this one: bad print of a talky black and white teen sci-fi thriller (with a notable cast); riffing is adequate but not outstanding; host segments are relatively weak, particularly segment three, where the arrival of Gypsy in a giant hand costume is a "WTF" ending to a labored bit.
- This episode was released by Rhino as a single.
- THIS episode, not episode 104, is the first time, following the theme song, that Cambot pulls out into the door sequence and arrives at the bridge of the SOL instead of cutting to Deep 13. This is the first episode (not counting episode 104, of course) in which, during the opening segment, Magic Voice announces "30 seconds to commercial sign," "Commercial sign in 15 seconds" and "Commercial sign in 5-4-3-2-1...commercial sign now." It's also the first episode where we can see buttons on the table.

- Joel explains the show's premise slowly, like he's talking to kindergarteners. He makes a point of gesturing to the buttons when Deep 13 calls. However, there are still no Bots present during the invention exchange.
- This show is the first time we see Joel pop a grape into his mouth after tapping the buttons. Joel would later explain that the Mads were doing a behavior modification thing by rewarding him with a treat for pushing the button.
- Joel starts to mention the "vacuflowers" during the invention exchange. Unless you had seen episode K01- INVADERS FROM THE DEEP (and only a few fans in the Twin Cities had, at this point), you would be totally lost.
- Segment 1 is a re-do from a sketch in episode K14- MIGHTY JACK.
- Crow's arms work during segment 1 and even Joel is surprised to learn that he can smell.
- The theater seats are, again, green.
- The role of moody teen Paul Lawrence is played by moderately successful teen idol Rod Lauren. His real name was Roger Lawrence Strunk, and in later life he became known as "the O. J. Simpson of the Philippines." Why? Okay, strap in...

In 1964, Strunk went to the Philippines to make a movie, and met Nida Blanca, a then-rising Filipina film star. The two became a couple and he married her in 1979 and he moved permanently to Manila. Blanca eventually became a huge star in her native land. She would appear in more than 100 comedy, drama, horror and action films and in more than a dozen television shows, and was a beloved show business personality.

On Nov. 6, 2001, Blanca's body was found in a parking garage, stabbed to death. The crime stunned the nation, and sparked a media frenzy in the Philippines. Suspicion immediately fell on

Strunk: Authorities believed he hired an assassin to kill his wife because she had threatened to divorce and disinherit him. Philippine justice dragged on for more than a year. The alleged assassin and his cohort at first admitted the crime, then recanted, claiming the confessions had been extracted by force. Strunk was about to be charged at last when word came that Strunk's mother in California was terminally ill and near death. In a move that stunned many, authorities allowed him to return to the U.S. to be with her. She died not long after he returned home and, a short time later, to nobody's surprise, he announced he would not return to the Philippines. Authorities charged him in absentia and mounted an extradition effort, but their presentation to a U.S. magistrate was a contradictory mess, and the judge denied it. Strunk had escaped Philippine justice.

He lived a low-profile life after that, but died on July 11, 2007, from a fall from second-floor motel balcony (which many observers assumed was a suicide). He was 67.

- Crow's apparently still sensitive about the whole "foreshortening" lecture Joel gave him several weeks ago, because he's still harping on it.
- This episode also has the first appearance of a "I thought you were Dale!" riff, which would become a staple of season eight shows.
- This episode also gives us the deathless line: "Dames like her always keep beer around."
- Trivia: Producer Joseph F. Robertson provided his own hand as the titular character.
- Stinger suggestion: Paul and the grumpy old man exchange awkward looks after Paul's failed murder attempt.
- Fave riff: "Wow! Look! She really IS smart!" Honorable mention: "And then the tape ran out."

Episode 107- ROBOT MONSTER (with shorts: RADAR MEN FROM THE MOON, Chapter 4: 'Flight to Destruction' and Chapter 5: 'Murder Car')
First shown: 12/23/89 (unconfirmed)

Short 1: (1951) The thugs kidnap Joan and take off with her in a small plane but Cody is in hot pursuit.

Short 2: (1951) Cody saves Joan but is shot down. The thugs blow another heist and are on the run again.

Movie: (1953) After invaders from space wipe out most of humanity, a surviving family confronts their robot nemesis.

Opening: Joel explains the premise
Invention exchange: The Mads demonstrate their methane whoopee cushion; Joel has the cumber-bubble-bund
Host segment 1: Reality vs. Commando Cody
Host segment 2: Crow and Tom play Robot Monster, but Joel misunderstands
Host segment 3: Crow and Tom trying to understand surrealism
End: J&tB's "tribute to Ro-Man" pageant baffles the Mads

Comments:

- It is with this episode, about halfway through the season, that the show really hits its early stride. You can feel them get more comfortable and begin to explore the premise they've created. This show has some very funny riffing, decent host segments and, of course, an iconic bad movie (and I don't like using that word much, but I think it applies here). It's one of the better episodes of the first season.

MSTIEPEDIA • 89

- It's my theory that, by riffing this movie, the Brains opened themselves up to the endless "When are you going to riff 'Plan 9'? questions. Somehow, in some people's minds, those two movies are intertwined (a little like how some people saw riffing "This Island Earth" as an affront to "The Day the Earth Stood Still").
- Joel once again explains the premise in the opening segment. I get the feeling that Comedy Channel wanted them to do this for the benefit of new viewers.
- The Bots are present during the invention exchange for the first time.
- Gypsy's light is still off.
- I must take issue with Dr. Erhardt when he says this movie stars "no one." Not really true. Maybe George Nader never went from B-list to A-list (due to personal reasons and the era this movie was made) but he was pretty well known. We've already encountered him in episode K18-THE MILLION EYES OF SU-MURU and we'll meet him again in episode 420-THE HUMAN DUPLICATORS.
- The theater seats are again green.
- Josh sneezes in the theater during the first short. Joel expresses some surprise at this, but Josh covers well. Trace just says "'zunt!" (Short for "gesundheit," I guess.) They keep going.
- When something that looks like a dartboard appears during the short, Joel's produces a giant dart. Tom Servo, perhaps fearful of what will happen to the screen, pleads with him not to use it.
- Elmer Bernstein, whose name Tom Servo seems to find amusing during the credits, went on to do some great scores (including "The Magnificent Seven" and "The Great Escape"). This one really isn't that bad, in fact.
- Yet more jokes at the expense of Isaac Asimov. I'd never noticed how often they do that in this first season.
- Servo's head explodes for the second time in the national series, during the first host segment, while thinking about bumblebees – followed by Crow and Cambot for the first and only time (I think).

- Segment 3 is a rethink of a segment in episode K11- HUMANOID WOMAN.
- This episode features the first of several references to a supposed dirty movie called "Yards of Leather." At the second convention, I asked The Brains if that movie actually existed or what? They all looked at me like I was crazy. Google is silent on the title.
- Thanks to the Urban Dictionary, I finally know what "the zacklies" are. Gross.
- Highlight: Joel's riotous narration of the love scene.
- The cave scenes were filmed on location in California's Bronson Canyon. That location was also used also in the filming of episodes 210- KING DINOSAUR, 311- IT CONQUERED THE WORLD, 315- TEENAGE CAVEMAN, 317- VIKING WOMEN, 319- WAR OF THE COLOSSAL BEAST, 404- TEENAGERS FROM OUTER SPACE and 701- NIGHT OF THE BLOOD BEAST.
- Stinger suggestion: "I cannot! But I must!"
- Fave riff from short 1: "What are the physics of a broken jaw, college boy?"
- Fave riff from short 2: "I think we've all reported to the moon at one time or another." Honorable mention: "I'm surrounded by idiots – of my own design!"
- Fave movie riff: "Okay, now tilt the camera down a little." Honorable mention: "Mother, keep digging graves. Better do two. This isn't going well."

Movie stuff:

1) The house foundation scenes were shot at a demolition site making way for Dodger Stadium.
2) The dinosaur scenes are from "One Million B.C.," and rocket scenes from "Flight to Mars."
3) Producer/director Phil Tucker tried to commit suicide after the film received awful reviews.

Episode 108- THE SLIME PEOPLE (with short: RADAR MEN FROM THE MOON, Chapter 6: 'Hills of Death')
First shown: 12/30/89 (unconfirmed)

Short: (1951) Krog sends the thugs to bomb a volcano, which causes widespread flooding, for some reason. Cody tracks the thugs to a diner, where a fight ensues and Ted is kidnapped. He soon escapes and Cody is after them again.

Movie: (1964) A sportscaster/pilot flies into Los Angeles and finds it deserted. He soon learns that reptilian monsters from beneath the Earth have conquered the city. With the help of a scientist, his two daughters and a marine, he mounts a counter-offensive.

Opening: Joel and Tom are sleepy, but Crow is a morning bot; Joel explains the premise again
Invention exchange: Joel is playing three-card monty with the bots when the mads call. His invention is cartoon eyeglasses; theirs is screaming cotton candy
Host segment 1: Crow and Tom take Commando Cody to reality court
Host segment 2: J&tB discuss how dumb the movie is, and suggest ways to make it better
Host segment 3: Inspired by the movie, the Bots fill the SOL with smoke
End: Joel bakes a pie, letter, the Mads are sarcastically happy

Comments:

- I'm not sure this one quite adds up to the sum of its parts. The riffing is about average for season one. The short, well, Commando

92 • MSTiepedia

Cody is wearing thin. And then there's the talky, foggy, completely nonsensical movie. I'd put this in the good-not-great column.

- This episode is included in Shout! Factory's "Mystery Science Theater 3000 Collection: Vol. XXVII."
- This is the first episode in which they add a blue tint to a black-and-white movie, presumably to help shadowrama be more visible. It's a practice that will continue into the fourth season.
- Joel is again in a robe (and so is Tom).
- Joel calls Tom Servo "Crow" and Servo corrects him.
- Joel calls the Mads "quasi-evil." Hmm.
- Again, both inventions are props from Joel's standup act.
- The theater seats are black again and they stay that way, thanks to the blue tint.
- Crow and Joel again duck out of the way so people can read the text at the beginning of the short. Again, Tom doesn't bother.
- Segment 1 is pretty much a continuation of the segment from the previous show, where they again rail against the absurdity of the way Cody's rocket belt supposedly works.
- Segments 2 and 3 do a good job of summing up most of what's wrong with this stooopid movie.
- Joel does the "Love-ly...love-ly" riff for the second week in a row.
- One thing about first-season episodes is that they seemed to be following the movie more closely than they would be in later seasons. At least Josh was. At one point in this episode, Servo points out: "Why are the guys carrying guns? They have no effect on the Slime People! We know that!" Leaving aside the fact that it's a major state park riff, it's hard to imagine that kind of a plot-intensive riff in later seasons.
- No Tom Servo in the closing segment.
- Stinger suggestion: The drunk looter in the theater.
- Fave riff from the short: "Come and get me! I'm a fuzzy little rabbit! I'm bring bad!" Honorable mention: "Hip? Not! Ick!"

- Fave riff from the movie: "Honestly, Bonnie, the slime you bring home." Honorable mention: "What it is, Doctah Bro?!"

Movie stuff:

1) The opening few minutes, with our hero flying in to L.A., do not in any way suggest that he is flying close to the surface of the ocean, which the characters later insist he MUST have done.
2) Our hero also says he "came through something rough." Again, the scene in which he is approaching the airport in his plane does not show this at all.
3) One of the dumbest lines of dialog ever: "Now, we've always known that there are fish in the ocean, haven't we?"

Episode 109- PROJECT MOON BASE (with shorts: RADAR MEN FROM THE MOON, Chapter 7: 'Camouflaged Destruction' and Chapter 8: 'The Enemy Planet')
First shown: 1/6/90

Short 1: (1951) The thugs have a new ray gun in a disguised truck, but Cody and Ted are after them.

Short 2: (1951) Cody and his team return to the moon and drive off with a cache of lunarium, but some moon men give chase.

Movie: (1953) In the far future — 1970 — the U.S. space program plans its first flight around the moon, but a commie spy plans sabotage.

Opening: Joel is cleaning the robots
Invention exchange: Joel shows off special paddles that let him juggle water, the Mads have invented the insect-a-sketch

Host segment 1: J&tB are playing Commando Cody and the moon man
Host segment 2: J&tB show off their line of neckties of the future
Host segment 3: SPACOM!
End: Crow and Tom are upside down reading letters

Comments:

- I'm going to give this one a good-not-great rating. The movie is just so much fluff, with very little substance and Commando Cody is really overstaying his welcome. The riffing is fine and the necktie and SPACOM host segments are first-season gems, but, even grading on the season-one curve, it's not that memorable.
- Uber MSTie Tom Noel has somehow unearthed a Cable Guide from the week this episode first aired and has confirmed the debut date, one of only two confirmed debut dates for season one.
- This episode is included in Shout! Factory's "Mystery Science Theater 3000 Collection: Vol XX."
- Joel's in a robe again in the opening, and so are both bots.
- The juggling water bit is from Joel's standup act, but I'm pretty sure the insect-a-sketch is new.
- This episode has "thin" shadowrama. Crow looks a bit strange.
- Fun moment in the theater: during a fight scene, Joel produces "Batman" (the 60s TV show)-style letters saying things like "biff!" A very Joel gag.
- Joel seems to know what the caller is telling Cody in the first short, and Servo is amazed.
- During the second short, J&tB sing the lovely Commando Cody theme song.
- Another funny bit in the theater: Joel holds up cue cards to help Dr. Bellows with his little speech about gravity.

- This ep features the first use of the riff: "By this time my lungs were aching for air." In fact, they use it twice, once in the short and again in the movie.
- The word "hexfield" pops up in the second host segment.
- I think this is also the first use of the little "buckawow" song, meant as shorthand to indicate a spot in an X-rated movie where, ahem, it goes from — um — a fiction movie to a documentary, if you know what I mean.
- And I think this is also the first use of the riff: "Get your shoes on, we're at Grandma's."
- An example of how casual this show is: There's a lovely closeup of Crow's hand (claw?) during "mail call." But it's too bad nobody has bothered to touch up the chipped-off paint.
- Creditswatch: "This episode is dedicated to the memory of Alan Hale Jr."
- Stinger suggestion: Brite Eyes writhes in super gravity.
- Fave riff from short 1: "It's me! It's always going be me. Whoever calls you, it's me!" Honorable mention: "So I'm just gonna hit you with this crowbar."
- Fave riff from short 2: "I can't believe we're trying to annihilate you! This is delicious!"
- Favorite riff: :::as Polly Prattles::: "You're over by a metric ton!" (Isn't it interesting how adding the word "metric" makes that riff funnier?) Honorable mention: "Spanking IS protocol in the high echelons of NASA."

Movie stuff:

1) This movie was initially intended as a pilot film for a TV series to be called "Ring Around the Moon." When science-fiction movies suddenly became popular, producer Jack Seaman added enough footage to the film to bring it up to feature length. This was done

96 • MSTiepedia

without the knowledge of writer Robert A. Heinlein, and he disowned the result.

2) It's interesting (to me, anyway) to compare "Project Moonbase," in which a sinister nation is worried about America's preeminence in space, and "Rocket Attack USA," (shown in season two) in which a worried America frets about a sinister nation's preeminence in space. Guess that's the difference between the optimistic world view of 1953 and the nervous world view of 1961. Did I just give somebody a poly sci/communications masters thesis idea?

Something else about that letters segment: Early in 2013, a reader wrote this to me: "When they read the letters at the end, one of the letters is from one Sam Litzinger in Hawaii. This caused me a short circuit because I hear this name almost every day. Sam Litzinger is an reporter/Washington anchor for CBS radio news. Same guy? According to his brief bio at CBS, he did attend university in Hawaii." So we asked Litzinger and got this reply:
"Ha! You've discovered my secret!
I used to watch MST 3000 all the time when I was supposed to be studying out in Hawaii. The highlight of my life so far (apart from meeting Lemmy from Motorhead!) was having my card read on the show.
Thanks for writing and reminding me of it.
Sam."
So there ya go.

Episode 110- ROBOT HOLOCAUST (with short: RADAR MEN FROM THE MOON, Chapter 9: 'Battle in the Stratosphere')
First shown: 1/13/90 (unconfirmed)

Short: (1951) Cody and Ted escape the pursuing moon men and make it back to the ship. They blast off and ... the film breaks.

Movie: (1986) In a post-apocalyptic future that looks a lot like Central Park, the cruel Valaria is the chief henchwoman of the all-powerful Dark One. But a rag-tag band of rebels is determined to overthrow them.

Opening: Joel explains the premise, then sings the human blues
Invention exchange: Joel demos his "nitro-burning funny pipe," The Mads have invented the stocking mask of the future (SM of F)
Host segment 1: Crow and Tom, in the "We Zone," make Joel do tricks
Host segment 2: Cambot's sitcom simulator malfunctions
Host segment 3: J&tB play Robot Holocaust, but Crow and Joel aren't having fun
End: Joel announces the "name the plant guy in the movie" contest and reads a letter

Comments:
- It's clear that, in 1994, Best Brains thought this is one of the better episodes of season one; it was the one of the ones they chose to show at the first Conventio-con, despite the fact that in general they were down on season one. And it was a good choice. The movie is bizarre and it's in color. The riffing is very strong for season one. The host segments are nothing to write home about, but they're not terrible either. All in all, lots of fun. And the line "It was after the apocalypse..." became a catchphrase.
- Magic Voice does not give the 30 second warning or the 15 second warning during the opening, only the final countdown.
- This episode is included in Shout's "Mystery Science Theater 3000 Collection: Vol XXV."
- Nobody's wearing a robe in the opening segment, for a change.
- The puppetry mechanism connected to Crow's jaw seems extra noticeable this week. Also, Crow seems to be clacking a lot.

- Another open flame in the invention exchange this week.
- The SM of F looks like something from Joel's standup act, but I'm not sure. I think the "funny pipe" is new.
- Another use of "By this time, my lungs were aching for air."
- The whole "the film broke" thing serves as our farewell to the "Radar Men from the Moon" series. I assume they discovered that the full short and movie together were a few minutes too long, so they decided to cut the short to the length needed. I don't really care that much, but it seems like there's a really long closing credit sequence at the end of the movie, where the riffs are a little thin, that might have been cut back instead. (However, there may have been a legal requirement to show the credits.) In the ACEG, Kevin also says they were sick of "Radar Men" by this point, so that may be the reason why the short got short shrift, as it were.
- Also note: They cut the entire opening credits for the short, which, of course, we'd already seen eight times. I don't blame them. YOU try to come up with nine sets of jokes for the same three minutes of footage. Eight was enough!
- Also, according to people who've seen the whole serial, the next installment is a recap episode, so it was now or never!
- After the film breaks Joel gets up from his seat and walks back to Cambot to investigate, giving us a rare sense of the empty space between the camera and the seat backs.
- For those who care, the Wikia page for this episode kindly provides a brief summary of what happens in the remaining installments:

"After Krog repeatedly fails to kill Cody, Retik comes to Earth so he can defeat Cody personally and oversee the plan to invade Earth. Krog's henchmen almost kill Cody's pals, but the bad guys are caught and arrested. Cody convinces the police to release the criminals so he can follow them to their secret hideout. Cody storms the villains' HQ, and eventually kills Krog and his two henchmen. Afraid of being caught, Retik takes off in his rocket ship. Cody uses

Retik's own giant ray gun to shoot at the departing rocket, destroying Retik and his plans to invade Earth." Whew!

- Joel does a turtle impression in the theater. Silly.
- I just want to note a weird coincidence. In this movie there's an evil robot named Torque (aka "Crusty"). In "Santa Claus Conquers the Martians" the bad guys have a robot named Torg. Then there's the evil henchman named TORGo... Then there's TOR Johnson... I think there's a lingusitics masters thesis in there somewhere.
- Segment 1 should probably have been shown later in the episode. We have no idea why Tom and Crow are dressed in furs and talking about the "We Zone" until later in the movie when we meet women in furs talking about the "She Zone."
- I do enjoy Joel's "crazy duck face," but it's too bad we don't get to see "snow storm in China," which reportedly is a stunning magic trick involving lots of confetti.
- "I kinda miss Earth, you guys." Poor horny Joel.
- Crow's never heard of George Clinton? What is he, a Gramercy Pictures executive?
- In the letter Joel reads, the little kid says his favorite riff is: "He's out of bang bang." Everybody draws a blank. I remember it: It was in a "Radar Men from the Moon" episode, when one of the characters' gun jammed.
- It's in this episode the we get the famous explanation as to why Servo wants Joel to carry him into and out of the theater (although over the years he made it in and out himself lots of times). As they leave the theater at the end of the movie, Servo says, "Hey Joel, you gotta come lift me over this heating grid." It isn't mentioned again until Mike's first episode, when Crow refers to it as an "air grate."
- The off-screen reason why they had to do this is: When they entered the theater, Joel/Mike could walk in, and Trace/Bill could slide over with Crow from the right, but Josh/Kevin had to be already sitting in Tom Servo's spot. So Joel/Mike had to carry Tom Servo in and hand him to Josh/Kevin, and carry him out at the

end. It does seem like Josh is crawling in with Servo in some of the KTMA eps, so it's unclear when they decided this would be the procedure.

- The winner of the "Name the plant guy" contest was announced in episode 104- WOMEN OF THE PREHISTORIC PLANET.
- CreditsWatch: Audio post production was handled by "IVL Post, Minneapolis" in this episode and again in episode 112.
- Suggested stinger: Neo stabs Crusty and then poses for a poster.
- Fave riff from the short: "Taste my steel, Jughead!" Honorable mention: "If the tank's a-rockin', don't come a-knockin.'"
- Fave riff: "I think somebody's forgettin' who's holdin' the pink slip, little lady!" Honorable mention: "Where IS the room of questions?"

Movie stuff:

1) Recognize that music during the opening and closing credits of the movie? It's the same music used in the movie in episode 706-LASERBLAST and several other Charles Band films (Band was the uncredited executive producer and the music is by his brother Richard).
2) Director Tim Kincaid (born Tim Gambiani) is also known as Joe Gage, a name he used as a gay porn director (and he is apparently a well-regarded one at that). A LOT of stuff in this movie starts to make sense when you know that.
3) Joel guesses that a particular shot was done in Central Park. He may be right. The IMDB says the locations were shot there, the Brooklyn Navy Yard and Roosevelt Island.
4) This movie makes the classic mistake of not letting us know ANYTHING about the protagonists, in an attempt to create a sense of mystery, I suppose. The result is that when our hero from the wastelands is battling Torque in the climax of the movie, we feel nothing. Even that stupid robot is a more sympathetic character.

MSTiepedia • 101

Episode 111- MOON ZERO TWO
First shown: 1/20/90 (unconfirmed)

Movie: (1969) On a colonized moon, the services of a disaffected former-astronaut-turned-"moon ferry"-pilot are needed by sinister tycoon and a woman looking for her moon miner brother.

Opening: Joel explains the premise and suggests viewers go get a nutritious snack
Invention exchange: Larry's hair is lifeless. Joel demonstrates his food teleporter; the Mads have invented celebrity mouth-to-mouth toothpaste
Host segment 1: J&tB perform a moon landing pageant
Host segment 2: J&tB conjecture about games of the future
Host segment 3: Crow and Tom fight over the women in the movie, in zero gravity
End: The bots play the "good thing/bad thing" movie review game and Joel reads a letter. Larry's hair is better.

Comments:

- I'm going to put this one, just barely, in the "good" column. The movie is just so goofy, but actually pretty watchable. The riffing is also quite good. The host segments aren't terribly funny, but they're passable.
- This episode was included on Shout's "Mystery Science Theater 3000: 25 Anniversary Edition."
- The bots are wearing robes in the opening, but not Joel.
- When Joel dances to the movie credits music, he jumps up on some sort of low platform to the left that is there in case anybody wants to dance, I guess.
- When Magic Voice attempts to announce "commercial sign in 15 seconds," her mic is off. You can hear her somewhere in the studio,

but she is very faint. It's back on for the final countdown. Either nobody noticed or they didn't bother to do it again.

- That twine attached to Crow's chin is again very noticeable.
- Joel once again explains the premise, using almost the exact same language as in previous openings.
- The Bots are uncharacteristically silent during the opening segment and the invention exchange.
- As the Mads call, Joel says: "Try not to look so happy, you guys." One of the interesting (to me, anyway) things about the first season is the way Joel didn't seem to be that upset about being stranded in space. It was only in later seasons that his character seemed to become more anxious to get back to Earth.
- Joel's invention is one of his lamer efforts, I'd say. You can pretty much see the mechanisms of everything. Or is that the point?
- Joel still has part of his invention exchange on his head when he comes into the theater.
- Josh reads that whole moon landing sequence in segment 1 like he had it memorized, but I asked him on Twitter and he said he wasn't that big of an Apollo buff – he just read the script they gave him.
- Also one minor fact in the host segment is wrong. The Eagle landed on the moon on July 20, not July 22.
- Crow is still wearing his helmet when he returns to the theater after the first host segment. Joel later removes it, causing Crow to yell "Ow! Ow!" It's those little touches that make Trace's performance so amazing.
- "I kinda miss the moon, you guys." Joel is still horny.
- Several times, the bots sing snippets of "The Wiener Man," a campfire favorite. I remember there was much fan chatter about this when it aired. It was mentioned in one of the early newsletters and there was an entry about the song in the FAQ for a while. There are a number of variations to the lyrics, but I think the most standard one (the newsletter notwithstanding) is:

I know a wiener man
He owns a hot dog stand
He gives me everything
From wieners on down.
Someday, I'll be his wife
And then we'll live the wiener life
Hot dog! I love that wiener man!

- We get another reference to "Yards of Leather."
- One of the waitresses on the moon base is played Carol Cleveland, who, the same year that she was in this, began making regular appearances on a little TV show called "Monty Python's Flying Circus."
- The down side of the higher resolution you get with a DVD is you can see little things you might otherwise have missed. Example: At the end of segment three you can see the string attaching the bottle to the glass. If one carefully pours down the wire, you can't see it, but Joel isn't quite that careful.
- Toward the end of the show, they come back from commercial and only Joel and Crow can be seen in the theater. After a few moments, Tom Servo pops up from the last seat on the left and heads over to his seat, saying: "Got my gum back." Ew.
- Gypsy's light is on at last! She again answers "Richard Basehart" when asked a question, and is again rewarded for it..
- Suggested stinger: Any portion of the floor show.
- Fave riff: "Fourth floor: Tyrannical tycoons, loose women." Honorable mention: "In space, no one can art direct."

Movie stuff:

1) It's interesting (to me, anyway), since I lived through that time period — to see an enactment of the future a lot of people considered almost inevitable right after the moon landings took place: that NASA would smoothly continue, colonizing the moon,

beginning passenger space travel, then mounting expeditions to other planets. I think if you went back in time and told the movie makers that, in the second decade of the 21st century, we haven't done any of it, they'd be amazed. (Though, as I write this, there are serious plans under way for a return to the moon.)

2) The movie takes place in the 21st century, so it's been at least 30ish years since the Apollo program. The bad guy says Kemp's "moon ferry" is 10 years old – so that means it was built in the 1990s at least. So, it's not like it's a leftover Apollo lunar module. So, why does it look exactly like a NASA lunar module? (I know, the real answer is probably because the filmmakers thought audiences would immediately recognize it as a space vehicle.)

Episode 112- UNTAMED YOUTH
First shown: 1/27/90 (unconfirmed)

Movie: (1957): Two hitchhiking sisters are sentenced to 30 days labor at a cotton farm run by a scheming, corrupt boss.

Opening: Joel explains the premise, again; Tom has a tape-worm
Invention exchange: Joel shows off the "never-light" pipe; the Mads have invented tongue puppets
Host segment 1: J&tB perform a pageant dedicated to Greg Brady
Host segment 2: Crow recalls when J&tB rigged up Cambot so they can see what Gypsy is thinking
Host segment 3: Gypsy's sick, and Tom is no help
End: Joel tries to explain the goofy guy from the movie, and reads some letters

Comments:

• The episode has some things going for it. The movie marks a real departure for the series: It's the first non-horror/sci-fi movie of the national series. (In fact, all the movies in season one, except this one, would have fit easily within the restrictions Sci-Fi Channel initially imposed on the Brains for season 8.) All in all, it's reasonably watchable, but the riffing is really only so-so and the host segments, like last week, seem to be either long marches to nowhere (segment 1) or disjointed messes (segment 3).

- This episode is included in Shout's "Mystery Science Theater 3000 Collection: Vol. XXIX."
- Crow still has the thick chin twine.
- Tom Servo states: "That's the only torso I have." That would not be true for long.
- Joel again tells the bots to "look downcast."
- The bots wince in pain when Joel strikes a match on them. Nice touch. And Joel doesn't seem to care! Why? Why were the bots created to feel pain?
- There was a certain type of MST3K fan who, when you asked them why they liked the show, would say something like "because that guy Joel was SO HIGH." Why that would be a positive attribute of a TV show escapes me, but that's just me. At an appearance more recently, Joel stated categorically that he was never stoned while shooting MST3K but, I gotta say, in host segment 1, he sure LOOKS it. I'm going to attribute it to Joel's acting skills.
- Joel also almost falls over as the segment starts (though, to be fair, there was only a very small platform behind the desk for the host to stand on – the rest was an open trench where the puppeteers stood; I once stood there, and I can attest to the fact that it would be very easy for even a completely sober person to accidentally misstep and almost fall).
- I was never that much of a "Brady Bunch" fan, so I don't really get why the detailed minutiae about the show they spout in segment 1 is funny. These season 1 "pageants" don't really stand up well to repeat viewings.

106 • MSTiepedia

- I wonder why they added the flashback element to host segment 2. Doesn't seem necessary and certainly doesn't add anything. To add time?
- Pre-movie LOTR reference: "Sauron's dark army?"
- Callback: "No dancing." (Crawling Hand); SPACOM! (Project Moonbase).
- We get several more uses of "Wonder what (s)he wanted..."
- Gypsy enters the theater for the first time (not counting KTMA) in this episode: Joel calls her into the theater to produce cotton in response to Tom Servo's query (apropos of NOTHING, by the way) about what real cotton feels like (though how exactly Tom Servo would "feel" the cotton is unclear – I know, it's just a show). Joel tells her to use her "teledyne vector" to perform this function, whatever that is.
- Gypsy's lips fall off during a very hectic segment 3. They keep going. Then when she spits out a new Tom Servo, there's no hand on his left arm. Either it wasn't there to begin with, or it fell off during the fall. They keep going.
- While we're more used to Joel stumbling over his lines, in the last half hour in the theater, Trace commits a doozy of a line flub with: "Hey, it's Grg-brg-grg-Greg Brady!" They keep going.
- With this episode, the MST3K "Fan Club" becomes the "Information Club" in the end-of-show announcement.
- Stinger suggestion: Goofy guy dancing.
- Favorite riff: "Wait...so you're my grandma, my sister, my mom ... did you marry Bill Wyman?" Honorable mention: "And who are all these guys on the floor?"

Movie stuff:

1) Ah, Mamie. Born Joan Lucille Olander, you might remember Mamie's appearance on the 1994 Turkey Day bumpers hosted by Adam West. You can read about her life in her autobiography

"Playing the Field." In 2010 she put an album out called "Still a Troublemaker." Mamie's now retired.

2) They may not have made a cotton picker out of him, but Tom's wrong: they WERE able to make a singer out of him. That's rockabilly star Eddie Cochran, playing a character named "Bong" (it was a simpler time). He was only 19 here, but sadly only a couple of years away from his death in a car crash at the age of 21. (Cochran holds the dubious distinction of being the youngest person to die in our MSTory database.)

3) "Untamed Youth" was condemned by the Catholic Legion of Decency, but reportedly it only increased the film's popularity.

4) Strange line from the movie: "I'll give ya an Italian haircut." Apparently it means slitting a person's throat. Problematic.

5) I think a brief explanation of the final musical number is called for: It feels shoehorned in, because it is. In 1957 (as this movie was being made) Harry Belafonte scored a HUGE hit with "The Banana Boat Song." The song was mostly a hit because of its different sound and of course Harry's charming singing style. But music promoters, as music promoters so often do, completely misread the public and decided that what the teeners wanted was calypso, calypso and MORE calypso. They didn't, and the whole fad folded in a matter of weeks, but not before Les Baxter jammed a little calypso number into this movie.

Episode 113- THE BLACK SCORPION
First shown: 2/3/90

Movie: (1957) Giant scorpions emerge from a Mexican volcano and go on a rampage.

Opening: The robots are throwing a party for Joel
Invention exchange: Joel has invented a man-sized party favor; the Mads have mutated

Host segment 1: J&tB attempt to speak Spanish

Host segment 2: Crow and Tom ponder the strange habits of Joel, failing to notice — until it's too late — that Gypsy is going through some changes

Host segment 3: The Bots' put on a puppet show; J&tB discuss stop-motion animation

End: J&tB read some letters; the Mads are starting to feel better

Comments:

- This is a fun, kind of middle-of-the-road episode. The movie is really not that bad; indeed there are moments where you really can get caught up in the story (though the romance between Richard Denning and Mara Corday is completely flat). The riffing keeps up with the movie, and it's pretty funny, which makes it, overall, a fun experience. But the host segments continue the trend of the last few episodes: they're mostly long setups that don't pay off.
- This episode is included in Shout!Factory's "Mystery Science Theater 3000 Collection: Vol. XXX."
- This episode is captioned for the hearing impaired! Yay, Shout! However, there are a few mistakes in the captioning.
- Nice spit take from Joel in the opening.
- Josh's make up in this show is remarkable! Quite a job. Faye Burkholder and Clayton James are listed as the makeup people in the credits. Kudos to whoever is responsible.
- There's a big goof by BBI in this episode: In the opening, Dr. F says the movie features special effects by Ray Harryhausen. It does not; the effects are by Willis O'Brien. In segment 3, Joel correctly describes Harryhausen as O'Brien's protege, even though he doesn't seem to be aware that O'Brien's work is featured in the film he's watching. In the early days, BBI didn't do much in the way research. I suspect that, until about season six, the closest thing

they had to a research library was a dog-eared copy of Leonard Maltin's Movie Guide.

- They do love that "Fentonville, east of Muncie" joke, don't they? We'll hear it several times in episodes ahead.
- Callback: "This is where they filmed Robot Monster!" (Actually, no.) "Scorpions like this always have lots of ice cold beer around." ("The Crawling Hand.)
- Joel and the bots produce giant wieners and hold them up to the screen as if they are toasting them on the footage of the volcano. At least I hope that's what they're supposed to be. I'm not quite sure the effect works.
- In the ACEG, Mike apologizes for the use of a peeing sound effect in episode 102. But he fails to mention the applause sound effect used every time Ramos is introduced in this ep. Who's supposed to be clapping, anyway?
- Gypsy's scorpion tail falls off in host segment 2. They keep going.
- Crow's Bing Crosby sounds a LOT like his Dean Martin, and vice versa.
- There's about five minutes in theater, right after segment 2, when they seem to do nothing but golf riffs. Not really sure why. The scenery in the movie doesn't really resemble a golf course.
- We get a couple of uses of the "SEEMED like [fill in the blank] … At first!" bit.
- CreditsWatch: Among the "additional production staff" is a new name: Elisabet Sandberg.
- Stinger suggestion: A shot of the Milling Around Festival.
- Favorite riff: "It's the Oaxaca steps sequence." Honorable mention: "Remember that bad thing we saw? It looked just like this. This is bad."

At the end of the closing segment, Josh simply says "Bye!" and walks off the set. And the first cast member departure takes place. Josh used to get short-shrift by many, but I think, thanks to his excellent work on Cinematic Titanic, that's changed. Looking back, Josh was clearly a gifted young man with a sense of humor and style well beyond his years. He certainly held his own in many ways with co-stars many years his senior.

The first season ended in the spring of 1990, and executives at the Comedy Channel assured BBI that a contract for a second season was coming ... but weeks went by and the check did not appear. A nervous period of waiting commenced. With no money coming in, nearly all the staff went on unemployment, the team spent their days kicking aimlessly around the studio and playing a lot of video games.

They also were making calls to various press outlets. One of those calls came to the features desk at the Philadelphia Inquirer and I overheard TV editor Jon Storm and TV columnist Lee Winfrey discussing it. Jon gave Lee the right of first refusal on the story, and when Lee heard that the interview would consist of several voices of the ensemble, he begged off. I remember him saying "I hate doing those group phone calls. I can never keep everybody straight."

Well. I had spent the spring and summer becoming a huge fan of MST3K, and I knew I could tell Joel's voice from Jim's voice from Mike's voice blindfolded. So I stepped up and pitched doing the story. Storm was wary but willing. He told me the piece would be on spec, meaning he would have to read it before he would pay me.

Jon gave me a press release with the phone number of the studio, and the phone number surprised me.

"Area code 612? " I asked. "Where's that?"

"Minneapolis." I was very surprised. Having seen months of Comedy Channel programs, almost all of which appeared to be being shot on a couple of floors of a New York skyscraper, I just assumed MST3K was being shot there too. I was looking forward to visiting the studio, since New York City was a two-hour train ride away. I really couldn't believe that a hip, hilarious show like this was being produced by Minneapolis clod-hoppers. I was much younger then.

So I called them, set up the phone call and I had a nice conversation with Jim and Joel (the crowd Lee Winfrey feared he would have to navigate actually didn't appear).

The biggest piece of news I got from the interview was that Josh was gone. During that fretful summer, Josh was growing more and more restless. He was not getting along with the rest of the cast, all of whom were at least a decade older than he. Jim attributed the split to "creative differences," but then Joel spoke up.

"Let me put it this way," he said. "He's 18 years old."

According to reports, Josh's biggest gripe about the series was that it was now being scripted. He had flourished in the easy-going, extemporaneous atmosphere at KTMA, but chafed at being held to a script. So, jumping before he was pushed, Josh departed for Los Angeles.

Success awaited, as both a writer and performer. MST3K fans watching "The Simpsons" would soon begin noticing a Josh Weinstein listed in the credits of that series, but it turned out it was not the same guy. To distinguish himself, our Josh chose a new professional name: J. Elvis Weinstein.

"I have no regrets," Josh said years later. "I'm glad I did the show, and I'm glad I exited when I did. Once the show moved to Comedy Channel, it became a very hostile environment for me to be in. Nothing good would have come out of me staying for anyone involved."

As for the article, Jon worked with me on it and everybody was happy with the results. And, someone very generous (Jon Storm, maybe) gave the article a "Knight Ridder Newspapers" byline. That meant that any of the publications in the large newspaper syndicate the Inquirer was a part of was welcome to use the article.

And some of them did. More on that later.

CHAPTER 4

With the departure of Josh, the BBI writing room was shorthanded. Mike had been promoted to head writer, and he had an idea for a writer who would fit right in, a comedian he had performed with many times.

FRANK

Frank (he was born Frank Jr., but changed it after his father's passing) is the son of a Pulitzer Prize-winning journalist and editor. Frank grew up in New York City, part of a family of five, where he spent some time as a standup comedian.
"It took me a while to get up the nerve," he recalled on a podcast, "but I did."

In the mid 1980s, he began to struggle with substance abuse and he decided to leave the city for rehab in Minneapolis. "Minnesota is very well known for its rehab facilities," he said. "Mary Tyler Moore and rehab centers."

But by the time his treatment was over, he had come to like the city and he was worried he might relapse if he returned to the comedy clubs of the big city.

"I wanted to stay away from New York, where I got into all kinds of trouble," he said.
He began doing gigs at comedy clubs across the upper Midwest. It was during this period that he struck up friendships with Mike, Trace and Bridget among others.

Frank was originally hired by BBI as a writer.

"They knew me and that I was funny," he said. "And they knew that I was a big film buff and that I had a lot of stuff in my head, which was perfect for what they were doing."

But Mike and the rest of the team suggested he try out for an on-screen role replacing Josh. They screen tested him and, as Frank put it, "apparently the camera loves me."

Frank's portrayal of the chirpy, fun-loving, off-the-wall "TV's Frank" was quickly revealed as a fitting foil for Trace's glowering, obsessive Dr. Forrester and the chemistry between the two performers became apparent almost at once.

Season two would bring other changes. For example, almost every first-season episode had been a science fiction or horror film. But in season two, with the network running out of usable science fiction films, the series would turn to other movie genres, most notably some very greasy and unpleasant biker movies.

Another change was completely revamped sets. Now, pasted into the hexagonal shapes that made up the walls of the SOL "bridge" set last season, were hundreds of little toys and found objects. Fans delighted in picking this or that recognizable shape out of the clutter in the background. And, to the viewer's left of the main bridge desk, an important new addition arrived: the Hexfield Viewscreen, through which Joel and his pals could interact with what would soon become a parade of visitors to the SOL's orbital path. In Deep 13, two other new characters were introduce: The Mole People, Jerry and Sylvia (named for the creators of Super Marionation shows like "Thunderbirds" and "Fireball XL5") who happily helped out around the place. Playing the Mole People were unpaid interns, broiling under the hot studio lights inside suffocating rubber masks.

With talented musician Mike now in command, music would become a larger part of the series. In one second-season episode, not one but two songs were presented, and the MST3K cast burst into song fairly regularly, belting out such gems as 'If Chauffeurs Ruled The World" and "The Godzilla Genealogy Bop."

Another serial would rear its ugly head: Three episodes of the dreary THE PHANTOM CREEPS, starring Bela Lugosi, would appear. And the last two episodes of the season would presage the season to come: They each featured a Japanese-made Godzilla movie.

Episode 201- ROCKETSHIP X-M
First shown: 9/22/90

Movie: (1950) A rocket ship expedition to the Moon is accidentally diverted to Mars, where the crew finds the ruins of a long-dead civilization.

The new season has a new theme song:

For episodes 101 through 512:
Lyrics: Joel and Josh Sung by: Joel and the Joels [Joel] Joel: In the not-too-distant future -- Next Sunday A.D. -- There was a guy named Joel, Not too different from you or me. He worked at Gizmonic Institute, Just another face in a red jumpsuit. He did a good job cleaning up the place, But his bosses didn't like him So they shot him into space. We'll send him cheesy movies, The worst we can find (la-la-la). He'll have to sit and watch them all, And we'll monitor his mind (la-la-la). Now keep in mind Joel can't control Where the movies begin or end (la-la-la) Because he used those special parts To make

his robot friends. Robot Roll Call: (All right, let's go!) Cambot! (Pan left!) Gypsy! (Hi, girl!) Tom Servo! (What a cool guy!) Crook! (He's a wisecracker.) If you're wondering how he eats and breathes and other science facts (la la la), Then repeat to yourself, "It's just a show, I should really just relax... ...For Mystery Science Theater 3000!"

Opening: The SOL has a new look; Joel is working on Tom and Crow has a toothache
Invention exchange: Tom gets a new voice and when Joel calls to the Mads they meet new trainee Frank; Joel shows off the BGC-19; Frank somehow has the same idea and is punished
Host segment 1: J&tB salute to the reporters of "Rocketship X-M"
Host segment 2: Joel gives a zero-gravity humor lesson
Host segment 3: J&tB are daydreaming when Valaria from "Robot Holocaust" visits on the Hexfield
End: J&tB disapprove of the movie, Joel reads a letter, Frank learns to push the button

Comments:

- And so, with the words "TURN DOWN YOUR LIGHTS (where applicable)" the next era of MST3K began. This episode is not on DVD, but it should be (I hear the rights issues are a nightmare). It's a quantum leap forward from season one, with an incredibly riffable movie, strong riffing all the way through and great host segments. A real winner and a series milestone.
- The stretch between the end of season 1 and the beginning of season 2 was 231 days.
- New things: The SOL set, the Deep 13 set, Frank, Tom's voice (Kevin), Jerry and Sylvia, Joel's jumpsuit (it's teal), a more-or-less final version of Tom Servo with several tweaks on the design, Alex Carr taking over as Magic Voice from Jann Johnson (except for Kevin filling in during segment 2) and the theme song has new visuals.

- Some connect this season to the show's move from The Comedy Channel to Comedy Central, but that's not really accurate. For the record, during the first run of season two, the show was still on The Comedy Channel. The Comedy Channel didn't merge with Ha! until April 1, 1991. (It was known for a couple of months as CTV, but there was a legal dispute over that name and they had to change it.) On June 1, 1991, it became Comedy Central. That was the same day season three of MST3K began. Season two episodes reran many times on Comedy Central, but I just wanted to note that when they debuted they were still on The Comedy Channel.
- Frank is terrific right off the bat and he brings a very different kind of energy.
- Dr. Erhardt is declared "missing." As proof, Frank holds up a milk carton with Erhardt's face on it. Younger folks may not understand that: back in the late '80s, milk cartons sometimes bore the faces of "missing" kids in hopes somebody would recognize them and report their whereabouts to authorities.
- Kevin takes over as the voice of Tom Servo, but for this and the next several episodes, he seems to be trying to sound a bit like Josh. It would be mid-season before he would truly relax and give Tom the voice we knew for the next nine seasons.
- A look at the credits confirms the swift rise to power and authority of one Michael J. Nelson. Hired less than a year ago to do "some typing," he has now gained Joel's and Jim's trust to such an extent that he has been named Head Writer.
- Tom's neck has extended before (during the "rock 'em sock 'em robots" bit, for one instance) but it now extends much further in the opening and invention exchange segments.
- The new counter at which J&tB stand is there at one moment, then miraculously vanishes a moment later when Joel demonstrates the BGC19. Then it's back again right before movie sign.

- The mole people are not yet working the camera in Deep 13. Dr. F. is controlling it via a button on a console later referred to as the "techtronic panel."
- Dr. F sounds a lot like Crow when he yells "What? NO!"
- Joel has movie sign alone and arrives in the theater with Tom and Crow already there.
- J&tB supply the lyrics to the "Rocketship XM" theme. It will not be the last time we get new lyrics to an insipid theme.
- "Once the rockets go up, who cares where they come down?" is a lyric by the great Tom Lehrer. (Look him up, kids.)
- Tom seems to go out of his way to say "Mike Nelson of 'Sea Hunt' fame." What other Mike Nelsons are there?
- The first host segment is wordy – almost overwritten compared to what we're used to – but very funny. It's a vast departure from the sort of segments we were getting at the end of season 1. But I wonder why is Joel reading the movie still's time code at the end of each of his lines. SMH.
- The second host segment is a true classic – one of the cleverest of the entire series – and it gives the viewer a small primer of the MST3K sensibility and worldview. From "The Flying Nun" to Gallagher, we get a sense of what the Brains think is funny and not funny. The only technical problem is that we never get a clear look at the floating wrench – Tom's bubble is in the way.
- Callbacks: "Spacom!" (PROJECT MOONBASE). "Dames like this always got beer around" (THE CRAWLING HAND).
- In segment 3 we get the series' first hexfield viewscreen visitor (Mike, in his first on-camera appearance) doing an impression of evil vixen Valaria from last season's "ROBOT HOLOCAUST." Folks who had not seen that episode must have been pretty baffled.
- The hexfield viewscreen is obviously still a work in progress: its opening appears to be a window shade, and then Mike just switches off a light at the end of the bit – but we can still see him!

- Then-current catchphrase: Hello, Federal!
- CreditsWatch: This is a big one. All the credits lists going forward will be based on this one. Mole person Jerry was played by intern Brent Peterson; mole person Sylvia was played by BBI staffer Alex Carr. "Head writer: Michael J. Mike" appears for the first time. Josh is, of course, gone from the writers list and Frank is added. The credit for "Joel Hodgson's Puppet Bots" is gone. Host segments "produced" by Jim Mallon. (For the rest of the season it would say "directed" by.) Trace is listed as "Special guest 'villian' (misspelled)" and it says "Introducing" Frank Conniff. Of course, the Dr. Erhardt credit is gone and Tom Servo's has changed.
- "Toolmaster: Jef Maynard" appears for the first time. Production assistant is now Jann L. Johnson alone (gone are Steve Rosenberer and Sara J. Sandborn). "Special Effects and Other Fancy Stuff: Trace Beaulieu" appears for the first time, as does "Additional Visual Effects: Industrial Plumbing and Heating." "Editor: Tim Paulson" appears for the first time. Under "Lighting," Ken Fournelle has been added. "Audio: John Calder" appears for the first time. Make-up: Faye Burkholder. Interns: Nathan Molstead, Tamra Lewis, Amy Kane, James Smith, Michelle Molhan and Robert Czech. "Video Services: Fournelle Video Production Services" appears for the first time.
- Special thanks: removed from the list are "KTMA TV23," David Cambell and Rick Leed and "Skyline Displays Inc." has been added. "Shot entirely on location at Best Brains Studios, Minneapolis," "Filmed in Shadowrama" and "Keep circulating the tapes" appear for the first time.
- Stinger suggestion: "Mahs! Extending us a velcome!"
- Fave riff: "I thought 'wormfood' was a bit strong, Lloyd." Honorable mention: "There's a Mr. 'Oh My God My Hair Is On Fire' on line one, sir."

Movie stuff:

1) Rocketship X-M" is considered by some to be a ground-breaking sci-fi movie, because it was the first American film to depict space travel seriously for an adult audience. It was made very quickly to beat George Pal's "Destination Moon" to the theaters, yet some consider it the better of the two. Its unhappy ending was unusual for its time (or today for that matter). The exterior Martian scenes were filmed in Death Valley, Calif.

2) I love the moment when the two scientists have to work out the problem with pencils – a process that one says will take hours. Ah, the days before calculators.

Episode 202- THE SIDE HACKERS
First shown: 9/29/90

Movie: (1969) A mild-mannered mechanic/pioneer in a new motorcycle "sport" runs afoul of a violent, megalomaniacal stunt rider and his scheming girlfriend.

Opening: Joel's been busy giving the bots a bath
Invention exchange: Joel introduces Gretchen the living slinky; Dr. F. has a slinky train body
Host segment 1: J&tB sing "Sidehackin."
Host segment 2: J&tB provide terminology for the sport of side-hacking
Host segment 3: J&tB have Rommel hats; JC and Gooch visit on the Hexfield
End: Joel croons: "Only Love Pads the Film," letters, Frank "will" push the button.

MSTiepedia • 121

Comments:

- In the past, this has never been a favorite. I know some folks love the biker movies, but they mostly leave me pretty cold. Still, in more recent viewings I liked it a bit better than I did in the past. Maybe it was because I finally followed the plot of the movie (such as it was). Maybe it was the nice clean print on the Rhino disk that helped make everything a little easier to follow. The songs are fun and the segments are entertaining, so, overall, it's somewhere between fair and good.
- This episode is included in Rhino's "Mystery Science Theater 3000 Collection, Vol. 3."
- Joel's jumpsuit is still teal.
- Gypsy has an eyelash.
- Boys with brothers (and any sisters who had to use the same bathroom) will get the "we were havin' sword fights" line. Ew.
- Apparently a mole person has taken over the camera work in Deep 13, but is still learning: Hence the confused camera work when we go to Deep 13 during the invention exchange. But we can also see two mole people on screen. So are there more than two mole people?
- The Rhino release of this episode came with alternate takes and outtakes. Perhaps most entertaining are the many, many takes for the invention exchange segment in Deep 13, where the back end of the slinky train prop seems to have given them no end of problems.
- Oddly, Dr. F. is, for some reason, performing the invention exchange experiments on himself. That would change.
- Crow's arm works in the opening.
- Cambot makes a rare movie riff, listing sidehacking scores.
- Before segment 2, Tom Servo attempts a little play-by-play, only to be frustrated by the fact that the sport is so new it doesn't have any terminology yet. Then, sure enough, in segment 2, what do

we get but terminology for sidehacking. You can pretty much see the genesis of the segment in the earlier riff. This sort of thing would happen in future eps, but they usually weren't as obvious about it.

- In a story that has been repeated by the cast many times (including in the ACEG), this was the episode where BBI learned to watch the whole movie before agreeing to riff it. Up to this point, apparently, they'd watched a little at the beginning of any movie they were considering, maybe skimmed a bit through the rest of the movie and made a decision. When they did that with this movie, they missed a brutal and graphic scene in which J.C. and his gang beat Rommel to a pulp and rape and murder his girlfriend, Rita.

- They tried to back out of doing the movie, but were told it was too late. So they cut the scene and did their best to write around it. (J&tB leave the theater to do segment 2 just before the mayhem begins, and when they return to the theater, the movie picks up as a bloodied Rommel wakes up from his beating.) During the morose montage of Rommel wandering the countryside mourning, Crow fills the audience in by saying: "For those of you playing along at home, Rita is dead."

- Callbacks: "There was nothing left after the ... Robot Holocaust." "Now that you're dead I can tell you about a thousand wonderful hours..." (ROCKETSHIP XM). "No drumming ... not allowed." (CRAWLING HAND). "Hikeeba!" (WOMEN OF THE PREHISTORIC PLANET).

- We get more choruses of "The Weiner Man," and "The Happy Wanderer."

- Catchphrases that came from this episode include: "That was number 5!" "He hit big Jake!" and the "It's pretty good!-It's not half bad!" interplay in the garage. And, although Ross Hagen never actually says it, the line "Chili peppers burn my gut," in a Ross Hagen-like growl, would be heard many times after this.

- The Hexfield has had a slight reworking. The window shade has been mounted on the bottom of the opening and it has some sort of mechanism to raise it at the end of the bit.
- When Joel sings his second song of the episode, It's interesting (to me, at least) that they made no attempt to rewrite the insipid lyrics sung in the movie, except for changing "...only love, only love." to "...only love pads the film." (Joel also sings it a bit in the theater.) Also, I wonder if the reason we are treated to ALL THREE verses of this dopey song is because they had to fill the time created when a chunk of the movie was cut.
- That, of course, is not a real keyboard Joel is "playing" in the final segment, and the real keyboard work, as always, is being done off-camera by Mike.
- Gypsy, wearing tambourines for earrings, joins Joel, Crow and Tom for the final number and steals the show, cracking Joel up with her contribution to the song.
- CreditsWatch: Dr. F is still a "special guest villian" (misspelled). Mole person Jerry is played by intern Nathan Molstead and mole person Sylvia is played by intern Amy Kane. J.C. was Mike, "Gooch" was Frank (the character in the movie's actual name is Cooch but Pataki seems to call him "Gooch" several times in the movie, hence the confusion.) Host segments directed (last episode it said "produced") by Jim Mallon. Toolmaster Jef Maynard is listed twice.
- Stinger suggestion: "NUM-BER EIGHT!"
- Favorite riff: "Even these oil fields seem to remind me of her. Can't put my finger on it..." Honorable mention: "You taste good too, but you're lips ... are ... drugged!"

Movie stuff:

1) It is implied that J.C. is some sort of motorcycle stunt performer, mostly because he wears a bespangled, Evel Knievel-esque outfit

in one scene. But we never see him do anything (other than fall off a side-hack several times in Rommel's back yard). I haven't seen the full movie, and maybe it was cut, but a scene of Rommel watching JC do his stunt act might have established the premise – and his megalomaniacal character – a little better.

2) You may be wondering: What in the world does "Five the Hard Way" (the original title of the movie) mean? Turns out they called it that in order to cash in on the Jack Nicholson movie "Five Easy Pieces," released earlier the same year.

3) The movie has a few hamfisted attempts at analogies to the Christ story, with Cooch in the Judas role betraying Rommel at the behest of J.C. (J.C.! Get it??) It's dumb.

Episode 203- JUNGLE GODDESS (with short: THE PHANTOM CREEPS, Chapter 1: 'The Menacing Power')
First shown: 10/6/90

Short: (1939) A mad scientist plans to sell his fiendish inventions – a huge robot, invisibility belt and exploding mechanical spiders – to foreign powers. In the opener, he fakes his death, then sabotages a plane carrying his enemies.

Movie: (1948) Hoping to get a reward, two pilots set out to rescue an heiress lost in the African jungle. They find her being worshiped by a native tribe.

Opening: J&tB are playing hide and seek with the elusive and inexplicable forces that control the universe
Invention exchange: Joel demonstrates his radio arm saw; meanwhile Dr. F.'s head is fused to a sax
Host segment 1: J&tB present the "Bela's OK Discoveries" infomercial; the Mads introduce the feature
Host segment 2: Joel demonstrates "gobos" using Cambot

Host segment 3: Two white devils visit on the Hexfield
End: J&tB in an episode of "My White Goddess," letters, Frank mimics Dr. F.

Comments:

- This one is just fair for me. The short is fun (though the print is really terrible) and movie is stupid but watchable. But the riffing is only really strong in spots, while in other places it drags. And I don't think much of the host segments.
- This episode is included in Shout's "MST3K Collection: Volume XXXI, The Turkey Day Collection."
- Tom's neck extends in the opening.
- Joel's jumpsuit is still teal.
- Once again the desk on the SOL conveniently vanishes when Joel needs more room for his invention, then reappears a moment later.
- Again Dr. F is performing experiments on himself. He would soon wise up.
- I suspect they chose to riff on "The Phantom Creeps" just so that Joel, Trace and Kevin could do their Bela Lugosi impressions. They all seem quite proud of them.
- Catchphrases from this episode: "How fortunate! It seemplifies everything!" "I'd love a hamburger sandwich and some french fried pototoes!"
- Callbacks: "The power of the dark one." (ROBOT HOLOCAUST). "Mahs! Extending us a velcome!" "We're on our way!" (ROCKET-SHIP XM).
- For those who don't understand segment 1, infomercials were brand new back then and I guess the Brains thought they were ripe for parody. The problem is that the sketch, in my opinion, has nothing clever or original to say about infomercials, and goes on about two minutes too long. Plus, unless you actually WATCHED infomercials, you wouldn't really get it. I always avoided infomer-

cials like the plague so I just didn't get it. By the way, the disc rolls right off the satellite dish and out of frame. They keep going.

- The Brains tried something different with this episode: Dr. F. introduces the short and, after it's over, during the next segment, we return to Deep 13 so he can introduce the main feature. They didn't do it much after this.
- Naughty riff: "Then I gotta wait a few minutes before I can leave."
- Segment 2 is very Ernie Kovacs-ey. You can see the early seeds of "The TV Wheel." It's not terribly funny, though some of the comments by the bots are fun.
- Segment 3 has Jim's first on-camera appearance (as "Imperialistic Alien #2"), and of course that's Mike, in his third Hexfield appearance, along with him. The sketch, however, is pretty dry. And I was annoyed by the toy gun Jim is using. The noise it makes sounds very little like a machine gun.
- This movie is only 62 minutes long, but apparently the Brains were forced to cut a chunk anyway: When J&tB leave the theater for segment 3, Mike, Bob and Greta are all peacefully coexisting around the campfire at night. When they return to the theater, it's daytime and Mike and Bob are in the midst of another fistfight.
- The ending sketch is cute, but, I dunno, they've already done several of these "unfunny sitcom with a laugh track" sketches in both KTMA and season 1. It feels like they're going over old territory. Also, note that Tom's arm works in that sketch.
- The ending sketch is the beginning of the story of how Crow ended up being called "Art" (mostly by Pearl, later in the series.) After the "My White Goddess" sketch, Joel imitates Jackie Gleason who, at the end of his TV show, would come back out wearing a dressing gown and bring out his cast members, also in dressing gowns, for another bow. One of those cast members, for many years, was Art Carney, and Gleason would shout his name with considerable gusto, as Joel does when he shouts "Art Crow!" Some little kid saw that and, not understanding the reference, just assumed that

Crow's name was Art. When he wrote them a letter, which was read in season four, he drew a picture of Crow and labeled it "Art."

- Frank mimicking Dr. F at the end sounds like an outgrowth of the way J&tB were mimicking Bob the white devil during the movie.
- CreditsWatch: Dr. F is still a "special guest villian" (misspelled). Mole person Jerry is played by intern Jim Smith. Jef Maynard again listed twice. "Introducing Frank Conniff" appears for the final time. The lyrics for the song "My White Goddess" were by Jim and Frank. Music by Mike. It is sung by "The Kevins" (which I assume means Kevin, overdubbing himself).
- Stinger suggestion: Witch doctor has an outburst, is shouted down by Greta and looks embarrassed.
- Fave riff from the short: "Put that lampshade on your head, tie femur bones around your waist and dance naked in the moonlight!" Honorable mention: "Burn the file on the electric dance belt and pick up my manhood – it's under the chair."
- Fave riff from the movie: "She thinks we speak English!" Honorable mention: "Phone THIS into Perry White!" and "We're already pretty guarded."

Movie stuff:

1) In "Mad Monster," the scientist was at least a patriot – he was planning to give his creations to the American military. Bela seems bent on selling his creations to … foreigners (gasp!).

Episode 204- CATALINA CAPER
First shown: 10/13/90

Movie: (1967) Two college boys enjoy Catalina Island sunshine, scuba diving and beach bunnies, while another boy's con-artist parents scheme to swindle a tycoon.

Opening: The bots say their prayers
Invention exchange: The Mads show off their "tank tops"; Joel has invented the tickle bazooka
Host segment 1: Joel vapor-locks as he remembers the '60s
Host segment 2: Tom sings an ode to the "Creepy Girl"
Host segment 3: TV's Frank's Tupperware party doesn't go well
End: J&tB chart the film and read a letter

Comments:

- The movie is a real departure for the show: a movie that was actually trying to be funny. They seldom tried it again, but that extra degree of difficulty is what makes the success of this episode so remarkable. This is a really fun episode. The movie is very watchable and most of the host segments (with one exception) are fun. It's a winner.
- This episode was included in Rhino's "Mystery Science Theater 3000 Collection: Vol. 1."
- Joel's jumpsuit is bright red this week.
- Frank does what I believe is his first "eyukaeee."
- During the Mads' invention exchange, as they are reeling in the target, the rope collapses. They keep going.
- Joel misquotes Firesign Theatre here. The actual line is "Fun's where the FAIR's at" (not "fear"). I guess he misheard them.
- Twice, Crow attempts another "By this time, my lungs..." riff, but Joel cuts him off. That's the kind of show this is: they'll actively forgo a joke – and then make a joke out of it.
- Joel has a memorable turn in segment one as he drifts off into a reverie about the '60s. The comment: "People smoked openly on 'The Tonight Show'" is just one of many gems. I wonder if the writers of "Mad Men" were watching. And Joel, I can relate about Woodstock. I was 12 and nobody was willing to drive me, either.
- Callbacks: "He saw big Jake" (SIDEHACKERS); Hikeeba! (WOMEN OF THE PREHISTORIC PLANET).

- Kevin really takes off in segment two with the marvelous song, "Creepy Girl." "C is for that feeling of uncertainty…!" It's really with this segment that we begin to hear the natural voice of Tom Servo.
- When the Creepy Girl is rescued by Tommy Kirk and runs up the beach to hide behind some rocks while she puts something on, I could swear that's the same set of rocks, from a similar changing scene from "The Crawling Hand." But I guess all rocks look alike, more or less.
- The "white male reality/Nazi/apartheid-loving people" jokes start off funny but wear a little thin toward the end. That said, there is sure a lot of white people in this movie.
- Unfortunately, segment three, with Frank giving a Tupperware party, is a clunker. Frank commits to the bit, and tries desperately to keep the momentum going, to no avail. I think part of the problem was the presence of Jerry and Sylvia. They're there so Frank has something to play off of, but they're just these expressionless, voiceless lumps and he has nothing to work with. Trace brings the funny at the end, but he can't save it.
- Joel mentions Crow's sarcasm sequencer – we'll get more info on that later.
- The ending segment – charting the film using the structure in Syd Field's Hollywood bible "Screenplay" – is amusing, mostly for the wacky descriptions of the characters and situations of the movie. But, it also goes on a little too long for the unsatisfying payoff.
- Joel mentions the "spiral-on-down" in passing. The last time he did that was in KTMA days. He also uses the word "MSTies" for the first time that I'm aware of.
- This episode would become infamous – and copies of it became collectors items – a few years later, when the rights to the movie expired and Comedy Central found they could no longer legally air it. It was the first movie that happened to, and it would not be the last.

- Incidentally, the historic SS Catalina, seen in early parts of the movie, had a slow, sad decline and in 2009 it was cut up for scrap despite efforts to save it.
- CreditsWatch: It's no longer "introducing" Frank and he and Trace are grouped together as "special guest villians" (STILL misspelled). Audio guy Fred Street appears for the first time. He will do audio off and on for them for many seasons. Jef Maynard listed twice for the last time. Clayton James begins a four-episode stint on hair and makeup. Jerry was played by intern James Smith and Sylvia was played by Robert Czech. The lyrics for "My Creepy Girl" are credited to "The Brains" so I guess it was a group effort. Music, of course, by Mike. There's also an additional notation: "Additional Special Thanks: Eli Mallon (Koochy-koochy-koo)." Guess he'd just been born. He'll get some screen time next season.
- Stinger suggestion: Jim Begg's "Ya got me!"
- Fave riff: "Hey, it's Gloria Estefan and the Catalina Deus Ex Sound Machina!" (One of the greatest riffs ever, that's FIVE JOKES IN 10 WORDS!) Honorable mention: "The youth of today, spent like so many shell casings on the battlefield of love." Also: "You were great! Now leave – out the back door!'

Movie stuff

1) I managed to locate John Gummoe, lead singer/founder of The Cascades, the Beach Boys-lite group that sings "A New World." I asked him if he remembered anything about making the movie. He said: "Mostly what I remember is that we did NOT want to do this song. It was arranged for us and we had no say-so. Piece of crap, as [MST3K] so aptly pointed out. And the movie was also pretty bad as well." By the way, that song was written by Ray Davies of The Kinks.

2) Tommy Kirk got his start on TV's "The Mickey Mouse Club," "The Hardy Boys" and in several successful films for Disney. His

future looked bright until another male teen threatened to publicize their affair. He was quickly dropped by the studio, and was left doing low-end stuff like this.

Episode 205- ROCKET ATTACK USA (with short: THE PHANTOM CREEPS, Chapter 2)
First shown: 10/27/90

Short: (1939) Ready for the synopsis? Strap in.

A disguised Zorka, believed by everyone to be dead, arrives at the site of the plane crash and learns his wife has been killed. Despite the fact that he caused the crash, he blames his enemies and swears to avenge her death. The pilot of the plane survived the crash but was put into a coma by the exploding spider. Dr. Mallory concocts a formula to revive the pilot, but it fails. Guessing there is some missing ingredient to be found in Zorka's lab, Mallory and military intelligence officer West go there, with reporter Jean Drew in tow. But Zorka beats them there, stocks up on supplies and escapes using his invisibility belt, though his assistant Monk is captured. West and Drew pursue Zorka and find his apparently abandoned car. West gets into the car and the invisible Zorka knocks him out and releases the brakes. As Jean looks on in horror, the car with the unconscious West inside careens down a hill out of control.

Movie: (1961) The U.S. sends spies to the Soviet Union to learn about an imminent missile attack, while trying to play catch-up with its own missile program. But failure on both fronts leads to a terrible conclusion.

Opening: Joel gives Tom a "haircut," then shows him the products he'll need to maintain it

Invention exchange: Joel has been working on a candy ribbon adding machine (Gypsy ate the Mexican jumping bean bag chair), while the Mads have invented water-polo foosball

Host segment 1: Joel explains The Charlie McCarthy hearings on un-American activities

Host segment 2: Joel is the host of a civil defense quiz show

Host segment 3: Joel's Russian counterpart visits on the Hexfield

End: J&tB explain why they're upset about the movie and read a letter; Frank suggests movies the Mads could send that wouldn't be so bad

Stinger: "Help me!"

- This is a great episode. It has three memorable host segments: the witty "Charlie McCarthy hearings," the clever "civil defense quiz show" and Mike, hilarious as the Russian counterpart. The short (as indicated by the complicated synopsis above) is action packed. The movie, on the other hand, drags in spots. But the riffing is very strong.
- This episode is included in Shout's "Mystery Science Theater 3000 Collection: Vol. XXVII."
- A first in this ep: Comedy Channel and BBI were getting complaints from viewers that Tom Servo's head was covering up too much of the screen, so they tried an experiment: they installed a skinnier version of the Executive Snack Dispenser (you can still see them at Mr. Bulky's) and announced that Tom had received a "haircut." The experiment would only last two episodes, thank goodness.
- Joel's jumpsuit is still bright red.
- Frank's "Ya got me!" is a callback to Jim Begg in "CATALINA CAPER."
- The water polo foosball thing is great but, because of the water, the foosball is floating higher than it would be if it was just rolling on the floor of the game, allowing the "players" feet to really get under it. The result is that the first time anybody connects with

the ball, it flies up and out of the shot. Frank retrieves it. They keep going.

- Despite a closeup of the prop, I didn't notice until I got to the Conventio-con, and saw the prop close up, that all the figures in the water-polo foosball game were tiny Dr. Forresters and Franks.

- Last week's installment of "Phantom Creeps" said this one would be called "Death Stalks the Highway," but it never actually says that in this episode. Chapter 2 is just called…Chapter 2. So, since it doesn't actually appear on screen in this episode, I am not including that title here.

- There's about 45 seconds of action in the beginning of this week's "Phantom Creeps" installment that is pretty much the same 45 seconds that was shown at the end of the last installment. Which means it's another situation where they end up having to write two sets of jokes for the same footage. But in one case they sort of fudged it: Crow does essentially the same Margaret Dumont joke in both versions. In one Crow says (in his best dowager voice) "Oh Captain Spalding!" In the other, Crow says, in the same voice, "But Professor Firefly!" Essentially the same joke.

- Naughty riffs: "Well, I got to third, if that counts for anything." And the classic "Good morning!" which they would use again.

- This is a good moment to clear up a common misunderstanding among some MSTies. In the short, a character whispers, "the driver is gone or he's hiding," in a very Ronald Reagan-like voice. Crow's response was to do his best Reagan impression and say "Welcome to Death Valley Days." For several seasons thereafter, whenever Ronald Reagan needed to be invoked, somebody (usually Crow) would do Reagan and say, "The driver is either missing or he's gone" or some such variation of the line. They did this so much that some fans began to believe that Reagan actually said something like this and that this was a direct reference to Reagan. He didn't. It wasn't. It was a reference to this moment in this short, where they were reminded of Reagan.

- Then-current riff: "Mallory..." "Yes, Alex?" A reference to then-hit TV series "Family Ties."
- I wonder who did those drawings in segment 1.
- Watch for two things as Joel carries Tom into the theater after the first host segment. First, you can see the silhouette of the stick attached to Tom as Joel hands it to Kevin. Second, Kevin apparently fumbles the handoff and Tom flops over.
- Whoa, slam on "Thicke of the Night" and Kip Addotta out of nowhere!
- Segment 2 really goes on and on. On the plus side, Gypsy falls over with a very satisfying clunk.
- Several times during the scenes at the Russian missile range, the slabs of concrete remind J&tB of the monolith scenes in "2001: A Space Odyssey" so much that they parody the eerie chorus in those scenes. Cracks me up.
- Callback: "The dark one awaits for the Robot Holocaust." And, a double: "The general is asking for hamburgers instead of chili peppers; they burn his gut (SIDEHACKERS). He'd really like a (as the woman in JUNGLE GODDESS) hamburger and some French fried potatoes!"
- Crow repeats the lyrics of a song called "Bombs Away" by The Police. I liked The Police, but that song didn't make an impression, so the reference went right by me.
- Another first: Thanks to one Mark Gilbertson, they've finally ironed out the Hexfield ViewScreen. It now sports a camera lens-like shutter, replacing that high-tech window shade technology.
- Segment 3 was recalled by a lot of fans when a Russian version of MST3K was discovered on YouTube.
- I can't say for sure, but I THINK the closing segment and the letter contains the last in a long series of slams on Isaac Asimov.
- The episode ends with the first-ever "stinger"–a short snippet, usually the oddest moment, from the film. For some reason they don't do one in episode 207- WILD REBELS, but after that it continues until the brief Observer takeover in season eight.

- CreditsWatch: A new element enters the credits this week: "Creative Pit Boss," a rotating job. This week it was Joel. Trace and Frank are again grouped together "special guest villians" (misspelled). Hexfield Viewscreen Designed and Constructed by: Mark Gilbertson. Sorri Andropoli: Mike. With this episode, the final credit "Executive Producers: Joel Hodgson, Jim Mallon" first appears.
- Fave riff from the short: "Stunned?? He took six bullets!"
- Fave riff from the feature: "That's why we've GOT TO CRUSH THEM!" Honorable mentions: "Oh that! My lederhosen just came back from the cleaners!" and "But underneath it was just like a bus ride in the 10th grade, if you know what I mean." Also, I love the little Road Runner "meep-meep" Joel does right before an explosion.

Movie stuff

1) Some of you young folks may be wondering who Art Metrano is, and why his name makes J&tB break out in song and dance music, accompanied by strange gestures. Metrano was a sometime standup comedian in the '60s, and he (briefly) hit it big with a silly, tongue-in-cheek bit parodying hack magicians. Soon every 12 year old in America (including yours truly) was doing it.
2) I love the line from the movie that slams cheese price supports. SOMEbody has issues...

Episode 206- RING OF TERROR (with short: THE PHANTOM CREEPS, Chapter 3)
First shown: 11/3/90

Movie: (1962) A seemingly fearless college kid must perform a ghastly task to be accepted into a fraternity.

Short: (1939) West bails out of the car before it crashes. Zorka, still invisible, steals another car and escapes. Everybody heads back to Zorka's, where the Feds revive Monk. Before they can take him in, the invisible Zorka rescues him and the two escape. Back in his secret lab, Zorka shows Monk the mysterious box holding his powerful formula. As Zorka tries to sabotage Mallory's research, Monk attempts to betray Zorka and make off with the box, but is nabbed by the Feds. As they drive him back to headquarters, one of the Feds starts to open the box, causing nearby power line towers to topple toward the car.

Opening: The bots trick Joel into thinking it's Movie Sign
Invention exchange: The Mads have an oversized "Operation" game, Joel shows off his "pin-bolus"
Host segment 1: J&tB do a commercial for The Old School
Host segment 2: Joel conducts an autopsy on Mr. Hoover
Host segment 3: The bots use subliminal suggestions as they complain about the movie; the Mads send a short!
End: J&tB react to the short; Frank sings "If Chauffeurs Ruled the World"
Stinger: "Weird. I guess that is the word for it. Weird."

Comments:

- This is a middling episode at best, with the highlight coming at the end as Frank belts out a classic song. The movie really drags everything down. Dumb, bad acting, dark, poorly cast … as Crow says in segment 3, it's a dog. The short doesn't help much either, though at least there's some action. The host segments – all of which are at least mildly amusing – really save this one.
- This episode was included in Shout's "The Mystery Science Theater 3000 Collection, Vol. 11."
- Joel's has returned to the teal jumpsuit.

MSTIEPEDIA • 137

- Tom Servo still has his alternate head.
- In the opening we actually see Joel jump into the hatch that we've been told leads to the "spiral on down."
- The "bonk!-thank you!" bit in Deep 13 is a Firesign Theatre reference. And for you members of the Church of the Subgenius, the Rev. Bob Dobson is also mentioned.
- One of the first things Tom does when they get into the theater is look the movie up in Leonard Maltin's Movie Guide. In these pre-World Wide Web days, I suspected that that book was one of their few movie research tools. It wasn't the only movie book they had, but they often seemed to default to Maltin.
- The bit at the beginning of the movie with the gate getting closer and closer is a classic example of how to make a dull moment in the movie into something at least moderately funny.
- Instant catchphrase: "Puma? Puma!"
- Callback: "Chili peppers…" (SIDEHACKERS) "Puma?" (Joel notes they're calling back to the same movie…) "It's the Power Station." (ROBOT HOLOCAUST)
- Naughty almost-riffs: Movie character says "It's going to start getting pretty sticky in here in a minute." The bots start to respond, but Joel stops them. Also: "Why are you sore?" (The bots whistle and try to sound casual.)
- Then-current word/concept: "Wilding."
- The second host segment is very funny–but a little gross and NOT to be watched while or immediately after eating!

And by the way, all these years later, having Garrett Morris as a speaker would not be that inexplicable.

- One issue I have with this episode is the conflicted message about the two overweight characters in the movie. The riffers mock the other characters for laughing at them – then they, the riffers, proceed to do fat jokes themselves. Later they become aggravated with the continued mockery in the movie, but, hey, writers, let's remember who called them "the fatties."

- Yes, the actors playing the college students are all in their 30s, and the first five or ten comments about it were pretty funny. The second 10 or 20 were mildly amusing. The 20 or 30 after that were a bit tiresome. They overdid it, is what I'm saying.
- Which brings us to a basic flaw of the movie: are the students depicted post-graduate medical students or are they undergrads? They appear to be med students (in which case they WOULD be older, though not THAT old) but the movie has them doing undergraduate things like rushing for fraternities and living in dorms. The movie can't seem to make up its mind is what I'm saying.
- And I would add: what's with the apparent "no girlz allowd" policy for the medical school? The college is clearly co-ed, so what's the deal? Sheesh.
- And what was with that out-of-the-blue swimsuit beauty pageant sequence (other than pure padding)?
- The third segment features the final time Joel asks the bots to play the "give me a good thing and a bad thing for ram chips" game that was a fixture of the first season. They don't really do it, just focusing on the bad things.
- This is the only episode in which the short follows the feature, necessitating an unusual return to Deep 13 during segment 3.
- Again, the previous episode of the short said this one would be called "Crashing Towers," but it doesn't actually appear on this short, so I am not including it in the title.
- And this is also the final episode we will get of "The Phantom Creeps."
- Frank really comes into his own with his first song, the memorable "If Chauffeurs Ruled the World" (featuring the classic Dr. F. line "Oh, push the button, Judy Garland!").
- CreditsWatch: For some reason the credits are very different this week: the font size is smaller and there is less spacing. Trace and Frank are grouped together under "also featuring" but the words "special guest villians" (misspelling and all) are missing. Jann

Johnson and Alex Carr get credits as "special guest writers." Trace was the "Creative Pit Boss." Frank wrote the lyrics to "If Chauffeurs Ruled the World," and Mike did the music. For some reason, the "Set Design" credit is not included this week. Randy Davis, who was the editor for all of season one, returns for this episode and never again. Fuller Productions is listed as the "online post-production facility," again it was used all through season one and then appears in this episode's credits and never again. I suspect those two credits are related.

- Fave riff from the movie: "Cause I'm gonna coat you with bear grease." Honorable mention: "Because he's got a squirrel in his stomach."
- Fave riff from the short: "Hmm. The plot gets weaker over here."

Episode 207- WILD REBELS
First shown: 11/17/90

Movie: (1967) A down-on-his-luck stock-car racer is recruited as getaway driver for a biker gang planning a robbery spree. He wants nothing to do with it until the cops ask him to go undercover.

Opening: Something's wrong with Gypsy but to find out what it is, Joel must shut down most of the ship's higher functions of the SOL
Invention exchange: Gypsy was just a little depressed but she's feeling better; the Mads unveil their hobby hogs; Joel shows off his 3-D pizza
Host segment 1: Joel explains that most famous intellectuals rode in biker gangs
Host segment 2: J&tB do a commercial for Wild Rebels cereal
Host segment 3: Joel and Gypsy have a nice little stroll, and he serenades her, a la the movie
End: Joel explains how to appreciate a bad movie, then he and bots start to party, much to Dr. F's astonishment. Joel reads a letter and Dr. F puts a partying Frank down for the night

140 • MSTIEPEDIA

Stinger: None.

Comments:

- I have to agree with the folks who say that this is the best of the three biker movie episodes in season 2. This ep is definitely a lot of fun. You've got a dumb but watchable movie, good and steady riffing and memorable host segments. All in all, plenty of KICKS!
- Joel, still in a green jumpsuit, is now sporting a goatee.
- This episode was included in Rhino's "The Mystery Science Theater 3000 Collection, Vol. 9."
- Tom Servo's regular head returns. No explanation is given.
- The opening explains Gypsy's role on the SOL, a bit that came in response to fan questions about her. In the ACEG they sheepishly admit that it was a little uncomfortable that the only female character on the show was distinctly cow-like. By the way, I never noticed before that Joel actually turns a little knob on the back of Gypsy's head in order to turn off the "higher functions."
- Trace and Frank are very funny in the invention exchange. Dr. F finally tries to get to the bottom of "eyukaeee," but nothing doing.
- Joel twice calls the theater the "Mystery Science Theater"–the first and last time he would do that.
- We get Gypsy's second appearance in the theater (her first was in episode 112- UNTAMED YOUTH) about ten minutes into the movie when somebody mentions "Voyage to the Bottom of Sea."
- Callbacks: "The driver is either missing or he's gone." "Thees will seemplify everything!" (both THE PHANTOM CREEPS)
- Segment 1 is a very funny sketch, including the great line "Everyone thought Joseph Campbell was tough, but that was just a myth."
- Segment 2 is an instant classic. Great line: "Like getting hit on the back of the head with a surfboard of flavor!"
- It's not in the credits, but that's Alex Carr as the voice of "Mom."
- Instant catchphrase: "That square bugs me!"

- Reportedly, this was an era at BBI when any character in any movie saying the words "I will..." was enough to get somebody shouting "I WILL KILL HIM!" as Sting did in the movie "Dune." They were obsessed with it.
- Joel says "J. Gordon Liddy." That's G. Oops.
- Segment 3 is just so adorable. Great line: "You know, I kinda feel like Mac Davis on 'The Muppet Show.' "
- The closing segment really gives viewers a primer the MST3k way to look at a movie.
- Joel says "...dark, tarry..." Hmm.
- A balloon explodes in mid-letter, the bots react in character and they just keep going.
- CreditsWatch: The font size and spacing are back to normal this week. Trace and Frank are, again, "special guest villians" (misspelled). This week's Creative Pit Boss: Jim. Jim's name, and Jann Johnson's name, appear along with Kevin's and Alex Carr's names, in the Post Production Supervision credit, for this episode only. After an episode off last week, Tim Paulson returns as editor and will remain in that job for the rest of the season.
- For some reason, this episode has no stinger. Maybe they just forgot. It was a new thing.
- My stinger suggestion: "That square bugs me..."
- Fave riff: "Personally, I like guys in clown suits." Honorable mention: "Here comes the sermon on the Gran Torino."

Movie stuff:

1) No gun dealer, no matter how naive or smitten, would ever load a gun for a customer.
2) The club where our hero meets the bikers was an actual place, a Dade County dive then called Trader John's.
3) The band playing in the background at the bar are "The Birdwatchers," a surf-rock band out of Tampa. Drummer Eddie Mar-

tinez died in the '80s. Lead guitarist Joey Murcia's whereabouts are unknown. As of a few years ago, keyboardist Bobby Puccetti was a party deejay in Florida and bassist Jerry Schills, who founded the group, lived in Dubuque, Iowa, and still played in a band. Lead singer Sammy Hall was a minister until he died in 2013. Schills, Hall and Puccetti reunited in 2012 to play a concert called "Geezerpalooza." I got an email from Schills, who said, "I don't remember much of the movie other than the whole 5 or 10 minutes we had in it took the whole damn day to film. We weren't the problem, it was just the way they do movies." Still, he says "It was an unforgettable time of our lives." I spoke to Hall on the phone for a bit. He also remembered that he was told to be there very early, and he was, but the filming still took all day. He also said he was the only one of the group who was actually called upon to act, "since I had to pretend I was playing the trumpet." Incidentally, the song they sing, "Can I Do It?"was never released commercially until a retrospective album came out in 1980.

4) The bartender is played by then-Miami radio deejay Milton "Butterball" Smith.

5) The driver of the lead cop car in the scene where the cops are pursing the bikers through the swamps is then-Miami radio deejay Dutch Holland.

6) Other than in the Marvel universe, I can't find a Citrusville, Fla. I believe Jupiter, Fla., stood in for it. There is a lighthouse in Jupiter, too, but it's unclear if that's the Jupiter lighthouse in the final scenes of the movie.

7) Also, the racing scenes were shot at the Palm Beach Fairgrounds Speedway.

8) J&tB take note of a really glaring continuity mistake early on, as the guitar is present on the car Rod is trying to sell, and a moment later it isn't.

MSTiepedia • 143

Episode 208- LOST CONTINENT
First shown: 11/24/90

Movie: (1951) A military/science team searches for a downed rocket atop a remote, dinosaur-infested mountain.

Opening: Coach Joel gives the bots a locker room pep talk
Invention exchange: The Mads unveil their exercise treadmill equipped with wheels, introduce the movie and give Joel movie sign against his will
Host segment 1: Hugh Beaumont, one of the four horsemen of the apocalypse, visits on the Hexfield with a message of unholy death
Host segment 2: J&tB's preachy "The Explorers" sketch bogs down
Host segment 3: J&tB see The Cool Thing and announce a contest
End: J&tB analyze the movie, Joel reads a letter, Dr. F declares victory
Stinger: "Well, thanks for straightening the whole thing out..."

Comments:

- This one is definitely a winner. Wacky movie, great riffing, decent host segments and, oh, did I mention ... rock climbing? Rock climbing.
- Joel, still sporting a goatee, is now in a never-before-seen cyan jumpsuit.
- This episode appears on Shout's "Mystery Science Theater 3000 Collection: Vol. XVIII."
- A message at the beginning of the Shout DVD apologizes in advance for the tape artifacts in their product. Apparently the official BBI copy was damaged or not stored properly. Upsetting.
- This is the infamous episode featuring, as previously mentioned, the mind-bloating "rock climbing" sequence. A couple of years after this episode came out, the sequence so moved one usenet

fan that he created a "rock climbing FAQ (frequently asked questions) file" that analyzed the "rock climbing" phenomenon within an inch of its life.

- During this season, J&tB's response to the movie was seen in a very black-and-white way – either Dr. F. "won" or Joel and the bots did. They never made this more explicit than in the opening segment here.
- However, Joel makes a little mistake in his pep talk: the episode two weeks ago was "Ring of Terror," not "Rocket Attack USA."
- Somebody actually attempted to market that Mad's invention. A video of it in action is (or was) on YouTube.
- Frank twice addresses the mole people, Jerry and Sylvia, who are apparently behind the camera in Deep 13.
- Joel never gets to do an invention exchange, but don't worry, the one he's holding, the sign language translator, will be used next week.
- Joel gets Movie Sign "against his will"–He refuses to enter the theater and appears to get an electrical shock to his tush. This is described as a "shock to the shammies" in episode 302- GAMERA, when Joel gets it again.
- Callbacks: "We're on our way!" (ROCKET SHIP XM) "Charbroiled hamburger sandwich and french fried potatoes!" (JUNGLE GODDESS) "Thees will seemplify everything!" (PHANTOM CREEPS) "Chili peppers, they burn my gut." (SIDEHACKERS) "That square bugs me! He really bugs me!" (WILD REBELS)
- That's Mike, of course, as Hugh Beaumont ("Cryptodad" in the credits) in yet another Hexfield Viewscreen appearance, in segment 1, and he's very funny, though the writing is excellent as well. This segment is a pretty good example of what is so wonderful about MST3K.
- Obscure KTMA reference I never got before: Joel riffs, "Maybe there was hand soap in the hydraulic fluid." A reference to a plot contrivance in the movie in episode K13- SST DEATH FLIGHT. Went right over my head in the past.

- Host segment 2 is probably inspired by the brief "asking for directions from the native" scene in this movie, combined with all the "white male reality" stuff from "Jungle Goddess." This may be the first "We're doing a sketch but it's not going very well" sketch? They'll do more sketches like it throughout the series.
- The "cool thing" bit in segment 3 is clearly inspired by the moment in the movie when the characters reach the top of the mountain, and everyone stands amazed at what they see, but they don't show us for a long time. Some of the entries they got from viewers were shown in episode 213- GODZILLA VS. THE SEA MONSTER.
- CreditsWatch: Trace and Frank are still "special guest villians" (misspelled). This week's creative pit boss: Kevin. The "Explorers Action Theme" written and performed by Mike. This was intern James Smith's last episode.
- Favorite riff: "Still talking to crap, monkey boy?" Honorable mention: "I never knew Mountain time was so slow!"

Movie stuff

1) Yes, the opening shot is the same shot used in "Rocket Ship XM." Lippert was nothing if not thrifty.
2) Actors do things in movies that real people would never do (unless they are very stupid). A pristine example is the cop in "Plan 9" who scratches his temple with the barrel of his gun. There's a moment like that in this movie: Would anyone really sit RIGHT on the edge of a dizzyingly high cliff, with their legs dangling over the side, like they do in the movie?

Episode 209- THE HELLCATS
First shown: 12/8/90

Movie: (1967): The brother and fiancée of a murdered detective infiltrate a drug-running biker gang.

Opening: J&tB have colds

Invention exchange: J&tB are feeling better thanks to vapor action, but it may cause flashbacks. The Mads are still enjoying the hobby hogs. Joel's invention is the sign language translator. The Mads just yell "NOOOO!" for reasons that never become clear.

Host segment 1: Tom's flashback: J&tB do Shatner with The Crawling Hand (from episode 106)

Host segment 2: Crow's flashback: Zero gravity humor lesson (from episode 201)

Host segment 3: Joel's flashback: Gobos lesson (from episode 203)

End: Gypsy attempts a diary entry; Crow and Tom mock her for it at first, but they soon admit they keep diaries too and everybody gets emotional. Joel reads a letter. In Deep 13, the Mads are emotional, too

Stinger: Trumpeter yells something unintelligible.

Comments:

- I laughed quite a bit the most recent time I watched this one, but I found I could only take this episode in short bursts of 10 or 15 minutes. The movie is just so meandering and pointless, and the retread host segments don't help. The movie is clearly cut from the same cloth as "GIRL IN GOLD BOOTS" (even "SIDEHACKERS" looks more professional), but the riffing is really pretty good, good enough to save this one from being truly painful. It's still not a standout episode or anything, but I had fun watching it – a little at a time.

- This episode was released (in DVD) by Rhino as a single episode in 2002.

- Just about every TV show has a cheesy clip episode, and this is MST3K's. In the ACEG, it is explained that most of the staff was going to be out of town, so the writing time was shortened and this is what they came up with. Mike calls it a "tribute to 'Family Ties'" (for the younger folks, that was an '80s TV show that seemed to have a lot of flashback episodes).

- Joel's jumpsuit is not a never-before-seen pastel green. The goatee is also still there.
- Joel mentions SPACOM, from "PROJECT MOONBASE."
- Joel finally gets to show off his sign language translator, which he wasn't able to present in the previous episode. The Mads, still enjoying the "hobby hogs" from the previous episode, offer no invention.
- In the bit in Deep 13 before the movie starts, you'll notice that it cuts off the INSTANT that Frank says: "I don't fink on soul brutha." The reason is that Frank could never say that line and look at Trace without cracking up (as seen in the "Poopie" reel). He finally managed to say the line straight and hold his laughter for about half a second, which was enough.
- During the funeral scene at the beginning, two guys are crouching behind a tombstone: a thin guy and a chubbier guy with sunglasses. The chubbier guy is director/screenwriter Robert F. Slatzer. Crow points out that the director is on screen, but when he says it, the other guy is being shown. At first I thought it might have just been bad timing, but later on they identify the other guy again as the director. So it's officially a goof by BBI. They got the wrong guy.
- Crow and Tom wear their robes in the theater for the entire show.
- Crow and Joel are very snippy toward each other early on in the theater, but then they re-enact a famous exchange from "Then Came Bronson" (which they felt it necessary to have Servo explain) and all is forgiven.
- Great moment when the shot moves to the gangster and his dog sitting in the convertible and all the riffers can do is laugh.
- Several times the bots reprise bits of the Weiner Man song.
- Callbacks: Several variations on "That was number 5!" (SIDE-HACKERS). Ross Hagen's name appears in the credits and there are numerous callbacks to SIDEHACKERS. Later, "He hit Big

Jake!" (SIDEHACKERS) and "Yew and your daughter are doomt!" (ROBOT HOLOCAUST)

- Kids, in the host segments, that thing sitting on the desk was known as a "typewriter." It was a very lo-fi word processor and had a REALLY slow internet connection.
- Servo notes that the flashback he introduces happened "before my voice changed."
- Note that Crow's arm works in segment 2.
- Toward the end of the movie, Tom spots a fire hydrant and makes a pass. Joel reins him in.
- In the closing bit in Deep 13, Frank uses a little AA lingo with the line: "work the steps, Doctor."
- CreditsWatch: This week's Creative Pit Boss: Joel. "Villians" still mispelled. Additional Music: Mike.
- Favorite riff: "Now Ross can put the star on the tree." Honorable mention: "They're all piano tuners." "I like to shoot heroin straight into my head." "Looks like she's into safe walking."

Movie stuff:

1) Some of the music for this movie was arranged and produced by well-regarded producer Richard Podolor (misspelled "Podlor" in the credits) who also produced Three Dog Night, Iron Butterfly and Steppenwolf. (By the way, there was a soundtrack album. Yes, there was.) The act Podolor tried to push in this movie was a group called Davy Jones and the Dolphins. Their career still went nowhere.

2) Incidentally, when Crow (wrongly, by the way) suggests that the Davy Jones of Davy Jones and the Dolphins is the same Davy Jones as the guy in The Monkees, Joel says "He would have been about 14 at the time." Uh, no. This movie was made in '67, a year after the Monkees TV show started. So, although Joel's reasoning is wrong, he's right: this group had nothing to do with The Monkees.

3) So, who were these guys? They were a group out of Connecticut founded in 1960 by a guy named David John Liska with his brothers Walt (bass guitar, he left the band in 1962) and Richard (who played steel guitar and keyboard). Also in the band at the time of "Hellcats" were lead guitarist Paul Bogel and drummer Bob Vilezanti (replacing original drummer John Urbanik, who left in 1965). In 1966 the four-piece band went to L.A. to record the songs for "Hellcats." They made a USO tour of Vietnam. When they returned to Connecticut they built a recording studio in New London called East Coast Sound Studios (no longer in existence as far as I can tell).

4) In 1970 the group was signed by Columbia Records, had their name changed to Crossroads and had a moderate hit with a song called "Shannon," but couldn't follow up. In 1974, David and Richard formed a bluegrass band called "Kentucky Wind" and toured for a while. In 1981, David moved to Nashville and wrote for various publishing companies. In 1991, David and Richard and their families moved to Nevada and formed a country-western group called "David John and the Comstock Cowboys." They were regulars at the Famous Bucket of Blood in Virginia City, Nev., but Richard died in 2010 and it's unclear how busy the band has been since then.

5) There's also music in this movie from a group called Somebody's Chyldren. The group was founded by David Clark Allen. I was able to email Allen and he told me their music got into the movie because it was promoted by their producer, a guy named Chance Halliday. Halliday had a few singles of his own, but Google is virtually silent, as far as I can tell, about his work as a producer.

6) I know, the plot's in tatters by the end, but when I watched it recently, I wondered how the biker gang knew to go to the docks and not the bad guy's office. It might have been cut for time.

7) Coleman Francis' drinking buddy, Tony Cardoza, produced this movie, so lots of Coleman's regulars are in it, along with some

150 • MSTiepedia

SIDEHACKERS alumni. Cardoza produced and appeared in all three of Francis' movies, which we'll encounter in later seasons.

Episode 210- KING DINOSAUR (with short: "X MARKS THE SPOT")
First shown: 12/22/90

Short: (1944) Careless New Jersey driver Joe Doakes finds himself in a heavenly courtroom, on trial for his vehicular misdeeds. His guardian angel is his only defense.

Movie: (1955) Two scientist couples are sent to investigate a mysterious new planet and are menaced by snakes, gators, giant bugs and other scary process shots.

Opening: Joel reads some beat poetry
Invention exchange: A crushed Dr. F. declares that he, "the pocket scientist," is his invention; Joel's accidental invention is the "incredibly stinky sweat socks."
Host segment 1: Crow asks: "Am I qualified?"
Host segment 2: J&tB introduce Joey the lemur
Host segment 3: Joel objects to the "Emotional Scientist" sketch
End: Crow and Tom complain about all the Lippert's movies, Joel shows off his theramin, Tom reads a letter
Stinger: Gator wrestling aftermath

Comments:

- This is a fun episode. Between the short, the goofy Lippert movie, Joey the lemur (he wasn't a lemur) solid riffing and a some memorable host segments, there's plenty to enjoy.
- This episode was included in Shout's "Mystery Science Theater 3000 Collection: Vol XXIII." Incidentally, I did not steal the

description of the movie that appears on the jacket of that episode. THEY borrowed MY description (see above), with my permission, of course. They said they just liked it.

- Joel's goatee is gone – but Crow and Tom are wearing them in the opening bit. He is still wearing the pastel green jumpsuit from last week.
- Sir Goofus von Drakesnot is a funny name.
- In the opening Dr. F. is seen working on an elevator in Deep 13. Like a lot of things on this show, it appears when needed then is forgotten about. It would reappear a few other times.
- Joel finally provided an explanation to the "hat party" reference, one that had been bugging people for years. It has to

do with magic conventions that he and his friends attended, which often had activities for wives of the attendees. At one convention there was a "hat party," and the blurb for it asked: "Will yours be the grandest of all?" or something like that.

- Neither the "pocket scientist" nor the "incredibly stinky sweat socks" are actual inventions, but the former is a very nice illusion and the latter is a pretty funny prop. So I will let them slide.
- With this episode we get our first real short, and it's clear immediately that this works much better for the show than the serials they'd been using. This isn't (I don't think) a classroom short, unless it was something Traffic Court made you watch after you got too many moving violations.
- Crow's inspirational speech in segment 1, including the brilliant, immortal words "Crush someone with an emotional word or an enigmatic look," is one of the funniest segments of the season.
- Callback: "That was number 2!!" (SIDEHACKERS)
- Yes, the gecko-Roman wrestling is the same footage from "One Million B.C." we've seen before. Also, Bronson Canyon was used for some exterior shots, as was done in many other MSTed movies.
- "I'm a pan-dimensional being" is a "Hitchhiker's Guide to the Galaxy" reference.

152 • MSTiepedia

- One of the highlights of this episode is the series of riffs in which Joel, in a gravelly voice, says "Hi, I'm Satan!" every time a snake appears. As these bits go on, they wander into a whole Kraft cheese thing, climaxing with Tom offering a very strange recipe, as announcer Ed Herlihy. Great stream-of-consciousness riffing.
- Segment two has, of course, the infamous "Joey the lemur" bit. Now, I like the "handmade" nature of the show as much as the next guy, but what the heck is going on with Joel? Was this planned? Did he just go off script for the heck of it? I have no idea what he's even saying half the time. In episode 611- LAST OF THE WILD HORSES (after Joel's departure) they do a very funny parody of this bit, implying that even they were baffled by it.
- Segment two, in addition to being weird, is also out of order. The "lemur" hasn't appeared in the movie yet. But it does seem like they are aware of it: Joel sort of backfills as they re-enter the theater.
- Great "Twin Peaks" reference: "The owl footage is not what it seems."
- Over the years, many fans have noted that the "lemur" in this movie is actually a kinkajou.
- Segment three is sort of another "we're trying to do a sketch but it's not going well" sketch. It was "meta" before (most) people said "meta."
- Naughty riff: "I'm gonna load up the steely dan."
- The closing bit is also a bit "meta." It's only been a few episodes since Joel did a presentation using the "series of sketches" and/or a musical tribute. They're already they're making fun of it?
- The letter that Tom reads is notable. It's, I think, the only time anybody on the show uttered the phrase "host segment." Tom pretends not to know what they are (though they're mentioned in the credits).
- CreditsWatch: This Week's Creative Pit Boss: Trace. "Villians" is still misspelled. Intern Nathan Molstad played Jerry the mole person. Additional music: Kevin and Mike.

MSTIEPEDIA • 153

- Fave riff from the short: "He said a silent prayer to Bongo, the god of gravity." Honorable mention: "...but I did find him down by the waterfront dressed in a Spartan costume."
- Favorite riff: "I'm Chirpy the mutant hellbeast, and I don't like this film." Honorable mention: "Relax?! There's a bee the size of a moose over there and you want him to relax??" and "There is a margin for shame, however."

Episode 211- FIRST SPACESHIP ON VENUS
First shown: 12/29/90

Movie: (1959) Scientists determine that an object bearing a garbled message came from Venus, so a multinational space mission travels to the planet to investigate.

Opening: Joel adjusts Tom Servo's sarcasm sequencer
Invention exchange: The adjustment goes well, maybe a little TOO well. Joel's invention is a junk drawer starter kit; the Mads can't find their invention in THEIR junk drawer, but they DO find Abe Vigoda
Host segment 1: Crow and Tom make a robot that speaks in foam; things get kinda foamy
Host segment 2: A menacing gorilla appears on the hexfield, but Tom soothes it with a song
Host segment 3: J&tB present a commercial featuring some possibly tasty(?) Klack recipes
End: J&tB offer their opinions of the movie: Crow liked it, it brought back memories for Joel and Tom gets so sarcastic his head explodes; letters; Tom revives and everybody is happy, which makes Frank happy and Dr. F. is nauseous
Stinger: The alphabet people wave good-bye
- Overall I like this ep, though portions of the movie make my head (and eyes) hurt a little. The movie is almost too watchable, a truly

bizarre vision of an international (but not necessarily any more competent) future and a genuinely alien depiction of Venus. The riffing is very strong: as we come down to the end of the season two, they really have a grasp on what they're doing and why they're doing it. The host segments are, as usual, a mixed bag, but there are definitely some highlights.

Comments:

- In the ACEG, Kevin says that after this one was over, "I for one had a good, long cry." I think that's a little harsh. As Crow says of the movie at the end, I kinda liked it.
- This episode was included in Shout's "20th Anniversary Edition."
- Joel's is back to the cyan jumpsuit.
- The opening features the well-remembered "sarcasm sequencer" sketch, featuring yet another dig at Best Brains' least favorite comic, Gallagher (now gone to that great comedy club in the sky).
- And speaking of riff targets who have passed on, that's Mike as "Abe Vigoda's back."
- A reference to "Roseanne singing the National Anthem" demonstrates the danger of topical humor. How many people even remember that incident?
- Segment one … sigh. I suspect they built the prop and then tried to write a sketch around it. Not much there.
- Host segment two, while generally lame, is highlighted by the golden Irish tenor voice of Kevin. When asked to sing at public appearances, he generally choses this little ditty. Inside the gorilla suit is a fellow named Crist Ballas. This was his first involvement with the show (according to the credits, anyway), but he went on to do hair and make up for 11 other episodes (mostly when Andrea DuCane couldn't make it, apparently).
- Somebody smarter than me tells me Joel's math problem is kind of a trick question and the answer is: any integer.

- Joel says "permersion" at one point. I think he meant to say "permission." They keep going.
- Obscure reference: Crow's mutters: "...strange figgahs, weird figgahs...," an homage to a memorable moment in The Marx Brothers film "Animal Crackers."
- Host segment three's clever but nauseating parody of the equally nauseating commercials often featured on TV's "Kraft Holiday Playhouse," is hilarious but a little gross. It also seems to be an extension of the Satan/Kraft commercials they were doing in the theater in the previous episode.
- Callback: I'm on my way! (ROCKETSHIP XM)
- Tom Servo's head explodes in the final segment. That hasn't happened in a while.
- CreditsWatch: This Week's Creative Pit Boss: Mike. "Villians" is still misspelled. The "Klack Holiday Parade" music was by Mike. Kevin wrote "O Sweet Mother o'Mine."
- Fave riff: "Any interest I had for them getting safely off the planet has been completely erased by a miasma of boring technical stuff!" Honorable mention: "At least we have our ewok suits to cheer us up." Astronaut: "I'm not getting you!" Tom: "I'm getting the Ha! Channel."

Movie stuff:

1) Polish physician and prolific sci-fi writer Stanislaw Lem wrote the novel, "Astronauci" ("The Astronauts") in 1951, and he helped convert it into the screenplay for "First Spaceship On Venus." But somehow it got away from him. After seeing the film, he repudiated it.

2) The characters keep referring to the "Tunga" meteor. Was "Tunguska" too hard to say? Also: When they get to Venus, the astronauts keep making these huge conjectural leaps that I really don't see a basis in hard evidence for. The little bobbly toy things are communication devices? They all seem so certain of this, but I

156 • MSTIEPEDIA

don't see why. The whole visit to Venus is like that: "I've made one small observation so it's obvious the whole planet works like THIS." Hey, maybe that's why ol' Stanislaw disowned it.

Episode 212- GODZILLA VS. MEGALON
First shown: 1/19/91

Movie: (1973) Godzilla and size-changing robot Jet Jaguar defend Japan from Megalon and alien cyborg Gigan, who have been sent by underground civilization Seatopia.

Opening: J&tB are in morning magazine show mode
Invention exchange: Both Joel and the Mads show off their easy-to-make Halloween costumes
Host segment 1: Crow and Tom argue over whose monster is more powerful
Host segment 2: Rex Dart, Eskimo spy!
Host segment 3: Crow and Tom pretend they're a certain well-known popcorn magnate and his grandson
End: Joel gives Crow and Tom new arms, the Jet Jaguar fight song is translated, the Mads are playing video games
Stinger: Godzilla takes the plunge.

Comments:

- A terrific episode, certainly one of the highlights of season two. Very strong host segments, very witty riffing and a reasonably watchable movie with plenty to riff on. It's also our first taste of the many Japanese movies to come next season.
- Joel has donned the maroon jumpsuit, which he will stick with until well into season three.
- The rights to the movie in this episode were apparently not properly cleared by Rhino when it released it as part of its Vol. 10 DVD

set, and Rhino was forced to withdraw the set. It later re-released the other three titles, along with the addition of episode 402- THE GIANT GILA MONSTER, in what it called "Volume 10.2."

- The opening bit is hilarious. I always wondered what Wanda Vacale's Whale of a Tale was all about, and why it would be of special interest to bachelors.
- The "explaining pain to Crow" bit is not new. Joel does the same thing to Gypsy in episode K03- STAR FORCE: FUGITIVE ALIEN 2 while trying to explain what taking drugs is like.
- The invention exchange is fun. Joel's "easy-to-make Halloween costumes" are straight from his standup act.
- The button on the desk breaks when Movie Sign hits the first time.
- Joel says "...before eating – uh, I mean after eating..." They keep going.
- Classic running gag: "These darn stairs..."
- Not really made clear in the host segment 1 is precisely what Tom and Crow are looking at that they don't want Joel to see. Looks like Polaroids. Hmm... (In the ACEG, Mike says they are "naughty pictures.")
- Host segment 2 is pretty random, but it's fun.
- Two KTMA riffs pop up: "That monster does not know the meaning of 'around' " and when somebody mentions evacuating, Joel says "sounds painful," something Crow said often in the KTMA season.
- Host segment 3 is a brilliant piece of work, but is now somewhat dated with the passing (in 1995) of Orville Redenbacher and the consequent end of the TV spots featuring him and his grandson Gary. Interestingly, it appears the sketch was somewhat prescient. With Orville's death, the younger Redenbacher does indeed seem to have disappeared into the night. (He's actually an attorney these days.)
- The final half hour of the show, with Tom and Crow as wrestling announcers, is great fun. "He's got a tree!"
- At the end of the movie, Joel explores the space between Cambot and the seats a bit, for the first time since "the film broke" in season one.

158 • MSTiepedia

- The end segment features the hilarious "English translation" of "Jet Jaguar Fight Song," as well as another open flame on set.
- The final bit in Deep 13 demonstrates the passion for video and computer gaming that was growing at BBI.
- CreditsWatch: This Week's Creative Pit Boss: Joel. This is the last episode that has the "Creative Pit Boss" credit. "Villians" still misspelled. "Rex Dart Action Theme": Mike. This was intern Tamara Lewis' last episode.
- Favorite riff: "He's got a tree! He's got a tree! This isn't the Godzilla we know!" Honorable mentions: "I know I'm supposed to be scared and all, but all I can think of is sweaty Japanese guys." "This watery manifestation of a vengeful, wrathful God couldn't have come at a worse time."

Movie stuff:

1) Ever wonder what the lyrics to the song REALLY are? Thanks to Marissa at the MST Discussion board, here they are:

Japanese:
Hito ga tsukutta robotto da kedo,
Jetto Jagaa, Jetto Jagaa,
Yatta, Jetto Jagaa
Yuke, yuke, heiwa o mamoru tame,
Minna mo odoroku yuuki wo miseru
Gojira to Jagaa de panchi, panchi, panchi
Nakuna, bokura mo ganbarou

English:
You're a robot made by humans, but
Jet Jaguar, Jet Jaguar,
You did it, Jet Jaguar
Go, go to protect peace

We are all surprised at the courage you show
Godzilla and Jaguar punch, punch, punch
Don't cry, let's do our best
Don't touch my bags if you please, Mr. Customs man. (Just kidding.)

Episode 213- GODZILLA VS. THE SEA MONSTER
First shown: 2/2/91

Movie: (1966): Searching for his brother who was lost at sea, a guy and his pals wash up on an island, guarded by crab-shrimp monster Ebirah, where some sort of evil paramilitary group has built an installation, unaware that Godzilla is asleep in a cave nearby. The brother turns out to be on an island nearby worshiping Mothra. Got all that?

Opening: Joel reads "The Velveteen Rabbit" and does all the voices
Invention exchange: Joel shows off his mind-controlled guitar, while the mads have doggie chew toy guitars.
Host segment 1: J&tB sing "The Godzilla Genealogy Bop"
Host segment 2: Joel succumbs to space madness and begins building very bad models
Host segment 3: Despite Joel's warning, Crow and Tom spoof the Mothra twins, only to meet Mothra on the Hexfield
End: J&tB discuss famous sayings actors didn't actually say and look through some "Cool Thing contest " entries; the Mads consider a corporate re-think
Stinger: Everyone bows down before Mothra

Comments:

- There's no avoiding comparing this to the previous ep, since they're both Godzilla movies. This one isn't quite the classic last week's outing was, but it's still lots of fun. The plot is a little more confusing, but I chalk that up to the editing by Film Ventures International. All the host segments are worth at least a few laughs, and the riffing is solid throughout.

- This episode is not yet commercially available (and seems unlikely to ever be).
- For the first time since Joel admonished Crow a few episodes back, he again goes for the Lloyd Bridges "By this time my lungs were aching for air" riff.
- For some reason J&tB wait for the FVI credits to be over before entering the theater. Was this something contractual, I wonder?
- Callbacks: "Rock climbing!" (LOST CONTINENT) "You and your friends the only creeps in this joint." (WILD REBELS) "Linda!" (WOMEN OF THE PREHISTORIC PLANET)
- Just for the record, what Joel is reading in the opening segment is nothing even remotely like the real "Velveteen Rabbit."
- Local reference: Somebody mentions Trip Shakespeare, a Minnesota-based band some BBI staffers knew.
- Joel actually sort of acts during segment two. Not that Joel isn't performing all the time on the show, but let's face it, Joel Robinson the character is not that far removed from Joel the guy. But in this scene he has to actually act like he's kind of crazy. He does a good job, I think!
- Then-current reference: Bhopal. Kind of a dark riff.
- I thought the "Karl Malden's nose!" line of the "Godzilla Genealogy Bop" was just a non sequitur, but this time I noticed a little random throw-away riff where they observe that Godzilla has a nose a lot like Karl's, which I guess is where that line came from.
- Incidentally, the "Godzilla Genealogy Bop" is one of those songs some fans forget, but it's quite a lot of fun.
- That's Mike as the voice of Mothra, of course, in segment 3.
- It seems like they wanted to have the Mothra prop blink, but couldn't come up with a mechanism, so they sort of shaded the light that was shining on his eyes. Didn't really work.

- Another then-current reference: "Cocooning," was one of those short-lived buzzwords that arose when the 200-channel cable universe arrived and just about every movie you could think of was on VHS, so people supposedly stopped going out and just stayed home taking in entertainment in their "cocoon." Wikipedia says it was coined by none other than Faith Popcorn, who was later parodied by the Brains.
- NOT-current reference, as Crow points out: "Thicke of the Night," a talk show hosted by actor Alan Thicke (father of recent pop star Robin Thicke).
- Trivia: The script for this movie was actually written for King Kong, but Godzilla was substituted when rights to Kong weren't available. What about Frankenstein?
- CreditsWatch: The whole "creative pit boss" thing is gone. "Villians" is still misspelled. Makeup lady Faye Burkholder must have tossed out some riffs that got used, because she was added to the list of writers for the first time since the KTMA era. Burkholder also gets a co-writing credit with Kevin on the "Geneaology Bop." Mole person Sylvia was intern Robert Czech and mole person Jerry was intern Nathan Molstad. And the "Squeeky" Toy Orchestra (the people providing all the additional squeaky-toy noises during the Mads' invention exchange) were Mike, Jef Maynard and Alex Carr.
- Favorite riff: "It's the Mothra Graham Dance Troupe." Honorable mention: "What a party! That last shot I saw crabs!"
- Early in 1991, in the middle of the second season, the Comedy Channel and its rival, Ha!, merged to become (after some confusion where it had to change its name) Comedy Central (hereafter called CC). While this was bad news for most of the series currently airing on the Comedy Channel -- very few of them made the transition -- it was good news for MST3K. Seeing MST3K as its signature series, CC executives wanted to lock in BBI, and

offered them a deal almost unheard-of in the industry -- three 24-episode seasons.

Delighted, the Brains signed eagerly, and returned to Minneapolis to a enjoy a rarity in the television world —long-term security. They set about grinding out episode after episode, and this was one of their most fertile periods.

Movie stuff:

1) What's the name of this movie?, you may be asking. Well, it was "Gojira – Ebira – Mosura: Nankai No Dai Ketto," in the original Japanese (translation: "Godzilla – Ebirah – Mothra: The Great South Seas Duel"). But it had other names in various incarnations, including "Ebirah, Horror of the Deep" (also "Ebirah, Terror of the Deep") when it was released in England, "Big Duel In The North" (also "Big Duel In the North Sea"), "Ritorno Di Godzilla" ("The Return Of Godzilla") when it was released in Italy and, for some reason, "Frankenstein Und Dis Ungehauer Aus Dem Meer" ("Frankenstein and the Monsters from the Sea") when it was released in Germany. Frankenstein?

2) This is our first FVI title. For those who don't know, Film Ventures International was a company that obtained the rights to films after the copyright expired, and then re-edited and re-marketed the film (sometimes under a different name, sometimes not). We'll get more FVI titles next season. By the way, the clips used during the opening credits are from "Son of Godzilla."

3) As the characters sneak into the installation, it's another classic case of a bad guy's building with hallways that have structures that stick out from the walls, making sneaking around easier. Only in the movies.

4) Ever wonder what the lyrics to the song REALLY are? Thanks to Marissa at the MST Discussion board, here they are:

Japanese:
Hito ga tsukutta robotto da kedo,
Jetto Jagaa, Jetto Jagaa,
Yatta, Jetto Jagaa
Yuke, yuke, heiwa o mamoru tame,
Minna mo odoroku yuuki wo miseru
Gojira to Jagaa de panchi, panchi, panchi
Nakuna, bokura mo ganbarou

English:
You're a robot made by humans, but
Jet Jaguar, Jet Jaguar,
You did it, Jet Jaguar
Go, go to protect peace
We are all surprised at the courage you show
Godzilla and Jaguar punch, punch, punch
Don't cry, let's do our best
Don't touch my bags if you please, Mr. Customs man. (Just kidding.)

PHOTOS

In his standup act, Joel billed himself as a "comic, magician and spy."

Jim made good on a campaign promise to "bring the Statue of Liberty" to the University of Wisconsin.

The bizarre short "Mr. B. Natural' was a fan favorite.

Scientista Dr. Clayton Forrester and Dr. Laurence Erhardt were the earliest "Mads."

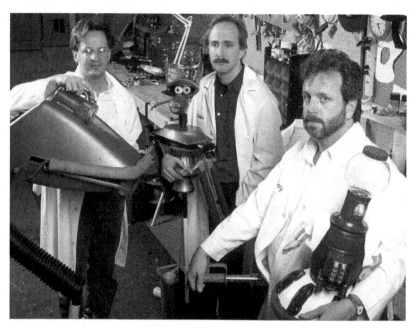

Building bots are, from left, Jim Mallon, Trace Beaulieu and Kevin Murphy.

Building sets are, from left, Jim Mallon, Kevin Murphy, Trace Beaulieu and new hire Michael J. Nelson.

Mad scientists Dr. Erhardt (J. Elvis Weinstein) and Dr. Forrester (Trace Beaulieu), as they appeared in the first Comedy Channel season.

Joel and the Bots, rough-housing.

Joel and the bots pose for a nice photo.

Frank's appearance as a trainee in Deep 13.

A wacky Comedy Central promotional image.

Mike Nelson cavorts with the bots.

The early KTMA set was rough.

Another fan favorite was "Manos" the Hands of Fate.

Crow, Mike and Tom, hangin' out.

A favorite sketch feature Mike as "Jack Perkins."

The image known as "Shadowrama."

The Amazing Colossal Episode Guide, ACEG for short,

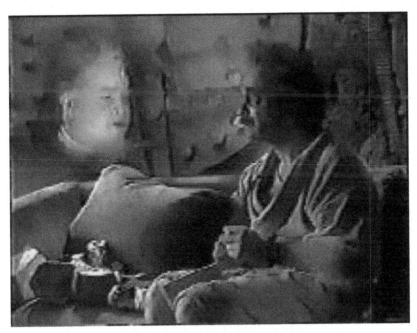

Trace plays a weepy Dr. F singing "Who Will I Kill."

The iconic "Spaghetti Ball."

The Comedy Central era "Mads."

CHAPTER 5

As they embarked on season three, they turned to material they knew was a riffing gold mine. The team ordered and re-riffed nine of the films that they'd riffed during the KTMA season, including five Gamera movies, the two FUGITIVE ALIEN movies, the mind-boggling TIME OF THE APES, and the incomprehensible MIGHTY JACK, all Japanese films imported to the U.S. by one Sandy Frank. Impresario Frank became the target of numerous barbs from the cast. One example: a lustily sung song in which Joel and the bots declared: "We wanna stick it to Sandy Frank/and sit on his chest/ and gob on his face/and make him cryyyy."

According to some reports, when Frank learned that he was being mocked by name on national television, he was not amused. The jibes would come back to haunt the series later.

For several of its other titles in season three, the team turned to the genre it would be best known for the classic 1950s quickies by Roger Corman and Bert I. Gordon, including THE AMAZING COLOSSAL MAN, its sequel WAR OF THE COLOSSAL BEAST, IT CONQUERED THE WORLD, EARTH VS. THE SPIDER, TEENAGE CAVEMAN and VIKING WOMEN AND THE SEA SERPENT. BBI would also return to TV movies, taking on two MASTER NINJA outings and the bland STRANDED IN SPACE.

For most of season three, BBI set up a see-saw rhythm in its movie choices: an American film, followed by a Japanese film, then back to a domestic title, and so on. To accompany the movies, when filler was needed, BBI shifted from the movie serials that had dominated the first two seasons to short one-reelers (most of which were provided by New York City-based film archivist Rick Prelinger), including a number of educational films with titles like "Using Your Voice," "Posture Pals" and "Appreciating your Parents." And, late in the season, their choice of an ill-considered promotional film made by a musical instrument manufacturer, entitled "Mr. B Natural," would turn out to be one of the highlights of the entire series. Episodes of season three began airing June 1st, 1991.

In late summer, the network and BBI agreed to have a marathon of the series on Thanksgiving Day, and the network requested "bumpers" that would run in between the episodes to pull the marathon together. BBI responded brilliantly, producing the now-classic bumpers in which Dr. F. attempts to conquer the world while Frank entertains Thanksgiving Day guests.

Helping to write the bumpers was a recent addition to the BBI staff, a local comic and writer named Paul Schersten, who went by the stage name Paul Chaplin.

PAUL

Paul was born and raised in the Chicagoland suburbs and received a Master's degree from the Humphrey Institute of Public Affairs.

He found his way to the Twin Cities comedy scene where he learned from different kinds of comics.
"Mostly," he recalled in an interview, "what I remember are all the guys who'd do the same basic set, time after time after time, hardly ever getting great laughs, hardly ever trying anything new. That's the challenge of stand-up: doing the same material many times in a way that it seems to be coming off the top of your head. I liked writing, though. It was just kind of a kick to see if you could come up with something that would make an audience laugh."

Paul had heard of MST3K but had never seen an episode when he was asked to try out.

"I knew Mike worked for it so assumed it had some value," he said. "One day Mike just approached me and said 'I'd like to talk to you about Best Brains' using the same tone of voice as someone saying "I'd like to talk to you about your insurance needs.' Joel once told me that he and Mike were intrigued by me because they saw me host an open stage that was horrendous from start to finish. Joel said he admired how I never gave up.

"I thought: oh, so this is what it means to write funny. Because in stand-up, you don't really have to write funny. It's 80 percent attitude with your average stand-up. It felt like I'd gone from Elizabethton [in baseball's Instructional League] up to AAA in one week."

Also contributing to the mix of new staffers was Mike's wife, who was still going by her stage name, Bridget Jones. She was what was known as a "home writer."

"They'd give me a tape of the movie, and I'd sit at home and write comments with the time codes," she recalled years later. "It was interesting doing it that way. When you're looking at it all by yourself, sometimes you're able to see things you wouldn't see if you were with a group in the writing room, while the movie is slowly choking the life out of you."

Episode 301- CAVE DWELLERS
First shown: 6/1/91

Movie: (1984) An evil overlord imprisons a wise man in order to learn the whereabouts of a powerful weapon. Ator the barbarian and his pals are determined to rescue him.

Opening: J&tB consider new names
Invention exchange: The renaming thing gets out of hand, while in Deep 13, Dr. F loses patience with Frank's "Mike Douglas Show" recreation; Joel's invention is a smoking jacket, while the Mads demonstrate robotic arm wrestling
Host segment 1: J&tB reenact the half-screen slo-mo credit sequence
Host segment 2: Joel explains how giving extraordinary names to ordinary things can dress them up a bit
Host segment 3: Joel gives a foley demonstration
End: J&tB rail against the movie, which pleases the Mads
Stinger: "Thong! The fish is ready!"

Comments:

- This one takes a little while to get going. It doesn't help that a big chunk of the first part of the movie is flashbacks to the movie this is a sequel of (which would be riffed in season 12). But once it gets into gear, it really is hilarious. The host segments are mostly in the more-clever-than-funny variety, but we're so comfortable with these characters by now, clever is usually enough. The movie, as Joel and the bots note in the ending segment, is a bit of a hard ride, but it's perfect for our experiments.
- One of the first things Joel says is: "Looks like we're back on, everybody!" implying that there's been some sort of break in communication. And, well, there had been, but not that long: The stretch between the end of season 2 and the beginning of season 3 was 119 days.
- This episode was included in Rhino's "Mystery Science Theater 3000 Collection, Vol. 2."
- It was with this episode that the real heyday of the series began. In the ACEG, Kevin notes it was the first of SEVENTY-TWO contracted episodes (in fact, they'd do at total of 96 episodes from this point before Comedy Central grew weary of them). It was

an almost unheard-of situation in the TV business, and you can almost feel them settle in for the long haul.

- That massive contract is perhaps the best evidence of how much CC officials considered this the network's "signature series." More evidence: June 1 was the day CC officially went on the air (after two months as "CTV"): this episode was one of the shows that ran that day.
- Many of the catchphrases that we'd hear again and again are heard for the first time in this episode, including "…later…later…," "bite me, it's fun!" "It's a graphic novel!" "they're kinda dumb and easy to kill" and "Go to bed, old man!"
- Dr. F. gives the whole "stranded in space" premise a boost by asking Joel, "How did you fare going through the asteroid belt?" (Apparently not well. Jeepers, ow.)
- Tom is wearing a fez. We'll never know why.
- The whole "Mike Douglas Show" bit (a decade before "Seinfeld" would explore similar terrain) establishes the "Man in My Little Girl's Life" as a piece of mental furniture for this show.
- In the invention exchange, arm-wrestler Dr. F. is wearing his baseball cap backwards in a homage to the movie "Over the Top."
- Oddest non sequitur: Joel says, "and…bring me the head of Gallagher!" apropos of nothing on the screen that I can see.
- Segment one just kind of establishes the premise then kills time. The credits are moderately amusing, though.
- Segment two feels very season two-ish: very wordy but funny.
- Segment three also feels like something out of early season two, akin to Joel's zero-gravity or gobos lectures.
- At the end of segment three, Trace does the voice of TV's Madam, but gets mixed up and makes Crow's mouth move for a moment. Oops! They keep going.
- Callbacks: "The driver is either missing or he's dead!" (PHANTOM CREEPS); "Pyuma?!" (RING OF TERROR) "I say it's foggy!"

(THE CRAWLING EYE) "It's the Aztec mummy!" "What's Your Dream?" (ROCKETSHIP X-M)

- Obscure riff: As the cave man eats human heart: "I wanna Barney Clark bar!" In 1983, Clark was the first person to receive a permanent, implanted artificial heart; he lived 112 days.
- Vaguely naughty riff: "It's the speedy delivery guy and has he got a package!"
- Great wordplay: "I think it's the Kurds." "And whey?" "Yes, way!"
- Tom's little "Ator's kite" song is great, and Joel's little harmony at the end really makes it charming.
- I just love that face Joel pulls at the beginning of that final host segment.
- How much Keeffe does this movie have? Miles O'Keeffe, perhaps best known for 1981's "Tarzan the Ape Man" with Bo Derek, apparently doesn't take his acting ability too seriously. He reportedly contacted BBI after seeing this episode and told them he loved it.
- CreditsWatch: Several changes have taken place in the credits. For one, former production assistant Jann Johnson is now production coordinator (while Alex Carr remained production manager–wonder how that worked). That's intern Christopher Wurst as the moleman Gerry, refereeing the robot arm wrestling. Wurst must have put his foot down during the making of this episode about how hot it was inside the mask: Gerry and Sylvia would never be seen again. Trace and Frank are no longer "Special Guest 'Villians' (misspelled)" as they were throughout season two. The lines "Special Effects and Other Fancy Stuff: Trace Beaulieu" have been removed, as has "Additional Visual Effects: Industrial Plumbing and Heating," which I suspect was just a joke anyway.
- The "Hexfield Viewscreen Designed and Constructed by: Mark Gilbertson" credit, which began with episode 205, is gone. New to the credits are technical supervisor Timothy Scott and manager of business affairs Heide LeClerc. And in the thank yous: Randy Herget has been removed and Bill W. has been added. The interns

were Thomas Alphonso, Cyn Eells, Tom Henderson and Christopher Wurst. Wurst also got a "Contributing writers" credit, along with Bridget. Also, the music during segment 1, which he titled "Jupiter," were written and arranged by Mike. I tweeted him about what "Jupiter" means and he replied, "that may have simply been the name of the tone on the keyboard."

- Fave riff: "Gomez! I've invented the wheel!!" Honorable mention: "You could drive a Mack truck through your cues! Tempo! Tempo!"

Movie stuff:

1) Before FVI got hold of it, this movie was called "Ator The Invincible." On video it was titled "The Blade Master." It was a sequel to "Ator the Fighting Eagle" (1983) and the prequel to "the Iron Warrior" (1986).
2) The clips used during the opening credits came from a sword-and-sandal flick called "Taur: the Mighty."

Episode 302- GAMERA
First shown: 6/8/91

Movie: (1965) In the first of a long-running Japanese movie series, a giant mutated turtle with super powers is accidentally revived from eons of hibernation and, of course, attacks Japan. Authorities, there and in the U.S., work to stop it. Meanwhile, young Kenny is fascinated by the beast.

Opening: Tom leads some warmup exercises
Invention exchange: Crow tricks Tom into the old "trust exercise" prank; Joel shows off his endless salad takeout container, but Frank's birdcage vacuum malfunctions
Host segment 1: Tom sings "Tibby, Oh Tibby"

Host segment 2: Crow and Tom hate Kenny, but Joel suggests a positive outlook, and proposes a contest
Host segment 3: The bots are playing beauty salon when Gamera visits on the Hexfield
End: Another look at the cast of the film, Joel reads some letters
Stinger: Eskimo says: "Bye..."

Comments:

- One of the things this episode-watching process does is compress the whole evolution of the show. If you watch all the episodes in order (more or less one a week), as I have done, it's been a little over four months since we watched episode K05- GAMERA, but for the Brains it had been two-and-a-half years since they watched it. But, wow, what a long way they have come in that time. This one, like last week's episode, is chock full of things that would be revisited again and again. The riffing is very funny and the movie is, well, it is what it is. Either you like this sort of movie or you don't. The segments are all at least good, and that brings the rating up a bit further. So this one may not be a home run, but it's a solid stand-up triple.
- Yes, Joel saw this movie during the KTMA season, but remember, this is all new to Trace. He was out of town last time. It's possible Kevin had to sit through some or all of this, I suppose.
- And although he was mocked a bit during the KTMA days, it's with this episode that they really stepped up the mockery of Sandy Frank.
- I believe both inventions are from Joel's standup act.
- The next episode, "POD PEOPLE," is famous for its "Chief? McCloud!" riffs, but did you catch the one here? "Goodbye, Chief." "Goodbye, McCloud." So it's clear this was a concept that was already percolating in the writing room.
- Callback: "No!" (CAVE DWELLERS). "No dancing, not allowed" (THE CRAWLING HAND).

MSTIEPEDIA • 183

- The phrase "In fear and hot water" is a Firesign Theatre reference.
- We haven't really had a complete song from Kevin since "Creepy Girl," and he's terrific once again – although Crow steals the show.
- Joel is carrying, and drinking from, a soda can during Tom's song.
- Following the song, back in the theater, Crow mercilessly pummels Tom with Tibby jokes and then Joel joins in, upsetting Tom so much he tries to leave–and he runs left! Very KTMA.
- If anybody ever sent replies to the "Kenny! What Gives?" contest, apparently they weren't funny enough to be included in a later show. It never comes up again.
- Goof: Tom Servo mentions Kenny's rocks before the "Kenny's rocks" scene in the movie. A lot of times they do a host segment that might have been more effective if it appeared in a different position in an episode, after whatever they're referencing takes place in the movie. This is one of those. But, in their defense, I suspect when you watch a movie five or six times in a given week you can lose track of when stuff happens.
- Then-current riffs: Tom does a Robin Leach impression. At the time, Leach's TV show, "Lifestyles of the Rich and Famous," was all the rage. Not so much, now and Leach passed away in 2018.
- Crow notes that the other international leaders are likely to listen to Japan "since you own their countries." Japan's "lost decade" put an end to jokes about how the uber-wealthy Japanese were buying up everything.
- I asked these questions when we did the KTMA version of this movie, but I still have questions
- Mike is hilarious as a smarmy Gamera, but unfortunately the gag "You'd know about pain–you've seen Spalding Gray" isn't quite as funny since Gray's death.
- Crow makes a bad pun about midway through the movie, and Joel casually rips Crow's arm off and tosses it across the theater!! He doesn't even let Crow retrieve it at the end of the segment! Later, he does it again! He's so strict!

184 • MSTIEPEDIA

- What causes him to do it a second time is when Gamera is being blasted off against his will, and Crow says, mockingly "Hey Joel, remind you of anything?" He and Tom then begin singing the opening theme song! This meta bit seems to enrage Joel.
- The Brains make no attempt to hide the fact that Tom's hand is taped to his head in the last segment. He even yells "Yowch!" when Joel pulls it off.
- In episode 208- LOST CONTINENT, when Joel gets "movie sign against my will" the official FAQ stated that the Mads gave him a "shock to the shammies." But that phrase wasn't used in that episode, and didn't appear until this one.
- "Gammera the Invincible" was the USA-released version of this movie, which included extra scenes with an American cast (Albert Dekker, most notably) filmed in America. The scenes add nothing … just more people talking about Plan Z. They're not included in the Sandy Frank version.
- CreditsWatch: One Lisa Sheretz is listed as a contributing writer for this and the next two episodes. Maybe she was a tryout that didn't take? Also: Colleen Henjum begins a "home writer" gig that will continue into season six. Audio was a rotating job this season: Fred Street did it in the last episode, John Calder did it this time and in the next two.
- Fave riff: "Oh, this is Pearl Harbor. How'd THAT get in there? Honorable mention: "So, extra crispy or regular?"

Episode 303- POD PEOPLE
First shown: 6/15/91

Movie: (1984) When some alien eggs hatch, it spells trouble for a pair of poachers, a vacationing singer and his entourage and an isolated family.

Opening: J&tB are having an arts chautauqua

MSTiepedia • 185

Invention exchange: After a brief scene from "An Officer and a Gentlemen," Joel demonstrates his monster chord; while the Mads have invented a public domain karaoke machine
Host segment 1: J&tB record "Idiot Control Now" and it stinks!
Host segment 2: J&tB present New Age music from Some Guys in Space
Host segment 3: "You are magic, aren't you, Trumpy?"
End: J&tB sing, "A Clown in the Sky"
Stinger: "It stinks!"

Comments:

- People adore this episode. In the ACEG it's described as a "fan favorite." But I gotta say this is number-one in my list of "sleeping pill" episodes. Don't get me wrong: the riffing is great and the host segments are ALL winners (which is a rarity). But the movie just puts me to sleep. Maybe it's all the fog and new agey music. I did make it through this viewing without dozing off, but I was getting pretty drowsy by the end.
- This movie was originally released in Spain as "Los Nuevos Extra-terrestres." For the American video release it was called "The Unearthling," but you might also have seen it titled "Extra-Terrestrial Visitors," "Tales Of Trumpy" or "The Return Of E.T."
- This episode was included in Rhino's "The Mystery Science Theater 3000 Collection, Vol. 2."
- Kevin croaks out the word "merchant" in the opening bit–they keep going.
- The blowed-up bots are the handywork of newly arrived Toolmaster Jef.
- Dr. F mentions the once-trendy clothing retail chain Chess King. They would be gone in four years.
- Frank addresses Jerry the Mole Person but we never see him.

- Despite the fact that the bots have just been badly blowed up, the regular bots walk into the theater a moment later. Joel covers by mumbling "Good thing we got those re-…um…those new heads on…"
- Film Ventures International used clips from a movie called "Galaxy Invader" for the titles. That movie would later be riffed by RiffTrax.
- The last time we had an episode with two songs was 202- THE SIDE HACKERS. We wouldn't get another one until episode 521- SANTA CLAUS.
- Callback: "Puma? Puma!" (RING OF TERROR)
- That's makeup lady (and occasional writer) Faye Berkholder as the recording studio assistant in Deep 13, her one and only appearance on the show. A lot of people thought it was Bridget for a long time.
- Kevin sort of coughs/clears his throat at one point in the theater. They keep going.
- During the wall of keyboards sketch, Crow has a bit of sammich on his beak. Another nice touch from Jef. Also –Why is Joel staring down at the floor while he's talking? Are his lines down there?
- A lot of people had no idea about the origin of that voice Crow does when he does Trumpy. "He's like a poh-tay-toe!" He's doing a vague impression of The Elephant Man from the movie of the same name.
- Also, a lot people had no idea who McCloud was. Dennis Weaver, we hardly knew ye.
- That said, they ran the "Chief? McCloud!" bit right into the ground. A running gag is one thing, but sheesh.
- Vaguely dirty riff: "That trunk could come in handy for hard to reach places!"
- Goof: When Joel says "Trumpy, you can do STUPID things!" in the theater, he's referencing a line by the little kid, Tommy, who says: "Trumpy, you can do magic things!" Unfortunately Joel does that

riff about 10 minutes BEFORE the Tommy says the original line. Another example of what happens when you watch a movie five or six times in a week. You can lose track of when stuff happens.

- CreditsWatch: Unbelievable: After two episodes where it didn't appear, "Special Guest Villians" (misspelled) returns. Starting with this episode and continuing through most of the season: "Host Segments Directed by Jim." And an important first in this episode: "Toolmaster: Jef Maynard." Mike and Kevin get the credit for "A Clown in the Sky." Trace gets a solo Art Direction credit (no Joel, for the only time during his tenure at the show). A new credit appears: "Post Production Coordination." It's Alex (already listed as "Production Manager") and Jann (already listed as "Production Coordinator"). Sheesh. Another new credit: "Prop Assistant." This week it's one Barb Oswald, who will get the gig in two more eps this season.
- Fave riff: "Hi! We're the cast from 'Straw Dogs.'" Honorable mention: "Hear that? Sounds like Norm Abrams being killed by a giant chicken."

Movie stuff:

1) The house in this movie is MUCH bigger on the inside than it looks like on the outside. It appears to have three or four guest bedrooms and endless hallways (and something completely crazy: a door to the outside in the bathroom off one of the bedrooms, through which evil Trumpy escapes after killing the girl in the shower).

Episode 304- GAMERA VS. BARUGON
First shown: 6/22/91

Movie: (1966) In the second outing of the movie series, a group of conspirators travels to a remote jungle island to retrieve what they believe is a giant opal. They're wrong: it's actually the egg of mythical lizard-dog creature, Barugon.

Opening: Crow and Tom argue the merits and drawbacks of computer interfaces

Invention exchange: The interface war continues; Joel demonstrates his animated soda can, while the Mads show off their disco cumber-bubble-bund

Host segment 1: Fast-talking Tom announces the "5000-piece fightin' men & monster set"

Host segment 2: Crow and Tom are Midwestern monster women eating at TGI Tokyo's

Host segment 3: Enjoying a simulated day at the beach, Joel tells Tom and Crow about the big celebrities in the movie, then vapor locks

End: Joel helps Tom and Crow read more about monster movies, Joel reads a letter, Frank has gotten Dr. F a book to read at the beach

Stinger: Opal guy seems happy

Comments:

- While not really a bad episode, after the previous justly famous outing this one's a bit of a letdown. On the other hand, compared to the LAST time they riffed this, back in episode K04, it's leaps and bounds better. The riffing is steady and funny, but there's not a lot that's memorable. The movie itself is strange, but reasonably watchable. And the host segments, typically, are a mixed bag.
- One nice thing about this monster movie is the absence of any sort of squeaky deranged kid.
- Following a repeat of this episode (some time in '92, I think), the user interface sketch sparked an actual "Mac vs. PC" flame war on the MST3K newsgroups. Ah, simpler times. And in case you forget how long ago this was, note that when this sketch was written, the now-long-forgotten Mac OS System 7 was still in the future

(though, by the time this show aired it had been released for about a month). And remember when people called PCs "clones"?

- Joel is very funny in the opening. His mannerisms and delivery are just great.
- In the opening, Tom is typing "wp51." He's running Word Perfect?
- At the beginning of the invention exchange, Crow calmly suggests rewriting the autoexec.bat file–a suggestion that probably sounds crazy to modern computer users.
- Also, early in the invention exchange, Crow's arm accidentally disconnects from his body and hangs from the desk. Eventually Joel grabs it and tosses it on the floor. They keep going.
- Frank's paltry bubble-making efforts are augmented by extra bubbles coming in from stage left.
- We get another look at Tom's "rockem-sockem-robot" neck extension. Only the most obsessive bot maker felt it necessary to include this function.
- Joel mumbles that the cumber-bubble-bund looks familiar…it should, they demonstrated a similar item in season one.
- Callbacks: Tom mentions "Jungle Goddess;" "a thousand wonderful hours" (ROCKETSHIP XM).
- Crow and Tom give us a little preview of segment 2 in the theater as they lapse into their Midwestern middle-aged lady voices.
- We have another case here where maybe a different host segment order would have worked better: Segment 1, which is very fun and frantic, by the way, mentions Barugon's ram tongue action – but we haven't seen it in the movie yet.
- The desk on the SOL was removed in order to shoot the photos for segment 1 and again for segment 3.
- Note the presence, in two sketches, of the partial air filter that was used in the "cheap Halloween costumes" sketch in season two.
- Segment 2 is a bit baffling. What is with the weird masks the bots are wearing? In the ACEG, Kevin calls the faces "awfully and inex-

plicably weird." So I don't even know if THEY know why they did it. I do love the dessert descriptions. Mike, and his tenure at TGI-Fridays, probably had a lot to do with that one.

- In segment 3, Joel recalls going to a drive-in "in Buffalo ...The Lucky Twin on Route 5." He probably means Buffalo, Minn., not New York. And I suspect he means Route 55 (which runs right through Buffalo) and he appears to remember the name of the theater wrong.
- There's a funny outtake to segment 3 in the poopie reel. (Help me!)
- Joel rips Crow's arm off again in the theater!
- Joel declares an official ban on the "By this time..." riff.
- The movie was originally titled "Dai Kaiju Keto: Gamer-a Tai Barugon" ("Great Monster Battle: Gamera vs. Barugon"); it was released in the U.S. as "War of the Monsters." You might also see it listed as "Gamera vs. Baragon (instead of "Barugon") . That's a typo stemming from confusion between Daiei Studios' monster Barugon and rival Toho's Baragon, which appeared in "Franken-stein Conquers the World" a year earlier. The two monsters are somewhat similar looking, but they are not the same monster.
- Creditswatch: Additional contributing writer: Jef Maynard. Guest "Villians" (misspelled) again. Two new credits appear: "Online Editor" (this week it's Tim Paulson); and "Audio Editor" (it's always Tim Scott). Barb Oswald is Prop Assistant again. Disco ball cour-tesy of: Teener's Theatrical Department Store." (It has since gone out of business.) Another new credit: "Additional Music Written and Arranged by." This week, and most weeks, it's Mike, but later in the season others will get it. The voice of Meryl Streep reading "The Velveteen Turtle" is not credited, but it sounds like Magic Voice, who was Alex Carr at this time.
- Fave riff: "Solipsism is its own reward." How true that is. Honor-able mention: "Hey, I listened to the diamond thing, but I'm NOT going to arouse him."

Episode 305- STRANDED IN SPACE
First shown: 6/29/91

Movie: (1973) Unsuccessful TV pilot about an astronaut who finds himself on a mirror-Earth, where the shadowy, oppressive "Perfect Order" rules.

Opening: Joel has turned Crow and Tom into a shooting gallery
Invention exchange: The shooting gallery is now in Apple Dumpling Gang mode; both Joel and the Mads show off variations of the "BANG!" gun
Host segment 1: Crow and Tom fight over their trading cards until Joel intervenes; he then shows off his "kids in court" trading cards
Host segment 2: Tom's baking cookies; Crow tells him about a nightmare that reminds Tom of Ward E, and they discuss their personal visions of what Ward E is like
Host segment 3: Joel is a TV movie villain, the bots are his henchmen
End: Joel and Crow try to sell "Stranded in Space" to producer Tom; Joel reads a letter, the Mads are TV movie villains and Dr. F foresees a promotion for Frank
Stinger: Bettina strikes Stryker.

Comments:

- I think Sampo's Theorem* is going to be in full force here, because, frankly, I'm not a big fan of this one, which means that I'm sure somebody will come forward to express their undying love for it. For me, the biggest problem is that the movie is as drab as a sinkful of dishwater. There's very little for the riffers to grab on to (though of course there are some great moments as always). All the host segments are worth a smile or two, but nothing is outstanding. A classic "meh" episode.

- This one's not on DVD.
- Joel explains the premise, this time adding some details we've never heard before, nor will ever hear again. He says, "As you can tell by the opening the Mads made..." and also says the Mads "sell the results to cable TV." The show seldom makes that much of an effort to explain itself.
- To wake the bots up, Joel throws glittery confetti. What is he, the Harlem Globetrotters? (Alternately, Rip Taylor.)
- Watch the plunger on the TNT prop as Frank presses down. They keep going. JEF!!
- Callbacks: Two uses of "hikeeba" (WOMEN OF THE PREHIS-TORIC PLANET) and several uses of "No!!!" (CAVE DWELL-ERS). Also: two references to SIDEHACKERS: "The most dramatic confrontation since Rommel met JC" and "that's pretty good!"
- My copy is from March of 1995, the "Play MSTie for Me" era. The OJ trial was in full swing and Comedy Central ran one of its "Just Say No J" promos twice.
- Instant catchphrase: "People used to laugh more then...there were concerts in the park..."
- Again, the order of segments isn't quite right: They've mentioned Ward E by the time we get to segment 2, but they haven't shown it to us yet.
- Tibby makes a return appearance in segment 3!
- At the end of the movie, a character introduces himself as "Tom Nelson" and Tom says "MIKE Nelson." That must have been baffling to viewers in 1991.
- In the ending segment, Tom says "letter latey." They keep going.
- Dr. F mentions Gizmonic Institute during the closer. First time in a long while.
- CreditsWatch: A guy named Bob King came in to do audio for this episode and only this episode. Tim Scott is listed as "on-line editor" for this episode only. Jann Johnson and Alex Carr are listed as additional contributing writers. Trace and Frank are still

"guest villians" (STILL being misspelled) and now Dr. F's name is misspelled "Forrestor." This was Lisa Sheretz' last episode as a contributing writer, and after this episode, home writer Colleen Henjum took three episodes off.

• Fave riff: "You'll always be a little girl." Honorable mention: "Sir, why aren't the Landers sisters in this meeting?"

* Sampo's Theorem states: "For every MSTie who believes that a given episode is the worst thing they've ever done, there is another who believes it is their finest hour."

Movie stuff:

1) You can see why this never went to series. His only way off the planet is via the Terra version of NASA. How many space launches are there? The guy says they have an active space program, but still. How likely is he to be able to sneak aboard a flight? If the plan they concoct in this episode failed, is some other plan likely to work better? It's an unworkable premise is what I'm saying.
2) Dated riff: Joel and Tom both mention "Photomat." The once-ubiquitous film developing retail chain is now long dead, put out of business by digital technology.
3) Before Film Ventures Intl. got hold of it, this was called "The Stranger." In their re-edit, they used clips from a movie called "Prisoners of the Lost Universe" during the credits sequence (RiffTrax would riff it in 2012.)

Episode 306- TIME OF THE APES
First shown: 7/13/91

Movie: (1974 TV series; 1987 compilation movie) A trio of young people take refuge in cryogenic capsules during an earthquake, and awaken in a world populated by intelligent apes.

Opening: Using Tom as a T-ball stand, Joel shags some flies to Crow, breaks a window and causes explosive decompression
Invention exchange: Gypsy fixes the hole and warns them not to do it again but of course they do. Joel shows off his cellulite phone, while the Mads demonstrate their miracle baby growth formula
Host segment 1: J&tB present: "Why doesn't Johnny care?" A film by Bell Labs
Host segment 2: J&tB present their version of "Inherit the Wind"
Host segment 3: Crow presents an "ape fashion minute"
End: J&tB sing the Sandy Frank song, Joel reads a letter, and in Deep 13, Baby pushes the button
Stinger: "Johnny, be careful." "I don't care!"

Comments:

- Back when we did the KTMA version of this, I wrote that the episode got "dragged down by the film, which is just a big giant carbuncle of a movie." Though it's much funnier, of course, I'm not a big fan of this version either. I based that statement on my memory of past viewings, but I gotta say, this time around was a pleasant surprise. I found myself laughing a lot and the movie, cut to incomprehensible ribbons though it is, moves along at a breezy, watchable pace. The host segments are all giggle-worthy too. It just goes to show you how your opinions of episodes can change over time.
- This episode is included in Shout's "Mystery Science Theater 3000 Collection: Vol XXII."
- During his second at bat, Joel's knocks off what's left of Tom's head. Ouch. They cover with a handy plastic coffee mug.
- Joel says, "You potched up the hole." They keep going.
- Crow's baseball glove falls off (you can see the duct tape) and Joel just rolls right with it.

- The baby is played by little Eli Kenneth Mallon, who is now all grown up.
- The miracle growth baby is sound guy Tim Scott, in the first of two appearances in that role.
- When they enter the theater after the opening, Tom is still wearing a coffee mug and Crow is still netless.
- Joel continues his strict style in the theater, AGAIN threatening to dismember Crow when he utters a pun.
- As we watch the monkey wake up, it sure sounds like Joel says "Shit." It might be "shoot" though.
- Crow asks Joel: "You said 'bowling ball' earlier. What did that mean?" Well, Crow, Joel was reacting to a shot of sun-bleached skull that looked vaguely like a bowling ball – albeit a white one.
- During segment 1, I love that Crow provides the projector noise, and that Tom misses a few sprockets, only to be nudged back into place by Joel. We have a few former A/V squad members on the writing staff, methinks.
- As they return to the theater after segment 2, Joel is carrying the cardboard standee of Judge Wap and sails it toward the screen saying, "Fly, judgie! Fly!" His Honor gets some good distance.
- Crow reenters the theater after segment 3 still wearing his hat.
- Tom's wearing a weird monkey mask during the final segment.
- CreditsWatch: Colleen Henjum moves from contributing writer to writer for this and the next two episodes. Additional Contributing Writers: Lynn-Anne Freise, Craig Tollifson, Tom Wedor, Jann L. Johnson, Alexandra B. Carr. And this is the first of 14 episodes in season 3 that a guy named Brian Wright did the audio. Dr. F and Frank are still "Special Guest Villians" (misspelled) and Dr. F's name is again misspelled "Forrestor." This is the last time in the Comedy Central era that Jim Mallon appears in the writers list.
- Fave riff: "Harder…" Honorable mention: "Home, where I comb my facey." "Johnny is a walking faux pas."

196 • MSTiepedia

Movie stuff:

1) As most of you know, this movie was cut together from an entire season's worth of TV adventures. If you watched the KTMA version, it was barely followable, but you could sort of find the thread of the action. But THIS incarnation has ALSO been cut for time by BBI and, intentionally or not, the result is a series of scenes, mostly action-y set pieces, that have little or no relation to each other. The overall final product is totally unfathomable. But, for riffing, it works.

2) Just a really dumb line from the movie: Somebody notes that earthquakes are possible but the Dr. Lee insists "nothing will happen suddenly." Wait, what?

Episode 307- DADDY-O (with short: "ALPHABET ANTICS")
First shown: 7/20/91

Short: (1951) A placid tour of the alphabet.

Movie: (1959) High-panted, cool-singing, truck-driving hepcat tangles with blonde bombshell, tries to solve his friend's murder and reluctantly becomes a courier for drug smugglers.

Opening: J&tB are marketing mad dogs gathered around the water cooler
Invention exchange: Dr. F is feeding the miracle growth baby; Joel shows off his air freshener mobile, while the mads demonstrate the alien teething nook
Host segment 1: Joel sings: "Hike Your Pants Up"
Host segment 2: J&tB reenact the drag race from the movie, with Joel getting killed a lot
Host segment 3: Joel is conducting a spit-take lesson, but the dumb guy from the movie keeps appearing on the Hexfield

End: Joel is studying the "Want some?" scene, Joel reads letters, and in Deep 13 the button doesn't work
Stinger: "Couldn't help ya if I wanted to, fella. Gym policy."

Comments:

- As the kids say, this episode is full of win (that is what they say, isn't it?). It is chock full o' awesome. It's got everything: a cheesy but watchable movie that even includes swingin' musical numbers, great host segments, riffing that starts in high gear and stays there and a memorable closing segment. A classic.
- This episode is included in Shout's "Mystery Science Theater Collection: Vol. XXXIII."
- If you're playing along at home, this was number 30 on that 1995 Comedy Central countdown.
- Those who say host segments in the Joel years were more often related to the movie were probably thinking of episodes like this one: Just about ALL the host segments are not only related to the movie, they're direct parodies or reenactments of scenes from the movie.
- Somebody actually marketed something very like the Alien teething nook. It didn't have the nipple, though.
- Again, that's Tim Scott as the miracle growth baby.
- The blue tint is back. Ugh.
- The short is the first of many educational shorts that would eventually become one of the most popular elements on the series.
- I love the way Joel imitates Dick Contino's rictus grin as he sings.
- That lyric about Corey Haim in "Hike Your Pants Up" got a bit less funny in 2010.
- In the reenactment of the race, it's interesting to note that Tom plays the guy and Crow plays the girl, for a change. It probably has to do with the placement of the guy and gal in the movie, but still, it's a rarity.

198 • MSTIEPEDIA

- When they re-enter the theater, Tom covers the absence of the cars they were wearing by saying "Good thing we were thrown clear of those cars!"
- Callbacks: "Ya got me!" (CATALINA CAPER) "Chili peppers burn my gut" (SIDEHACKERS) "Hey that's from Catalina Caper!" "The driver is either missing or…" (THE PHANTOM CREEPS) "I don't care!" (TIME OF THE APES)
- Segment 3 features the first use of the hexfield viewscreen since episode 302. That's Mike, of course, as the clueless Bruce.
- During segment 3, Tom's Carmen Miranda hat almost falls off. Joel straightens it and they keep going.
- Little letter writer Christina, 7 when she wrote to the show, is now (assuming she is okay) over 30.
- The crowning glory of this terrific ep is the famous "broken button" bit, a gem people remembered for years. Unfortunately, in later years a lazy Comedy Central did not respect the bit and actually ran voice overs during it – an incident that sparked one of several major online protests among fans.
- The closing bit also features an uncredited mole person.
- CreditsWatch: Jim moves from writer to contributing writer for the rest of the season. Paul Chaplin joins the list of contributing writers. "The Pants Up Song" is by Mike and Kevin and Mike did the "baby music." Trace and Frank are still guest "villians" (misspelled) and Dr. F's name is still misspelled "Forrestor."
- Fave short riff: "But he's got a brain like a chick pea!" Honorable mention: "It's the Georgia juvenile correction system."
- Fave feature riff: "On my ANKLE, like I SAID!" Honorable mention: "Do you like the names of lots of fish?"

Movie stuff:

1) Okay, Dick lost his license, but he doesn't need a driver's license to race cars on private property, right? It's a plot hole.

MSTIEPEDIA • 199

2) The lady in the club does look a LITTLE like Lou Reed from the "Transformer" album. It's kind of a stretch, though.

Episode 308- GAMERA VS. GAOS
First shown: 7/27/91

Movie: (1967) In third outing of the long-running Japanese movie series, the giant flying turtle monster faces off against Gaos, a shovel-headed bat-monster with the ability to shoot laser beams. Caught between the two monsters are some nearby villagers, who want to stop the construction of a highway through their land (or at least get a good price when they sell it). The grandson of their leader is young Itchy who, after Gamera saves him, becomes an instant expert on both creatures.

Opening: The bots are pretending they are raspy-voiced celebrities and Joel joins in
Invention exchange: Gypsy does her impression of the NBC Sunday Night Mystery Movie. The mads show off their self-image printers, Joel demonstrates his fax tissue dispenser
Host segment 1: Joel presents an arts and crafts project, but Crow and Tom are no help
Host segment 2: The "Gamera-damerung" never gets off the ground
Host segment 3: Ed Sullivan presents "Gaos the Great"
End: The bots suggest other ways to snuff Gaos and request ideas from the viewers
Stinger: Comic relief guys get scared.

Comments:

- I'll admit I was dreading this one. After my encounter with it during the KTMA season, I remembered it as a long slog. What a pleasant surprise. It's really a lesson for me not judge a season 3 episode by its KTMA antecedent. The riffing is sharp (though it sags a bit in the middle), the host segments are generally fun and the movie was more watchable than I was worried it was going to be. All in all, lots of fun.

- This episode was included in Shout's "Mystery Science Theater 3000 Collection: Gamera Vs. MST3K" (aka Vol. XXI).
- For those keeping score, this was number 52 in that 1995 countdown.
- Joel blows his reading of the name "Brenda Vacarro." They keep going.
- Joel is VERY funny in the opening sketch. Of course, most of the people mentioned in the sketch are now dead, because they all got their raspy voices from smoking which, you know, killed them.
- This will not be the last time the "NBC Sunday Mystery Movie" is mentioned.
- I've always suspected that the mads' invention was largely a way that Jim could invest in some large-format printers and then write them off.
- The noise we hear as the printer images are revealed sounds like a dot matrix printer, which they probably had sitting around in the office. I suspect Trace and Frank are just unrolling the images by hand.
- That's not to say it isn't a funny sketch. Dr. F's self-description is great.
- Joel's invention is dependent on the then-current nature of fax paper. Two decades later, with plain-paper fax machines having almost completely taken over (and then fax machines quietly vanishing), younger viewers might not even know what he's talking about (or even know what a fax machine is).
- This is as good a place as any to mention that quite a few of the little "Play MSTie for Me" bumpers CC ran during the summer of 1995 were, simply, wrong. One example came in this episode, in

a message that Joel "was 10 in 1967." No, he wasn't. The author of all or most of these cards was a MSTie who had managed to make friends with somebody in the Comedy Central scheduling department, and soon became quite useful to online MSTies by regularly posting largely accurate lists of which episodes were going to air. He apparently gained CC's confidence enough that he got tapped for the gig of writing these bumpers. But there was no fact-checking, apparently.

- Callback: "Rex Dart, Eskimo Spy." (GODZILLA VS. MEGALON); "It's pretty good!" (SIDEHACKERS)
- I think this is the first episode featuring the phrase: "You look at it, I'm bitter"?
- Then-current reference: "Arsenioooo Haaaall!" (Woof! Woof! Woof!)
- The "arts and crafts" segment is a classic, with a TON of great lines. And, Joel, I believe you about the mucilage.
- Joel, usually quite the stickler about puns to the point of ripping parts off the bots, says: "I thought this was ferris wheel's day off." The bots glare at him. Hypocrite!
- Joel re-warns Tom about Anthony Newly impressions.
- Naughty line: "Have you ever seen 'The Last Emperor', sister?"
- Joel uses the phrase "deus ex machina," not for the last time.
- I like the way Gypsy chuckles at the phrase "Gameradamerung." As Mike mentions in the ACEG, that segment had a lot of set-up for a two-second bit.
- Tom is still wearing his Gameradamerung costume when he reenters the theater. After all that setup, I get it.
- Kinda dark riff: "Take one down, write piggy on the wall..."
- Gamera climbs on Gaos's back and Tom says: "You're a big ol' hog!" Yikes!
- Then-current riff: "Just like when Gary died." (It's a "thirtysomething" reference.)

202 • MSTiepedia

- I wonder how many young viewers have any clue what that Ed Sullivan sketch is about. I do love the way Joel slaps the plates together over and over, as if it's supposed to demonstrate something.
- In the last segment Tom is again wearing the hat he was wearing in segment 3.
- Did anybody write in to the "Ways to Snuff Gaos" contest? Like with the "Kenny. What gives?" contest, they never read any of the entries, if they got any.
- CreditsWatch: Trace and Frank are still "guest villians" (misspelled) and Dr. F's name is still misspelled "Forrestor." Someone named Karen Lindsay does the first of nine eps as online editor. A Lori Schackmann was prop assistant for only this episode. Mike wrote the plate spinning music, which he entitled: "Opus 4, Number 23, Plate Spinning Song"
- Fave riff: "Grace Jones takes one to the head–she can't take it there!" Honorable mention: "I wish to play with clay now!"

Episode 309- THE AMAZING COLOSSAL MAN
First shown: 8/3/91

Movie: (1957) Exposure to an atomic blast causes an army colonel to become a giant.

Opening: Crow and Tom hide out in their super-secret cardboard fort
Invention exchange: The mads have created a plant that reviews music; Joel shows off his idea for non-permanent tattoos
Host segment 1: Joel helps the bots learn the right thing to say to the relative of a horribly disfigured nuclear accident victim
Host segment 2: Joel agonizes about being a 50-foot man

Host segment 3: The bots wonder what they'd ask Glen, then he visits
End: J&tB suggest other things Glen could've done, Joel reads letters, Dr. F. has a giant hypo and it's aimed at Frank
Stinger: Glen laughing 'til it hurts

Comments:

- The movie is well-remembered, and we meet so many AIP regulars. But in terms of bringing the funny, I have to give it a good-not-great rating. The movie is strangely captivating, and I think the writers kind of got caught up in it. There are some great riffing moments, but it's just not solid throughout.
- This episode was released and then almost immediately recalled by Rhino. If you have a copy, you have a rarity.
- Callback: "The HU-man" (Robot Monster). And lots of "No!" (Cave Dwellers)
- The plant guy, aka "Robert Plant," was Kevin's first on-screen performance on the show. The character would return in Turkey Day bumpers.
- As they leave for a break, Crow departs, then comes back for one more riff.
- Naughty riff: "Sorry, wrong bone growth."
- It was popular back then to call A&E the "all-Hitler Channel." This was before A&E spun off their massive library of World War II documentaries, mostly to The History Channel.
- Joel is hilarious as Glen, the 50-foot man. "Aah! No!"
- In "Daddy-O," Crow asks "Do you know the names of lots of fish?" In this ep, Tom asks "How many fish can you name?" Funny both times.
- During that sketch Tom's arms work! Crow even asks him about it!
- In the lab scene, they do three consecutive riffs hammering the idea that some cosmetic companies use animals such as rabbits to test their products. It's one of the few times I can recall them

doing three variations of essentially the same joke right in a row. I do love Crow's great little voice as the rabbit, though.

- We haven't seen J&tB daydreaming at that window since episode 201- ROCKETSHIP X-M.
- Mike is also great as Glen.
- Joel is still holding the Barbie from the earlier sketch later on.
- Precognition by J&tB (or, the segments are not in the proper order): In segment three they mention Glen in Vegas, when we haven't gotten to that part of the movie yet.
- Tom makes a pun and Crow warns him: "That kinda talk'll get your arm ripped off." From one who knows.
- As the movie ends, and the "The End" card comes up, J&tB respond with "Or is it?" I wonder if they knew, then, that they were going to do the sequel?
- CreditsWatch: Collen Henjum, who has gone back and forth between "writer" and "contributing writer," goes from writer to contributing writer for the rest of the season. Tim Scott is back as online editor. Trace and Frank are still guest "villians" (misspelled) and Dr. F's name is again misspelled "Forrestor."
- Fave riff: "That, and 'aaaaaah!'" Honorable mention: "John Philips Sousa's life is flashing before his eyes!"

Movie stuff:

1) This movie has an incredibly long shot with nothing happening and nobody in frame – we just look at a door for a good 12 seconds. J&tB make the most of it.
2) The movie's single strangest idea (and that's saying something): the notion that the heart is "made up of a single cell." Did they think audiences were going to buy that?
3) I enjoy the window fan shadow when they are supposed to be in the helicopters, obviously trying to convey to the audience that

they are flying. Pro tip: a real helicopter blade, going fast enough to keep the helicopter up in the air, would not make a distinct shadow like that. If you are in a helicopter, and you see that kind of shadow crossing your body, it means you're plummeting.

Episode 310- FUGITIVE ALIEN
First shown: 8/17/91

Movie: (1978 original TV show episodes; 1986 compilation movie) Alien marauder Ken becomes a fugitive from his home planet, then joins the Earth spaceship Bacchus 3 to fight against his former masters. Meanwhile, his girlfriend Rita is sent on a deadly mission.

Opening: Old Joel Robinson had a farm?
Invention exchange: The mads demonstrate their eye, ear, nose & throat dropper; Joel has invented a musical chair and there's a special guest in Deep 13: Jack Perkins!
Host segment 1: J&tB stage a hat party
Host segment 2: Joel forces Crow and Tom to reenact a scene from the movie
Host segment 3: Crow and Tom are confused by the movie, so Joel helps out using Syd Field's "Screenplay."
End: Joel explains his buttons and reads a letter, in Deep 13, they're still torturing Jack Perkins.
Stinger: "AHAHAHAHA....you're STUCK HERE!"

Comments:
- Wow, this was really a watershed episode. There's so much going on here. The sketches are all great, the movie is mind-boggling and the riffing is everything you want from an MST3K episode. It's an instant and enduring classic. Plus, it's full of phrases that immediately became part of the MSTie lexicon, from "You're stuck

here!" to the merry tune, "He tried to kill me with a forkliiiiift...."
One of the best.

- This episode was on Shout's "Mystery Science Theater 3000 Collection: Vol XXIV."
- Love the opener. These folks have been around farmers and they know farmer talk. Tom's "help ussss!" is priceless.
- Mike is also hilarious as Jack Perkins. Jack would return, and not just in Deep 13. The character of "the host" who introduced the "MST3K Hour" shows was loosely based on Jack, though he was never explicitly called Jack Perkins. By the way, word is the real Mr. Perkins reportedly found Mike's impersonation as hilarious as everybody else did.
- Hopelessly dated line: "He's in more trouble than 'Hudson Hawk' at the box office!" It seemed like a big deal at the time.
- Call forward: Tom mentions "Marooned."
- The "Marooned" mention comes as part of a succession of bits Tom and Crow do in the theater when they pretend they are scif-fi geeks. Geek culture is now robustly defended by the members of its community. I wonder if anyone who considers themselves part of that community has (had?) a problem with these bits?
- Vaguely dirty lines: Joel: "I wanna die in the thong section of Victoria's Secret!" Also: "Speaking of punishing mercilessly .... rowrrr!"
- Literary riff: Tom: "Biff!" Crow: "Happy!" SOMEbody's read/seen "Death of a Salesman."
- This episode may hold the record for the most callbacks? Among them: "Third planet from the sun shall be called...Earth" (Women of the Prehistoric Planet); a reference to the "geometric nucleus" (Cave Dwellers); "It was after the...Robot Holocaust;" "I was in Time of the Apes!" "...and a good friend" (Rocketship XM); "Trumpy, you're stinky!" (Pod People) "Hikeeba!" (Women of the Prehistoric Planet.) "Hey, like the Wild Rebels!" "This must be

the [fill in the blank]...I've heard them talk about...so much... lately?" (Gamera); "Rock climbing, Joel." (Lost Continent).

- Crow has a right to be concerned in segment two. Didn't Gypsy have a six-foot foam scorpion stinger hanging off her butt during episode 113- THE BLACK SCORPION? There's a precedent, is what I'm saying.
- I noticed something this time about the "forklift" song. The first time they sing "This is the chase, Rocky and Ken," they do so before the movie reveals that it was Rocky driving the forklift (though Ken immediately suspects him and says so).
- When Joel punches the bots in segment 2, note how VERY GENTLY he punches them. He knows how fragile they are.
- Joel is great in the closing bit. "That's portion control. Next question."
- CreditsWatch: Trace and Frank are still guest "villians" (misspelled) and Dr. F's last name is still spelled "Forrestor." Special Make-up: Crist Ballas and Glen Griffin. I'm guessing they were needed for Mike's Jack Perkins getup. This was Faye Burkholder's last episode doing regular hair and makeup.
- Fave riff: "Uh, you're crying on my bombs." Honorable mention: "Oh, those are bugs. They wash right off."

Episode 311- IT CONQUERED THE WORLD (with short: THE SPORT PARADE–SNOW THRILLS)
First shown: 8/24/91

Short: (1945) A newsreel spanning the globe to bring you the constant variety of winter sports, (including "she-ing" and "she-horing.")

Movie: (1956) With the aid of a deluded Earth scientist, a Venusian pickle creature uses bat thingies to take control of humanity.

Opening: Joel tries his hand at ventriloquism, with Crow as his dummy

Invention exchange: The mads show off their hanged man costumes; Joel has invented the "Sony Sea-man"

Host segment 1: Tom narrates "The Winter Cavalcade of Fun"

Host segment 2: J&tB share sarcastic banter over dinner

Host segment 3: With time to kill, J&tB sing a song about celebrity siblings with the same last names

End: J&tB rewatch Peter Graves' speech, Crow, Tom and Gypsy each read a letter, the Mads rewatch Peter Graves' speech

Stinger: "He learned too late that a man is a feeling creature…"

Comments:

- I'll start with the good news. The short is great fun, with great riffing. All the host segments, even the oddball song in segment three, are entertaining. And the movie is, well, what can you say? It's classic Corman.
- Now the bad news: the riffing just kind of limps along, with only occasional bright spots. State park jokes abound. As with "Amazing Colossal Man," I think they kind of got caught up in the movie a little. So there's fun to be had in this episode, just not as much as I would have liked.
- This episode is not on commercial DVD and maybe never will.
- For you younger folks, "Star Search" was sort of the '90s version of "America's Got Talent." Amusingly, Geechy Guy (a repeat contestant on "Star Search"), is STILL seeking fame: he also appeared on AGT.
- Joel's mannerisms as the ventriloquist are classic. The random movements are done to distract you from looking at the ventriloquist's lips. Joel was into ventriloquy since he was a boy (he came to school on picture day with his dummy), so he knows all the tricks.

- In Googling around, I actually found a reliable site that gave me a definitive year – 1945 – for "Snow Thrills," one of the few shorts we hadn't been able to put a date on.
- Callback: "That's not half bad!" "She's givin' it back to you!" (a paraphrase from Sidehackers) "Chili peppers burn his gut." (also Sidehackers).
- Triple callback: "Thong? Ator? Puma?" (Cave Dwellers and Ring of Terror) I half-expected to hear "Chief?" next.
- Naughty line: Announcer: "It's the biggest one-man thrill in Jack Frost's show." Joel: "I know a better one…" The bots are scandalized.
- Then-current reference: "I'd rather watch 'thirtysomething.'" (Second "thirtysomething" reference in two or three episodes.)
- Joel again warns Tom about Anthony Newly impressions.
- They again do a "Helloooo baaaaaaby…" joke during a plane crash. A little dark.
- My copy is from Turkey Day '94, and includes a commercial for the video game "Burn Cycle," for Magnavox's cd-i game platform. Remember THAT short-lived product?
- During the song in segment 3, Tom again does his Tom Waits impression.
- Also, about the song: The joke is that they claim to be naming celebrity siblings with the same last name, but they are actually naming people with the same last name who AREN'T actually siblings (i.e. Mary Tyler and Roger Moore). I hate to break it to whoever wrote the lyrics (the credits do not specifically name the person), but Julia and Eric Roberts ARE siblings.
- Somewhat obscure riff: "Not the craw, the craw!" (A "Get Smart" running gag.)
- The closing repetition of the speech can be explained by Joel's earlier admission that the show was a bit short that week.
- Bot stuff: Is this the first time they've used the word "hoverskirt"? Also: In the final segment Joel, also takes a moment to explain Gypsy and her role again.

210 • MSTiepedia

- Crow and Joel get out of the way so Tom can read the number off the side of the jeep.
- This movie was remade for television by director Larry "Attack of the the Eye Creatures" Buchanan as "Zontar, The Thing from Venus."
- CreditsWatch: Karen Lindsey is back in the credits as online editor. Clayton James does the first of 11 stints as hair and makeup person. Additional contributing writers for this episode were Jef Maynard, Jann Johnson, Alexandra Carr and Timothy Scott. I suspect that credit happened when one of them wandered into the writing room, said something funny and they kept it. Trace and Frank are still "guest villians" (misspelled) and Dr. F's last name is again misspelled "Forrestor."
- Fave riff from the short: "Get in, old man, you've seen enough." Honorable mention: "Yeah, well, you're full of skit."
- Fave riff: "Venus? You know: no arms, nice rack..." Honorable mention: "She's just going to slip into something a little more clinical."

Movie stuff:

1) This movie is our first taste of oeuvre of one Roger Corman. Dr. F. introduces it as one of his best and that may be true. But he also says "it's really really really bad," and I don't think that's true. It's not a "good" movie, of course, but it's not really a bad one either. Its chief defect is that it was clearly made on a very low budget. But, despite that, Corman coaxes some really pretty good performances out of people who would go on to be known as pretty good actors. In addition, the story, while silly in some places, is almost gripping in others. We'll see many worse movies, including some from Corman, is I guess what I'm saying.

2) The Venusian costume was lobster red. It was nicknamed "Big Beulah" by its creator, Paul Blaisdell, and "Denny Dimwit" by

the screenwriters. Other names given by the cast and crew were the "Tee-Pee Terror," "the Cucumber Critter" and "The Carrot Monster." When she was a guest at an MST3K convention, Beverly Garland recalled that she kept telling herself that it wasn't finished, that they were still working on it, that it would get better. But of course, it never did. Chocolate syrup served as the Venusian's blood. Always ready to reuse props, Corman used the bat-thingies again in "The Undead."

3) Once again, the exterior shots were done at Bronson Canyon, which was also used for exterior shots in the filming of seven other MSTed movies.

Episode 312- GAMERA VS. GUIRON
First shown: 9/7/91

Movie: (1969) In the fifth movie of the long-running Japanese monster series, two boys accidentally hijack an alien spaceship and fly to a dying planet, where they encounter two evil women and knife-headed monster Guiron.

Opening: Crow and Tom are playing "school lunch"
Invention exchange: The mads show off their racy Rorschachs, Joel has invented a collapsible trashcan
Host segment 1: J&tB sing the Gamera song (with English lyrics)
Host segment 2: Joel's "sawing a robot in half" trick gets ruined
Host segment 3: J&tB do a pageant about Richard Burton, based on the kid in the movie's vague resemblance
End: the Gamera song again (with fake Japanese lyrics); meanwhile, Michael Feinstein is headlining in Deep 13
Stinger: "What a monster!"

• Wow, this episode is so much fun. It's my favorite Gamera outing for sure, and just a really fun MST3K episode all around. It has great riffing, and all the host segments are at least worth a smile. And then there's the movie itself, a truly zany outing (featuring the inimitable Cornjob) made all the zanier by the hamfisted dubbing. Much fun, and no traffic accidents.

- This episode was included in Shout!Factory's "Mystery Science Theater 3000 Collection: Gamera Vs. MST3K" (aka Vol. XXI).
- Note the MST3K lunch boxes (sold by the Info Club; now no longer available) in the opening segment ... Frank has one too!
- I'm not sure what's funny about Joel's invention. Seems pretty useful, actually, and a while back somebody started making and selling them.
- Did you notice the season one-style table slap! What happened to the buttons?
- The awful, awful dubbing in the press conference scene early on makes for a gaspingly funny few minutes of riffing.
- References to things completely forgotten: "The New Munsters" and "Superboy." Sheesh.
- Crow gets roughed up by Joel in the theater after deploying several puns in a row.
- Callbacks: The space ship is "funny flying." (ROCKETSHIP XM) "... so much... about ...lately?" (GAMERA) "And he's givin' it back to you!" (SIDEHACKERS) "Rex Dart" (GODZILLA VS. MEGALON)
- There's a funny in-joke when the bots point out a starfield created by putting "a bunch of Christmas light against a wall" and talk about how really cheesy that is. That, of course, is exactly how BBI did it.
- Joel rolls with the punches again: In the theater, as the Gamera song begins, Crow's arm falls off. Joel just reattaches it and they keep going. Crow's arm falls off again in the next segment and Joel pops it back on again. They keep going.
- The lyrics to the song in the first segment kind of restate the premise. I wonder if they were they getting notes from the network asking them to restate the premise more.

- One curious lyric in the song is when, explaining the kinds of riffs they do, J&tB sing: "So we hi-keeba all over the place and talk of a thousand wonderful days." The first example is a pretty good description of a typical riff, but "talk of thousand wonderful days," a callback to a line in "ROCKETSHIP XM," has maybe been referenced twice since then. Did Mike (who, the credits say, wrote the song) really think that was a typical example of a movie riff?
- The whole notion of a twin earth on the opposite side of the sun (which we previously encountered in "Stranded in Space") pops up for a moment in this movie and is then forgotten.
- Tom and Crow come into the theater still wearing their hats from the host segment 2; Joel removes them. Crow has no net for the entire theater segment.
- During the flashback, we get a few minutes of a Gamera movie MST3K didn't do (it's "Gamera vs. Viras").
- One of the kids says, "wait a minute..." and Tom says "You're not a cop!" Both Tom and Joel express their love of that joke. It's a reference to a scene from the Mel Brooks movie "High Anxiety" I'd completely forgotten about.
- Zappa fans loved to hear "Weasels ripped my flesh! Rizzz!!"
- Instant catchphrase: "I'm feeling really good!"
- Vaguely dirty riff: "Wait, touch me here while you do that!"
- The Richard Burton sketch is pretty dumb, but it's saved by Trace's great impression. Also, it was definitely written in pre-internet days, when they could have easily looked up info on him (such as that he was born Richard Walter Jenkins).
- I think this is the first time Crow has called himself "Crow T. Robot"? Joel seems surprised by it.
- Also, Joel amusingly refers to himself as "the sleepy-voiced narrator."
- Toward the end of the movie, there's a riff in which Tom rattles off a bunch of New York-area subway stations. Gotta figure that was provided by Frank.

- This is also the episode with the infamous "most obscure reference ever": "Stop her! She's got my keyboard!" (By the way, it's often quoted – including by cast members – as "...Mike's keyboard..." but that's not what is said.)
- In the closing segment, J&tB sing the Gamera song AGAIN–this time in fake (and mildly racist, it seems to me) nonsense words intended to sound like Japanese. I'm not sure I get the point, but it's wacky!
- Mike is hilarious as Michael Feinstein, but wow does he ever hit a sour note at one point.
- CreditsWatch: Trace and Frank are still "guest villians" (misspelled) and Dr. F's last name is still misspelled "Forrestor." Brian Wright returns for the first of five eps as audio guy. Someone named Carolyn Sloat was a prop assistant for this episode only. Sometimes hires don't work out. For Thomas Alphonso and Tom Henderson, this was their last show as interns.
- Which brings us to a special treat, courtesy of a MSTie named Lisa Wakabayashi (with assistance from her mom, thanks ladies): The Gamera Theme Song translated (the Japanese lyrics are, obviously, phonetic. The English lyrics are in parentheses after each line.)

Verse 1

Gamera, Gamera (Gamera, Gamera)

Ikasuzo, Gamera! Ikasuzo, Gamera! Ikasuzo, Gamera! (So cool, Gamera! So cool, Gamera! So cool, Gamera!)

Nichi, Getsu, Ka, Sui, Nichi, Getsu, Ka, Sui (Sunday, Monday, Tuesday, Wednesday, Sunday, Monday, Tuesday, Wednesday)

Nikkoh saegiru, Akuma no niji da (Shadow the sun, evil's rainbow)

Reitoh kaiju, kurunara koi! (Frozen monster, dare to march!)

Haneta-zo, tonda-zo. Go! Go! Go! (Jumped, flew. Go! Go! Go!)

Kaen funsha de yattsukero (Destroy with jet flame)

Ikasuzo, Gamera! Ikasuzo, Gamera! Ikasuzo, Gamera! (So cool, Gamera! So cool, Gamera! So cool, Gamera!)

Verse 2
Gamera, Gamera (Gamera, Gamera)
Ganbare, Gamera! Ganbare, Gamera! Ganbare, Gamera! (Hold out,
Gamera! Hold out, Gamera! Hold out, Gamera!)
Getsu, Ka, Sui, Moku, Getsu, Ka, Sui, Moku? (Monday, Tuesday,
Wednesday, Thursday, Monday, Tuesday, Wednesday, Thursday)
Gekkoh yaburu, satsujin onpa (Overcome the moonlight, super sonic)
Mach kaiju, itsudemo koi! (Monster mach, come anytime!)
Hikatta, yoketa-zo. Go! Go! Go! (Burning bright. Go! Go! Go!)
Kuwaete hanasuna, Fukitobase. (Bite hard and blown away)
Ganbare, Gamera! Ganbare, Gamera! Ganbare, Gamera! (Hold out,
Gamera! Hold out, Gamera! Hold out, Gamera!)

Verse 3
Gamera Gamera (Gamera, Gamera)
Tsuyoi-zo, Gamera! Tsuyoi-zo, Gamera! Tsuyoi-zo, Gamera! (So
strong, Gamera! So strong, Gamera! So strong, Gamera!)
Ka, Sui, Moku, Kin, Ka, Sui, Moku, Kin? (Tuesday, Wednesday,
Thursday, Friday, Tuesday, Wednesday, Thursday, Friday)
Kasei ka, Kinsei, dokokano hoshino (Mars, Venus, any other stars)
Uchu kaiju, nandemo koi! (Come monsters from the universe!)
Kitta-zo, Tsuita-zo. Go! Go! Go! (Stabbed, shoved. Go! Go! Go!)
Kaiten jet de, taiatari (Tackled with circling jet)
Tsuyoi-zo, Gamera! Tsuyoi-zo, Gamera! Tsuyoi-zo, Gamera! (So
strong, Gamera! So strong, Gamera! So strong, Gamera!)
- Fave riff: "We're from the padding department! Where's the plot
  hole?" Honorable mention: "You know, guys, it just dawned on me
  how weird this film is."

Movie stuff:

1) A moment from this movie that always has me in stitches is
   the whole "Hello! Thank you!" routine. A classic case of taking

216 • MSTIEPEDIA

something innocuous in the movie and exaggerating it for brilliant comic effect.

2) This is the movie with the memorable "Gamera on the high-bar" moment, later used in the opening. I am a little surprised it wasn't used here as the stinger.

Episode 313- EARTH VS. THE SPIDER (with short: 'SPEECH – USING YOUR VOICE')
First shown: 9/14/91

Short: (1950) Prof. E.C. Buehler explains how to be a good public speaker.

Movie: (1958) A teen discovers her father has become a meal for a giant spider, which then attacks the small town where she lives.

Opening: Crow hosts Tom in "Inside The Robot Mind."
Invention exchange: The Mads have invented the cheese phone, while Joel shows off his CD blow drier
Host segment 1: J&tB read through Crow's screenplay, "Earth vs. Soup"
Host segment 2: A rehearsal of J&tB's rock band Spidorr brings a visit, on the Hexfield, from the custodian of 7th galaxy
Host segment 3: J&tB discuss Creeple People and other dangerous but fun toys
End: Crow and Tom present their reports on Bert I. Gordon, Tom reads a letter, Frank is sick
Stinger: From the short, "Don't worry, we've had him put down."

Comments:

• As we begin the second half of this season, there is a lot to love about this one. Hokey movie, classic short, familiar faces, great riffing, great host segments. This is one of those "firing-on-all-cylinders" episodes.

- It seems like they had season one and Josh Weinstein on the brain during the making of this episode. In the opening bit, the Mads reprise the season-one catchphrase "Thank you!!" then look embarrassed. Later, as the deputy (who looks a little like Dr. E) is devoured by the spider, Joel yells: "Dr. Erhardt! No! So that's what happened to him!" (a reference to the fact that Dr. E's fate was never really spelled out when he was written out of the premise). And at the end, in another homage to season one, Joel offers ram chips to the bots as rewards, something he has not done in ages.
- Jerry and Sylvia get a mention in the opening.
- The short became an instant classic, with instant catchphrases like "Plenty of lip and tongue action." I think it really showed them the riffing potential of this kind of short. This could have been one of those episodes where the short overpowered the movie, but they managed to rise to the occasion with the movie as well.
- Incidentally, the speaker standing by the American flag is none other than Herk Harvey, director of this and four other MSTed Centron shorts (he's perhaps best known as the director of the infamous stinker, "Carnival of Souls.")
- Callbacks: "...and a good friend" (ROCKETSHIP XM), "Joe Doakes..." (X MARKS THE SPOT), Crow sings "Hike your pants up..." (DADDY-O), "the spider is either missing or he's dead!" (PHANTOM CREEPS)
- After the spider attack in the opening, Crow says, approximately, "Heyhepullhefilalayvava." They keep going. By the way, once and for all, THAT is Merritt Stone driving the truck and being killed by the spider in the beginning of the movie.
- I love how, in segment 1, Crow's "lips" move while the others read their parts. Classic Trace.
- A little Firesign Theatre reference, I think, when Joel says "Oh Porgie no!" while reading through "Earth vs. Soup."

218 • MSTiepedia

- I just love Joel's skeleton voice. "I'm famished!"
- Gross riff: "Does your dad like bran?" Ew.
- Tom Servo twice pronounces Gary Busey's last name "bussy" instead of "byoosie." I wonder if Kevin had not heard of him. They keep going.
- Joel brings up, and then defends the reputation of, the Ashwaubenon High Jaguars, from his real-life Wisconsin high school.
- The ELP bashing is interesting. That feels to me like it comes from Mike.
- Geek alert: In the Rocket Number 9 shot, the spaceship is a badly disguised TOS Klingon battle cruiser model. I'm so embarrassed that I know that.
- This would not be the last time Mike played a janitor...
- Mike says: "What the Hector Alonzo is goin' on?" I think he meant Hector Elizondo. They keep going.
- As Paul points out in the ACEG, the second host segment is in the wrong spot. But they seemed to know it at the time: as they're coming back to the theater Joel says: "I don't know what that janitor has to do with anything." Later, when the janitor finally appears, Joel says: "Ohh! THAT's how it fits in."
- An odd moment as they re-enter the theater, Joel says "We're comin' out of the game thing." In some of the outtakes that have come to light in recent years, we sometimes see them reminding each other what host segment just appeared in the show. Filming schedules were such that host segments were filmed on one day and theater segments another day, so it was sometimes easy to forget where all the pieces fit in the puzzle. I think that's what Joel was doing here, but they didn't bother to start over.
- I can't find it on the Web anymore, but there used to be an odd web site by a guy who was REALLY into the Thingmaker and Creeple People (discussed in segment 3). The page had a transcript of segment three, because he found it so moving.

- Segment 3 is weird – for most of it, they seem to be championing these toys and blaming the "careless" kids who got them taken off the market, but then Joel ends it with a saccharine little homily about the toymakers of tomorrow. I don't get it. I'm not quite sure what's supposed to be funny about that. Maybe they were just desperate for an ending.
- Note the "Movie Sign!" bumper sticker on the desk in the ending segment.
- There's an interesting "call-forward" to "Beginning of the End" in Crow's report. Had they seen it? It was two seasons away.
- CreditsWatch: Paul Chaplin becomes a full-time writer. Tim Paulson is back as online editor. Cindy Hansen begins her stint as an intern. Someone named Mary Flaa does the first of two shows as hair and makeup person. Trace and Frank are still "villians" and Dr. F's name is still spelled "Forrestor."
- Fave riff from short: "Here's George Patton, a patriot and into high-grade weed." Honorable mention: "We've had him put down."
- Fave riff: "Everybody's afraid of these crane shots!" Honorable mention: "We've got bugs!"

Movie stuff:

1) Character Mike mentions wanting to see Bert I. Gordon's "Attack of the Puppet People." You can see the lobby cards for it in the background, and a poster appears outside the theater. Lobby cards and posters for the movie in episode 309- THE AMAZING COLOSSAL MAN also appear, not-so-subtly.
2) Originally titled, "The Spider," this movie was retitled to cash in on the name of another successful movie with a similar title, 1956's "Earth vs. the Flying Saucers."

Episode 314- MIGHTY JACK
First shown: 9/21/91

Movie: (1968 TV series; 1987 compilation movie) A top secret organization, called Mighty Jack, makes use of a giant submarine, called Mighty Jack, to battle terrorist organization Q.

Opening: Something horrible has happened on the SOL ... face!
Invention exchange: The Mads show off the formal flipper; J&tB demonstrate ear-shaped earmuffs
Host segment 1: The bots show Joel their Mighty Jack pet food commercial
Host segment 2: The bots put Joel in the blinding light compartment
Host segment 3: Joel goes off the deep end while suggesting underwater movie ideas
End: J&tB sing "Slow the Plot Down!" and Frank's quoting Melville, arr.
Stinger: He died as he lived ... lovin' his work.

Comments:

- I'm going to put this in the "good-not great" column. The Brains are on such a roll at this point in the season that even a bolus like this movie can't stop their momentum. There are a few slow/quiet patches in the riffing and segment 3 is a bit strange, but there's a lot more to like in this episode than dislike.
- This episode appears on Shout Factory's "Mystery Science Theater 3000 Collection: Vol XXII."
- For one of only two times until he would leave the show, Joel is NOT wearing the standard maroon jumpsuit he's been wearing since episode 212. It's kind of a pastel green.
- The opening is a lot of fun. "I'm blind! That thing cut me!" cracks me up every time.
- Jerry the Mole person gets another mention.

- Another use of the then-hot phrase: "Hello, Federal!"
- At the beginning of the invention exchange, you may be wondering why there is Velcro on the bots' heads. You soon find out.
- Yikes, those awful pictures at the beginning of the movie. Bleah.
- Yes, Joel, the joke was a little racist, or at least language-ist.
- Callbacks: Puma? (RING OF TERROR) Also: "That's pretty good!" (SIDEHACKERS) "Glenn Corbett! (STRANDED IN SPACE) "Hikeeba!" (WOMEN OF THE PREHISTORIC PLANET) "You're stuck here!" and "He tried to kill me..." (FUGITIVE ALIEN) and "It's Gamera!"
- Segment 1 is just so conversational and laid-back, it's a great example of their unique style of humor.
- Obscure riff (for me, at least): Riffing on the horn stuff in the musical score, Servo rattles off the names of several horn players I recognized. But Teo Macero I had not heard of. Now I have. See, this show teaches you things!
- Segment two is a real gem, one for the highlight reel. "You have GOT to be KIDDING me, Crow!"
- You can tell this episode was written only a few months after the end of the first Gulf War. It features a lot of buzzwords and phrases from that era, including "collateral damage" and "baby formula factory."
- Vaguely dirty riff: "I was just daydreaming." Also: Movie: "Full thrust!" Crow: "Really!?"
- Regional riff: There's a reference to Tommy Bartlett, the Wisconsin impresario responsible for several attractions in the Wisconsin Dells. You pretty much have to have vacationed in the Midwest to get that one.
- Joel follows right up on the "Earth vs Soup" bit from last week.
- Joel mentions Shake-a-Pudd'n. As a kid, I loved Shake-a-Pudd'n. Or maybe I just loved the commercials. I forget.
- The "Slow the Plot Down" song is a classic. Note the way the camera rocks slightly as they sing. Makes me a little nauseous.

222 • MSTiepedia

- CreditsWatch: Mary Flaa completes her two-episode stint as hair and makeup person, and was never seen or heard from again. Trace and Frank are still guest "villians" (misspelled) and Dr. F's last name is still misspelled "Forrestor."
- Fave riff: "Meanwhile, back on the Greasy Bastard..." Honorable mention: "Oh, my aching imperialist dogs!"

Movie stuff:

1) Like "Time of the Apes" and "Fugitive Alien" before it, this is the first and last episodes of a TV series season, with a little connecting filler thrown in. Initially I, like Crow, could barely even retain a memory of anything that I had seen in it. The movie seemed to self-erase in my memory as I watched it. It took many viewings to get any sense of what the damn thing was about, or for any of it to stick in my memory.

Episode 315- TEENAGE CAVEMAN (with shorts: 'AQUATIC WIZARDS' and 'CATCHING TROUBLE')

Short 1: (1955) Water skiing thrills from Florida's Cypress Gardens.

Short 2: (1936) Wildlife bully Ross Allen threatens ecosystems, endangers animals and generally terrorizes the Florida Everglades.

Movie: (1958) A rebellious teenage caveboy questions the clan's rules and yearns to explore the land beyond the river.
First shown: 11/9/91

Opening: It's dreary rainy day on the SOL and J&tB are bored. Magic Voice has some suggestions for activities
Invention exchange: J&tB present their creative ipecacs, the Mads try to unveil their invention, but end up in a brawl

Host segment 1: J&tB present "Catching Ross"
Host segment 2: The Mads are still fighting
Host segment 3: Joel explains to the bots how there were conservatives and risk-takers throughout history
End: The bots are dressed as the mutants from the movie, Joel reads a letter, the Mads are patching things up with a cup of kindness
Stinger: Watch out for that ... tree!

Comments:

- It's a rare two-short episode and that's just one of the delights of this episode. The movie is Corman at his corniest, and it brings out the best in the riffers, and the segments are a lot of fun too. A standout episode.
- This episode is not yet available on DVD.
- My copy is from Turkey Day '94, with Robert Vaughn appearing in the window of Adam West's microwave during the introductory bumper.
- J&tB have one of their longest conversations with Magic Voice during the opener.
- The invention exchange has the memorable ipecac bit, followed by the truly classic battle of the Mads.
- As Frank and Dr. F prepare to mix it up, Frank makes use of the classic "Road House" line: "Take the train."
- The riffers did a lot of variations of the line: "Just throw that stuff in back, I kinda live outta my car." In the water skiing scene it's: "Just throw that stuff in the back. I kinda live off my shoulders."
- Where I used to live, we knew a couple who were actually named Bob and Connie. I made them a special sound file of Crow saying, in his best announcer voice: "Bob and Connie really enjoy life." They did, too, and as far as I know they still do.
- Now we come to the infamous "Catching Trouble" short, featuring such casually cruel footage that J&tB felt they must immedi-

ately take revenge in the following host segment, which became an instant classic. I love Joel's cry of "We went to camp together! He hates me!"

- Memorable moment: Joel has one bear cub call another bear cub "Greg." Tom then turns to him and asks, incredulously, "Greg?"
- A character in the movie mentions "the thing that gives death with its touch" and the riff is "Penny Marshall?" Yow.
- Joel seems to be parodying his own season-two segments in segment 2. That stack of artist's renderings has become shorthand for "Joel has a boring idea for a presentation."
- There's a moment in the theater when Tom Servo applauds. ...um...
- Note the Star Trek fight music playing during second fight scene. Also note the classic Mannix/James Kirk disarm, the cry of "HiKeeba!" and a slam on Beetle Bailey outta nowhere.
- Isn't it fun when you get a riff for the first time, even after you've seen the episode several times? I had one of those this time, when Tom sings o/` "Heeeeerrrrre he iiiiiis, your komodo draaaaagon-nnn" o/` which I suddenly realized was a reference to the movie "The Freshman."
- Segment 3 is not really funny, just kind of thoughtful. But I like when Tom Servo says "Well, they were right about THAT!" Which is true, and kind of negates the point Joel is making.
- For some reason Crow's net is on the counter during segment 3.
- Vaguely dirty riff: "He invented the quiver." "So did SHE!"
- Callbacks: "You know right now I could go for a char-broiled hamburger sandwich..." (Jungle Goddess), "Plenty of lip and tongue action," (the Speech short), "I'm Trumpy!" (Pod People), "Thong, the fish are ready!" (Cave Dwellers), "Chili peppers burn my gut" (Sidehackers) and "This looks like a job ... for Mighty Jack!"
- At one point, when actor Ed Nelson appears, Joel recognizes him and points out that he's there. A state park joke.
- There's a Firesign Theatre reference as Tom, as the old survivor, says that something "scared everybody."

- This makes twice in two episodes they have used the Odd Couple line: "bad meat or good cheese."
- CreditsWatch: Faye Burkholder returns for two eps as hair and makeup person. Trace and Frank are still guest "villians" (misspelled) and Dr. F's last name is still misspelled "Forrestor."
- Fave riff from first short: "They just snap clean away!" Honorable mention: "This has got litigation written all over it."
- Fave riff from the second short: "Ross tries to towel away the evil, but nothing doing." Honorable mention: "Oh, there just happened to be a camera under the water…"
- Fave riff from the movie: "Um, like, do you know any Tull?" Honorable mention: "So, how many toasters did we get?"

Short stuff:

1) The two shorts are both essentially commercials for now-extinct Florida tourist traps that closed down in the 1970s, as the popularity of Walt Disney World drove a lot of other Florida attractions out of business. Founded in 1936, Cypress Gardens, in 2011, reopened as Legoland.
2) Ross Allen's Florida Reptile Institute was in Silver Springs. It's gone now, but you can still visit Ross Allen Island.

Movie stuff:

1) Wondering what the Helsinki Formula is and why they keep mentioning it? It's a supposed baldness cure that actor Robert Vaughn used to pitch. Sadly Vaughn died in 2016, forever dashing my hopes of a "Man from U.N.C.L.E." reunion with David McCallum.
2) The parrot-like costume is left over from "Night of the Blood Beast," and was worn by uncredited actor Ross Sturlin. Sturlin also helped make and wore a leech costume in "Attack of the Giant Leeches."

226 • MSTIEPEDIA

3) Screenwriter R. Wright Campbell was capable of better: he got an Oscar nomination for his screenplay for 1957's "Man of a Thousand Faces."
4) Once again, stock footage from "One Million B.C." makes an appearance.
5) Exterior water scenes were done at the Arboretum in Arcadia, Calif. Other exterior shots were filmed at Bronson Canyon, of course.

Episode 316- GAMERA VS. ZIGRA
First shown: 10/19/91

Movie: (1971) In the (sigh) seventh outing of the long-running Japanese monster movie series, aliens from a distant planet, called Zigra, send a spaceship, called Zigra, commanded by a strange creature, called Zigra, to Earth with a plan of world domination. Opposing him is a pair of concerned marine biologists, pesky brats Kenny and Helen and, of course, giant turtle monster Gamera.

Opening: J&tB are having a root beer kegger to celebrate the last Gamera movie
Invention exchange: The Mads have invented Three Stooges guns; Joel has invented the Crow-ka-bob; Frank spoils Dr. F's surprise
Host segment 1: The bots have built a scale model of Gamera
Host segment 2: The bots present their shoe box dioramas
Host segment 3: Kenny and Helen visit on the Hexfield
End: J&tB present different ways to sing the Gamera song
Stinger: Fish boy talks to himself.

Comments:

• It isn't my favorite Gamera movie (that would be "Guiron") but this one is plenty strange and very riffable, and the guys do a great job. The host segments are fair to good.

- This episode is included in Shout!Factory's Mystery Science Theater 3000 Collection: Gamera Vs. MST3K (aka Vol. XXI).
- The Shout DVD menu notes something I never noticed before – there's a preponderance of Monty Python references in this one, for some reason.
- At the beginning of the invention exchange segment, Joel hits the piñata a little too hard, I think, and it spins around and empties the "guts" contents, with the opening facing away from the camera. Joel quickly reaches in and taps it so it spins back around, and we can still see some guts hanging out, so we get the joke, but we never got to see what we were supposed to see. They keep going AND they used this take!
- "I'd take the pizza off the ceiling" is a reference to a commercial at the time. I can't find it on Youtube.
- It must have taken some practice for Trace and Frank to line up those guns so they would meet.
- Tom makes a raspberry, and Joel notes that Tom has no fleshy parts with which to make it.
- Sandy Frank probably didn't appreciate the assertion that his IQ is 13-and-a-half.
- In the segment with the Gamera model, you can see some "guts" leaking out the bottom from behind the door before Joel opens it.
- Joel says "Oh, Lisa..." before opening the "guts" door. "Green Acres" reference?
- Then-current riff: There's a deserved slam on once-prominent KKK leader David Duke, but how many people even remember him now?
- The appearance of the Japanese version of the Monty Python "It's!" guy seems to go nowhere, as does the whole "who gets to buy the fish" subplot.
- During the sketch with the dioramas, a table has been added to the set in front of the normal desk. It looks like it was something out

of the prop shop – there's spray paint patterns on it that they didn't even try to cover up.

- As Joel brings up Tom's diorama, Tom and Crow have some lines, but Joel completely plows right over them with his own dialog. Joel also says "Steven Bing…er…Steven King." They keep going.
- It's a nice touch that Cambot goes through the diorama door.
- Callback: Tom sings the WILD REBELS song. Also: "McCloud!" ("POD PEOPLE").
- Tom again does an impression of Dr. Erhardt saying "Enjoy!"
- A glaring mistake (among many) in the dubbing: Lana says she is going to feed the kids to the dolphins, but the animals in the tank before her are whales.
- Obscure reference/pun: "That terrapin is stationary." The right Deadheads will get it.
- In the host segment with the hexfield, the model of Gamera is, well, lame. By the way: this is Bridget's first appearance on the show.
- The whole sequence where Gamera rescues the crippled bathysphere (which people in the movie keep calling a "bathoscope"), and delivers it on shore like Lynn Swann scoring a touchdown, which we saw in the KTMA version, is missing here. Tom notices.
- Suggestive riff: "You know, Gamera's never seen the mohel…"
- I love Gypsy's bullet bra in the ending segment.
- The final, harmonized version of the Gamera song seems to be all Kevin, overdubbed.
- Creditswatch: The mole people "roadies" behind Dr. F. and Frank are Kevin and Jef. There's also a "special thanks" to St. Paul Harley Davidson. Maybe for Trace's and Frank's getups? Once again "villians" is spelled wrong and Dr. F's last name is misspelled "Forrestor."
- Fave riff: "And, uh, maybe you could dust up here some time!" Honorable mention: "Wait, I found some more oxygen in a drawer.

We're fine." and "Fish Argument Theater will be right back, but first, a scene from Plot Convenience Playhouse."

1) As I noted when we watched this on KTMA: I don't really understand the anti-science message that floats through the movie. The two dads are biologists. Doesn't that make them scientists? And are scientists actively polluting the sea? So why are scientists the problem?

2) As I also noted then: I have seen this movie a dozen times now and I still cannot make heads or tails out of the weird Zigra monster up on the shelf in the alien spaceship. It looks a little like a skeksis from "The Dark Crystal," but what's with the billowing cobwebs?

3) Also from the KTMA comments: How did "your Earth science" pollute a planet 400 light years away? I ran that back and listened to it again and that's definitely what he says. Doesn't make any sense.

Episode 317- THE SAGA OF THE VIKING WOMEN AND THEIR VOYAGE TO THE WATERS OF THE GREAT SEA SERPENT (with short: THE HOME ECONOMICS STORY)
First shown: 10/26/91

Short: (1951) Four college girls major in home economics in college.

Movie: (1957) Viking women set sail to rescue their men who have been enslaved by barbarians.

Opening: Consider the lowly waffle
Invention exchange: Joel continues to consider waffles; the mads demonstrate their meat re-animator, Joel shows off an iron that turns waffles into pancakes

Host segment 1: Joel has reprogrammed the bots to love waffles and asks them to suggest new uses for waffles
Host segment 2: "Waffles!"
Host segment 3: Willy the Waffle gives a spirited defense of waffles
End: The Waffle song, Dr. F is "re-animating" Frank
Stinger: "But you don't understand! I'm a PRINCE!"

Comments:

- Let me just say: waffles. Things get into the heads of the writers during the course of doing an episode, and sometimes it just leaks out. I think this is one of those times. All in all, this one is lots of fun. The movie is, if such a thing is possible, even lamer and sillier than "Teenage Caveman" and the riffing is solid. As for the host segments, well: waffles.
- This episode was included in Shout!Factory's "The Mystery Science Theater 3000 Collection, Vol. XXXIV."
- In the theme song, the clip from "The Crawling Eye" that has been part of the intro since the first season has been replaced with Godzilla's tail slide attack from episode 212- GODZILLA VS. MEGATON.
- Dr. F calls Joel "Aunt Jemima" twice in one segment.
- Trace's expressions during the invention exchange are priceless.
- Tom and Crow both make LOTR references at the beginning, though Crow says "I'm ashamed I know that."
- Callback: Tom rediscovers the Creepy Girl (CATALINA CAPER). It's a calamity! (GAMERA VS GUIRON) "The law is the word..." (TEENAGE CAVEMAN)
- In segment two, after Joel delivers his line, he throws the plate up in the air, and then has to duck out of the way of it. They keep going and they used the take.

- Tom and Crow are already in theater when Joel arrives after segment 2.
- How many now-middle-aged people had the problem of not being allowed to stay up and watch "Love, American Style"? I know *I* did.
- As has been chronicled, the Willy the waffle bit is based on the "CASE OF SPRING FEVER" short, which they watched during this season but never riffed until season 10.
- Joel's line "We got a party to go to" at the end of segment 3 is a "Laugh-In" reference.
- Crow still has his Willy the Waffle outfit on when entering the theater after segment 3.
- Then-current reference: Rosie Ruiz.
- The show ends with a great song, but how come there's no "lyrics and music" credit for it in the credits. Guess it was a group effort?
- CreditsWatch: Andrea DuCane came in to do makeup for the only time this season. Trace and Frank are still "villians" and Dr. F's last name is still misspelled "Forrestor."
- Fave riff from the short: "Kegs will be tapped. Men will be used." Honorable mention: "...while Kay struggles with basic motor skills."
- Fave riff: "...and no time to figure out how we saw all that!" Honorable mention: "Not a chest hair among 'em" and "I'm Todd the Baptist!"

Movie stuff:

1) In far shots, the sea serpent was actually special effects guy Irving Block's finger, covered with clay, with a fin stuck on it. Really. And, of course, this is yet another Corman movie largely shot in Bronson Canyon.

2) Oh, and: despite what is says in the ACEG, Jonathan Haze does NOT play the prince.

232 • MSTIEPEDIA

Episode 318- STAR FORCE – FUGITIVE ALIEN II
First shown: 11/16/91

Movie: (1978 original TV show episodes; 1987 compilation movie)
The further adventures of the crew of Earth spaceship Bacchus 3:
They try to destroy a super-weapon and Ken finally confronts his
former leader.

Opening: Tom and Crow discuss the nature of puppets
Invention exchange: Tom and Crow compete in a "name-that-puppet" quiz show, with Joel as quizmaster. In Deep 13, the Mads have
invented big noses, while Joel shows off his big head
Host segment 1: Tom Servo is dead! Joel and Crow rush to save him
Host segment 2: J&tB present the Captain Joe action figure
Host segment 3: J&tB sing: "The Fugitive Alien medley
End: Crow and Tom are hoping to influence the Mads' movie
choices; Joel asks the bots how they would design the ultimate evil
person; Joel reads letters; Frank defends Tom T. Hall
Stinger: "Captain, I've got it fixed! It's all working again!"

Comments:

- I know if they hadn't done this, fans would be complaining about
  that "to be continued" at the end of the first one, but, jeebus, did
  we really need more of this? The first "Fugitive Alien" ep is one
  of the most beloved episodes of the show, no question. This one,
  well, it's more of the same, and it starts to wear a little thin (for me,
  at least) in the last hour or so. Even Servo sings "We realize you've
  had your fill..." Still, the host segments are great, so overall I'm
  going to go with a "fair" rating.
- This one was included in Shout!Factory's "Mystery Science Theater 3000 Collection: Vol XXIV."

- This is the last of the Sandy Frank KTMA re-dos (though no fan copy of the KTMA riff of this movie is known to exist). It is also the end of this season's see-saw, back-and-forth pattern – one Japanese outing, one American film, etc. From here the season goes is strange new directions.
- During the quiz show bit (which is kind of reminiscent of those season-two segments with the artists renderings) Joel – reading off a card I think – says he wants the bots to guess the "genius" of each puppet. I think he meant to say "genus." Tom Servo quietly corrects him and they keep going.
- I love Joel in full quizmaster mode: "Kukla… Kukla…"
- For a long time, I wondered what that was in Joel's hand when he's wearing the Big Head. Then it hit me – it's his lavaliere mic, which the Big Head would probably have interfered with.
- Trace seems to have more fun with the big noses than Frank. He just loves making it waggle ever so slightly.
- Joel wears the big head into the theater, then hurls it aside.
- As soon as the movie starts, all the old riffs come rushing back: "Rocky!" "Again!" "Rita!" "Meter Maid!" And forklifts galore. I don't think I should call these "call backs." More like retreads.
- Joel forgets Tom when entering the theater after segment 1. Tom reminds him and he goes back to get him.
- Callbacks: "A girl!?" (VIKING WOMEN) "Hikeeba" (WOMEN OF THE PREHISTORIC PLANET)
- After Joel sings his song in segment 3, Tom quietly comments: "What a lunatic, huh?"
- There's more Sandy Frank bashing in this one, especially the final verse to the song in segment 3.
- Tom does a lot of singing in this one.
- Then-current reference: "Farfegnugen."
- Complicated and now-quite-dated riff: "I'm George Bernard Shaw in Baghdad – I'm under a table and I'm writing 'Candide.' " This is a Swiss army joke.

- This show marks the first reference to Leonard Maltin's Movie Guide, I think.
- To any adult, that first letter Joel reads, from an Eddie Hogan of New Jersey, is worrisome. I wonder what happened to Eddie. It's also a pretty pristine example of the unintended downside of Joel's "sleepy" character, which a lot of kids mistook as some sort of endorsement by the show, and by Joel in particular, of being a stoned slacker. You can tell the kid was expecting that his comments would be met with approval, not a concerned suggestion that he get into breakfast.
- CreditsWatch: Clayton James is back at hair and makeup. Additional Music: Lyrics: Kevin. Trace and Frank are still "villians" and Dr. F's last name is still misspelled "Forrestor."
- Fave riff: "'Course it pierced his colon...'" Honorable mention: "He's getting a tattoo with a Busy-Buzz-Buzz."

Episode 319- WAR OF THE COLOSSAL BEAST (with short: 'MR. B. NATURAL')
First shown: 11/30/91

Short: (1957) A shrill, androgynous succubus urges a gawky middle schooler to take up a musical instrument.

Movie: (1958) When giant Glenn from "The Amazing Colossal Man," now a deranged and disfigured monster, is spotted in Mexico, his worried sister tries to save him.

Opening: J&tB come up with new names for Mex-American food combos
Invention exchange: The Mads have invented the breakfast bazooka, while Joel shows off his between-meal mortar
Host segment 1: Tom and Crow debate the topic "Mr. B. Natural: man or woman?"

Host segment 2: J&tB are singing the Big Head song when Glen revisits
Host segment 3: Joel presents "KTLA predicts!"
End: Joel offers the bots samples of his special bread, Joel reads a letter then Glen reads one; Frank gets another breakfast shot at him
Stinger: That's a happy king?

Comments:

- If there was ever an episode where the short outshines the feature, this is it. That being said, this was one of those times where I was expecting to struggle through the movie but was pleasantly surprised. Instead of the dull slog I remembered from previous viewings, I found it pretty entertaining and the riffing was pretty consistently good. The host segments are more good than bad as well. This really is a fun episode all around.
- Ah, Mister B. Calling it a classic short isn't enough. It is probably the most famous of all the shorts the show presented and maybe the most watched 20 or so minutes of the entire series. I practically have the thing memorized. (Note: I admit to stealing the phrase "shrill succubus" from the ACEG. It's just too perfect a description.)
- In the segment 1, Joel says "bogart" instead of "robot." They keep going.
- The military guy says the river below Boulder Dam is "a mile deep in some places." Wait, WHAT??
- The Big Head makes another appearance in segment 2.
- The gibberish Joel shouts at the end of segment 3 comes from the chaotic labels of a product known as Dr. Bronner's Magic Soap – still available at your local health food store, and at drbronner.com.
- Callback: McCloud! (POD PEOPLE)

- This is one of two MSTed movies (522- TEENAGE CRIME WAVE is the other) that ends at L.A.'s Griffith Observatory.
- CreditsWatch: This was intern Cindy Hansen's last episode. Trace and Frank are still "villians" and Dr. F's name is still misspelled "Forrestor."
- Fave riff from the short: "Mom, Dad? Tell me you heard that!" Honorable mention: "Forget music! I wanna dance!"
- Fave riff from the movie: "My nurse fell down his throat!" Also: "Hee-haw, it's Sam Wainwright!" and "Sir, you just described ME!"

Short stuff:

1) The short is in horrible shape. Mr. B's arrival in the kid's bedroom has been spliced out, for example. It was probably hilarious, and therefore somebody cut it out of the print and kept it for his or her own collection of goofy footage. A lot of classic moments in movies have been lost to anonymous "collectors" savaging the only remaining copy of a particular movie. That being said, thanks to RiffTrax, we now know that a pristine, un-chopped-up copy of the short exists – it's the one they used when RiffTrax re-riffed it and MST3K later ran it in the Gizmoplex.

2) The short was filmed at the Waukegan (Illinois) Elementary School and Miami (Ohio) Sr. High School.

3) Betty Luster, who played Mr. B, had a brief TV career in the early 1950s. Her first TV job was on the CBS show "Sing It Again" (1950-51), which was a game show similar to "Name That Tune." Her second TV gig was on the NBC show "Seven at Eleven," which was only on the air for one month in 1951.

4) For a long time I wondered what the target audience of this short was. It couldn't be the kids — they're presented like clueless dorks. It couldn't be the school music teacher — they already know all this. Then, it hit me: It's for the PARENTS! The music

teacher probably was paid to show this during parent-teacher night.

Movie stuff:

1) Why didn't they keep Glenn sedated once they got him into the hangar? (I know, they wanted to have the exciting escape scene).
2) Of course, this movie is known for the 30 seconds of color at the end, triggered by Glenn grabbing the power lines. Did Bert I. really think this was going to help the movie somehow?

Episode 320- THE UNEARTHLY (with shorts: 'POSTURE PALS' and 'APPRECIATING OUR PARENTS')
First shown: 12/14/91

Short 1: (1952) An elementary school teacher holds a posture contest.

Short 2: (1950) A young boy needs to learn how much his parents do for him, and that he should help out around the house.

Movie: (1957) A mad scientist uses nefarious methods to acquire subjects for his bizarre experiments.

Opening: The bots are making a "funny" submission for "America's Funniest Home Videos" and Crow gets the worst of it
Invention exchange: Crow is gnarled, but he likes it. The Mads demonstrate their "hard pills to swallow," while Joel shows off his everyday products named for celebrities
Host segment 1: Crow and Tom present: "Appreciating Gypsy"
Host segment 2: With the help of the Video Toaster, J&tB present the many faces of Tor Johnson

Host segment 3: Tom and Crow create a "Unearthly" board game, but Joel gets hung up on reading the instructions
End: J&tB enjoy using their "Dead End Kids patois," Joel reads a letter using the lingo, and even the Mads get into it.
Stinger: "Time for go to bed!"

Comments:

- This is really a case where the shorts save the episode. Both shorts are fun and the riffing is great. But once the movie starts, things bog down. The guys make fun of Tor for a while, then they start kind of free associating (mixing in some state park jokes), then they fall back on the whole Dead End Kids patois thing. But the riffing never really takes off. Most of the segments are good, which helps drag the rating up a bit as well.
- Oh, the irony of an "America's Funniest Home Videos" parody. Little did Trace suspect he would be drawing a paycheck from it in less than ten years.
- The Mads' invention is my all-time favorite IE. Trace and Frank are brilliant.
- Although there were episodes in the first season that had two episodes of "Radar Men from the Moon," this is only the second time in the history of the series that we have had two shorts (the first was 315- TEENAGE CAVEMAN). They did it one more time in season six.
- At a RiffTrax Live show in 2015, they riffed a short that, according to the credits, was an updated version of "Appreciating Our Parents."
- The Rhino version had alternate takes of the host segments. It was always interesting to see which take they chose and which ended up on the cutting room floor.
- Dr. F says "Enjoy!" like Dr. Erhardt again.
- Short 1 was one of those instant classics that just struck a chord with the fans.

MSTIEPEDIA • 239

- Tom seems scandalized by Joel's reference to VPL.
- Crow is still gnarled when they go into the theater, but during short 2 he says "I better go freshen up," walks off, about three riffs go by without him, and then he returns good as new.
- During segment 1, there's a shot of the SOL bridge piled high with junk. Many of the items are past invention exchanges.
- At the end of segment 1, Gypsy breaks the button.
- In segment 2, the "artists renderings" make another appearance, only to be immediately rejected. Also in segment 2, Tom says "perfap...er...perhaps." They keep going.
- Some techies may be amused by the appearance of an early version of the Video Toaster. It must have been fun to use but, from a present-day perspective, it doesn't seem that impressive. Maybe they were just not very good at it using it, but most of the images are pretty fuzzy and hard to make out.
- Instant catchphrase: "Time for go to bed!"
- In segment 3 there's a little Tom Servo figure among all the crap on the table. Where'd that come from?
- Tom and Crow are already there when Joel arrives back in the theater. Another example of Tom making it to the theater on his own.
- CreditsWatch: Barb Oswald was prop assistant for her third and last time this season. She'd be back for a couple of episodes in season four. Jef Maynard gets credit for "Paint Box Artistry" which I assume means he was able to figure out the Video Toaster better than anybody else.
- Fave riff from short 1: "She should just go home to bed." Honorable mention: "Yes, very much so."
- Fave riff from short 2: "Well, I isolated that nucleotide today..." "Honorable mention: "Dad pulls the lever at the big house."
- Fave riff from the movie: "Stop fighting and give me some skin!"

Episode 321- SANTA CLAUS CONQUERS THE MARTIANS
First shown: 12/21/91

Movie: (1964) Determined to bring Christmas to their home planet, Martians kidnap Santa Claus.

Opening: Crow and Tom are looking at Christmas catalogs
Invention exchange: The Mads demonstrate their wish squisher; J&tB offer up their own misfit toys
Host segment 1: J&tB sing: "A Patrick Swayze Christmas"
Host segment 2: J&tB look over tapes of cheesy Christmas specials
Host segment 3: J&tB read their Christmas essays
End: Caroling, stocking time, Joel reads a letter, meanwhile in Deep 13, the Mads are also exchanging gifts
Stinger: Bad martian's derisive laughter

Comments:

- This one is a genuine classic, and for a lot of MSTies it's as much a part of the holiday season as "White Christmas" or "It's A Wonderful Life." All the host segments are gems. The riffing is solid throughout. It's also another one I have almost completely memorized. But as good as it is, as much fun as it is, as much as "A Patrick Swayze Christmas" has become a yuletide tradition, well, I'll just say it: Both the RiffTrax and Cinematic Titanic riffs of this movie are funnier. That said, this one's guaranteed to get you in the holiday spirit.
- This episode was included in Rhino's "Mystery Science Theater 3000: The Essentials."
- This episode was the one they were working on when a crew from Comedy Central arrived at the studios to shoot footage for the documentary "This is MST3K." Unfortunately, that led to several misunderstandings among some fans. MSTies had been told that

bots painted black were used in the theater sequences, but in the special we could see that the regular bots were being used. "What gives?" a lot of fans asked at the time. The answer: The regular bots had been altered slightly with Christmas additions, and so those were used in the theater, this one time, for continuity's sake, rather than the usual black bots. It's just unfortunate that cameras were there to capture it.

- The invention exchange segment starts very abruptly, directly in Deep 13 rather than having the usual SOL intro. Perhaps they just hurrying for time.
- Frank seems to think kids would like to get what he calls a "video cassette cartridge game," which I don't think is actually a thing. I assume he is talking about Sega or Nintendo but those four words are not the way to describe them.
- Note that they have a tree in Deep 13 but it's not decorated.
- The image above was the best one I could get for this movie, because this version has no title card. The version you can download at Archive.org also has no title card. For a while I thought this was the only print available, but the RiffTrax and Cinematic Titanic versions DO have the title card. So, a much cleaner version exists.
- There are a LOT of then-current topical references in this one: C. Everett Koop … "Twin Peaks" … the Thomas hearings … "Gates has been confirmed" … the notion that Drew Barrymore is a little kid … Eric Heiden … Donna Rice … and the first of several references to long forgotten commercial character, "Bonnie, your Time/Life operator."
- At one point Servo says to Droppo: "You're the Gilligan of your time." Um, sorry, Servo, but this movie and "Gilligan's Island" both came out in the same year.
- Callbacks: "Puma?" (RING OF TERROR) "…the ROBOT HOLOCAUST…"

242 • MSTiepedia

- Right before they start singing "A Patrick Swayze Christmas," Joel says "Paul..." Apparently that was meant to be a David Letterman impression, but almost NOBODY got it.
- That's Mike on the keyboards.
- Note the reference to "suggestive refueling sequences" – we'd get more in season 6.
- In segment 2, Joel seems to be "reading" the undersides of unpackaged VHS tapes. What could possibly be written there? They couldn't have taken two minutes to fabricate little packages? Oh, and Burl Ives has since died.
- Frank's present has little Shadowrama tape on it.
- Fave riff: "Tonight I'm a space pirate! Permission to come aboard!" Honorable mention: Martian: "Crush him!" Tom Servo (robot voice): "You were adopted!"
- CreditsWatch: For some reason, this episode has a whole herd of "additional contributing writers": Lynn-Anne Freise, Tom Wedor, Craig Tollifson, Bob Schrad and Christopher Whiting, whoever they are. It should be no surprise that the music and lyrics for "A Patrick Swayze Christmas" were written by "Road House" aficionado Mike. Trace and Frank are still "guest villians" and Dr. F's last name is still misspelled "Forrestor."

Movie stuff:

1) The movie reportedly was filmed in some abandoned airplane hangars near the Roosevelt Field Mall in Long Island, New York.
2) About Pia. For those who don't get the "Golden Globe" reference, in 1982 Pia Zadora, who as a child played little Girmar, stunned Hollywood when she won a Golden Globe in the "best new female star" category for her bland performance in a terrible little movie called "Butterfly." Hollywood whispers had it

that her rich husband, many decades her senior, bought her the nomination and award through much publicity – and possibly other methods. Hollywood cringed again when she and her husband bought the former estate of movie legends Mary Pickford and Douglas Fairbanks Sr. and she promptly started gutting and modernizing the historic home. That said, Pia does appear to be moderately talented, and apparently has a self-deprecating sense of humor, as shown in when she accepted roles in the movies "Hairspray" and "Voyage of the Rock Aliens." As Joel says in the Cinematic Titanic riff, "You know, I remember thinking that the fact that Pia Zadora was in this was hilarious, but now I can't remember why."

Episode 322- MASTER NINJA I
First shown: 1/11/92

Movie: (1984 TV episodes; 1991 combined movie) An occidental ninja, searching for his long-lost daughter, joins forces with a mush-mouthed drifter to help save an airport, and then a nightclub, from thugs, while evading the ninjas who have been sent to kill him.

Opening: The bots build a model muscle car, and it's a bad influence on Gypsy
Invention exchange: The Mads demonstrate their boil-in-a-bag IVs, while J&tB show off their pop-up books for adults
Host segment 1: Crow presents "The Van Patten Project"
Host segment 2: J&tB brawl to Master Ninja's many theme songs
Host segment 3: J&tB explore other kinds of nunchuks
End: Song: J&tB sing the "Master Ninja Theme Song" while Joel reads a letter; Frank gets even with Dr. F
Stinger: "To them it's some kind of ritual"

244 • MSTiepedia

Comments:

- I'm going to fall back on the "good-not-great" assessment for this one. The movie is reasonably watchable while being very riffable (did nobody have the nerve to tell Timothy to slow down and enunciate?). Most of the segments are fun (though the nunchucks one goes nowhere), and the stupidity of the movie brings out some solid, if not dazzlingly brilliant, riffing.
- This episode was included in Shout's "Mystery Science Theater 3000 Collection: Vol XX."
- In the invention exchange, the script does not call for them to open the "Naked Lunch" book – so the prop guys didn't bother making something that opens. Unfortunately, that makes it not look very much like a book.
- Callbacks: "He learned too late that man is a feeling creature..." (IT CONQUERED THE WORLD); "I'm a ninja warrior!" (paraphrase of a line from "VIKING WOMEN.")
- Crow's crack about "check your career!" came before Timothy became a very successful and award-winning director.
- I like the way Crow ZOOMS out of the theater as he heads into the segment 1, hurrying to prepare his presentation.
- One small problem with segment 1: Timothy is not Dick's son. He's Dick's half brother.
- In the theater segment after segment 1, Crow's net falls off. They keep going.
- They mispronounce Clu Gulager's last name twice.
- We get another reference to "Bonnie, your Time/Life operator." This commercial must have permeated somebody's consciousness.
- Host segment precognition: At the end of segment 2 we see Frank, with top hat and cane, saying "It's show ti-..." We have no idea what he means until we return to the movie and get the second plot about the aging hoofer.

- The second episode – er, I mean, portion – of the movie presents yet another modern night club with an enormous dance floor on which dancers perform but do NOT take off their clothes (see "Flashdance" a prime example). I contend such places DO NOT EXIST. Most night clubs, if they have live shows, have a TINY stage so they can jam as many tables in as possible. And NOBODY dances for an audience in a night club and keeps their clothes on.
- Segment 3 features yet another plea for people to write in, (remember "ways to off Gaos"?) and once again we never hear anything more about it. Did nobody write in?
- CreditsWatch: Frank's name appears along with Mike in the "additional music" credit. There's also an additional contributing writer: Mike Gandolfi. Trace and Frank are still "villians" and Dr. F's last name is still misspelled "Forrestor."
- Fave riff: "Hey mister, your ninja's dragging!" Honorable mention: "I just passed wind in my suit. I ask you, as a point of honor, give me a second."

Movie stuff:

1) The exact year of this "movie" is unclear. Trans World Entertainment came out with VHS tapes in 1985 that featured these two episodes and it's called "Master Ninja I," but I don't know if they'd been stitched together to form a movie, or whether Film Ventures International did that when they came out with their version in 1991. In the end I decided to go with the copyright date on the screen.
2) These two episodes aired on NBC on Jan. 20 and Jan. 27, 1984. The series was called "The Master." The individual episodes were titled "Max" and "Out-of-Time-Step," respectively.

3) In the first barroom scene, after being harassed by the sheriff, Lee proceeds to trash the place. Why? What did the owner of the bar do to Lee to deserve all that damage? Does the sheriff own the bar? If so, it's not established.

Episode 323- THE CASTLE OF FU-MANCHU
First shown: 1/18/92

Movie: (1969) Evil mastermind Fu Manchu has a new plot to destroy the world, but his arch-nemesis Dr. Nayland Smith is on the case.

Opening: J&tB sing "We're on the Satellite of Love."
Invention exchange: The bots have developed a useful telephone transducer chip, while all Joel has is the big head (again); The Mads demonstrate the Joe Besser "Stinky" Bomb
Host segment 1: Crow decries "The Miss Saigon Syndrome," J&tB become distraught, which pleases the Mads
Host segment 2: The Shriner flying carpet sketch collapses into weeping; the Mads are delighted
Host segment 3: The bots are inconsolable, Joel tries to cheer them up with the story of Fu-Manchu, but the pain is too much; the Mads celebrate
End: J&tB are utterly beaten, the Mads toast their victory but then get a little too cocky
Stinger: Monkey pile on the castle guard!

Comments:

• I know, I know, this movie is terribly painful. I'm sure there are some among you for whom it is just too painful. But I'm just going to come out and say it: I LOVE this episode! The host segments are uniformly funny and the riffing is top-notch. In a perverse way, this would be an excellent starter episode, since it's one of the shows that most explicitly deals with the premise of the Mads trying to drive J&tB crazy with bad movies. The movie, no question, is terrible: it's drab, confusing, clumsy and poorly shot. And I imagine the cuts the Brains made didn't help matters. But compared to some of the movies we'll get later, it seems like a breeze.

- This episode is included in Shout!Factory's "Mystery Science Theater 3000 Collection: Vol XXIII."
- The opening is one of the best ever. My daughter, as a youngster, fell in love with that song and sang it constantly for about two long weeks, especially the "dumpy overlords" line and the part about not wearing underwear. To a 7-year-old, that's great satire.
- By the way, the song is loosely based on the theme song of a 1960s Saturday morning cartoon show, "The Funny Company." They even steal the line "Stories! Songs! Toys!" The line at the end, "Warriors of the World–by Marx!" apparently refers to ads for the "Warriors of the World" line of toy soldiers from all historical eras, by toy maker Marx.
- Joel's line "…uh, I'll be right back" in the invention exchange segment was sampled by some MSTie and it became a very popular – and useful – chat room sound file.
- Local reference: the piano bar at Nye's.
- We get the third and last appearance of the Big Head.
- Dr. F. lights the fuse on the Stinky Bomb and the sparks look like they almost put Frank's eyes out. Yeesh.
- Then-current references: "Filmed in Oakland" (a reference to the massive firestorm that hit the city in 1991); Crow parodies the now-forgotten "Lifestyles of the Rich and Famous," and also mentions "Doogie Hauser."

248 • MSTiepedia

- VERY naughty riff from Joel: "I didn't mean to but, uh, the new seat covers..." Tom and Crow are scandalized.
- Crow mentions "The Seven Faces of Dr. Lao." It would come up again.
- J&tB enter the theater with their Shriner costumes on. Joel removes his, then Crow's, then turns to remove Tom's fez, and either can't do it or thinks better of it.
- Callbacks: "Glen Manning get off that dam!" (Amazing Colossal Man), "I can remember a thousand wonderful hours..." (Rocketship XM), Tom hums the Catalina Caper theme, Hikeeba (Women of the Prehistoric Planet).
- Who drew those "artist's renderings"?
- In the theater, at different points, both Tom and Joel get irritated at Crow and tell him to shut up or stop. Kinda testy!
- Love the slam on Toastmasters (an organization full of very nice people who think they're witty, but usually aren't).
- CreditsWatch: Kevin's name appears along with Mike's under "Additional Music Written and Arranged by." Maybe he helped on the opening song?
- Favorite riff: "Look at this shot. They should never have let Shatner direct!" Honorable mention: "Feed him to the clam!"

Movie stuff:

1) The ship sinking footage at the beginning is from 1958's "A Night to Remember." And the whole opening section of this movie was spliced in directly from "The Brides of Fu Manchu." So it's twice-reused footage.
2) The dam bursting scene is footage taken from a 1957 movie called "Campbell's Kingdom." You can even see stars Dirk Bogarde (green checked shirt) and Stanley Baker (red shirt) in the footage.

Episode 324- MASTER NINJA II
First shown: 1/25/92

Movie: (1984 TV episodes; 1991 combined movie) An occidental ninja and his mush-mouthed pal help a feisty union organizer, and then help stop a gang of terrorists.

Opening: J&tB are an improv group
Invention exchange: The Mads have invented a conveyor belt buffet, while J&tB have created a (hopefully) self-perpetuating hamster habitat
Host segment 1: The bots design their own custom vans
Host segment 2: Crow is General Timothy Van Patton
Host segment 3: Tom has a new subroutine that allows him to pair detectives with their appropriate pets
End: Joel shows off the Van Cleef dress-up doll and reads a letter; Frank makes a heartfelt plea for the return of "The Second Hundred Years"
Stinger: Lee! Take it easy with the hamster!

Comments:

- And so, season three comes to a close with a middling effort. This one has some stretches with solid riffing, and other stretches that are less strong. It has one of my favorite host segments and some forgettable ones. All in all, it will pass the time, but it's nothing remarkable.
- This episode is included in Shout! Factory's "Mystery Science Theater 3000 Collection: Vol XX."
- In the "improv group" bits, there's a lot of jargon only professional comedians who have done improv would know ("going to your

where," "you negated me", "yes, and"). I think a lot of ordinary folks would hear that stuff and go "huh?"

- I'm guessing the hamster-loving hero of the movie led to the idea for Joel's invention, while the conveyor belt in the canning factory sparked the Mads' invention.
- I like the way Cambot goes right through the terrarium at movie sign.
- The two episodes in this movie were "State Of The Union" (which originally aired Feb. 3, 1984) and "Hostages" (which aired Feb. 10, 1984).
- Again, Joel makes a special mention of Michael Sloan.
- As they're digging the grave in the movie, Crow goes completely off the rails with his Cryptkeeper impression. Joel and Tom are ready to kill him.
- "MENDOZAAA!!" is a nice little nod to "The Simpsons."
- It's pretty clear the Brains cut the movie for time, and the cuts were so noticeable they felt the need to have the bots mention the edits.
- Callbacks: Several "Hikeebas" and "Charles Moffett: feared not" (RING OF TERROR); "Ator! No!" (CAVE DWELLERS) "Ya got me!" (CATALINA CAPER), "McCloud" (POD PEOPLE).
- Segment 3, where Tom pairs detectives with appropriate pets, is a classic, the kind of sketch that made MST3K so beloved: Clever, well-written and off the wall.
- Tom does a great little song at the end.
- At one point, BBI was talking about doing "Master Ninja 3." Cooler heads prevailed, I guess.
- Tom yells "FOUCAULT!!!" at the end of the episode–hope the censors didn't have a fit.
- CreditsWatch: After almost a whole season of "Host segments directed by Jim," for this last episode of the season, Mike directed.

Additional contributing writer: Mike Gandolfi; additional special thanks: St. Paul Harley Davidson (not sure why). Trace and Frank are "villians" for the last time. Dr. F's last name is still spelled "Forrestor."

- Fave riff: "The wizard's not in!!" Honorable mention: "It's great we can joke about now that his hips are crushed."

CHAPTER 6

1992 dawned, and by spring, BBI had begun working on season-four episodes, which began running on June 6th. Joining the writing team was a talented actress, comedian and the pride of Circle Pines, Minnesota, a small town outside of the Twin Cities when she was a kid, these days a full-fledged suburb.

Mary Jo Pehl
As a teen, Mary Jo worked as a babysitter and was allowed to watch the TV in the house, and most of the time this was Friday and Saturday nights.

"There were four channels on the TV and one of them was the late night movie that was usually horror or sci-fi," she recalled in a recent interview. "And I loved those bad black-and-white movies, like 'Teenagers from Outer Space.' "

When she grew up, she was working several low-paying gigs and supplementing her income doing standup comedy, when she was approached, like the rest of the writing team, one evening at a comedy club. She'd met the cast members, and spent time with some of them on the road traveling together to gigs at the string of comedy clubs that had sprung up in the upper midwest.

"I had done comedy with the people who started the show," she said. "We all knew each other. We shared a sensibility of comedy." But she had never seen MST3K, for one basic reason: she didn't own a TV. "So I didn't really understand it until I got asked to audition for it. They gave me clips on a VHS cassette and I watched it and wrote some riffs, and got invited to attend a writing session. The first time in the writing room, I thought: I am home. Who knew there was a job like this where you could get paid to watch TV?"

But in the beginning, Mary Jo, who had just been let go from six previous jobs, was anxious to keep her head down, which she did. It was Bridget who took Mary Jo under her wing and helped her get her footing.
"Every day I would laugh my head off," she remembered. "It spoiled me for life in the real world. I know I'll never experience anything like it again."

That spring and summer, the staff began to get a number of very positive reviews in the media. Prominent among those reviewers was Washington Post staff writer Tom Shales, whose acerbic articles had made him one of the most powerful critics in the nation. His review was a rave.

Calling the show "patently irresistible," he called on readers to "throw a fit" if Comedy Central was not offered by their cable provider. "It is, in short, a joy, a treasure, a golden voyage of discovery, a sweet-natured celebration of human fallibility." He later appeared on NPR, again praising the show.

"We finally got press," Joel recalled years later. "That year, we were one of People Magazine's Top Ten Shows of the Year. When you get people saying, 'this is great!' it helps get you to the next level."

BBI was running reasonably smoothly, busily cranking out a season that some fans point to as their most consistent and memorable.

As the episodes began to air, BBI became aware of a new way to hear from and communicate to its fans -- something called the internet. It was about that time that early pioneers of the internet scene began to set up online communities devoted to the series. The newsgroup alt.tv.mst3k was already in existence, and one occasional poster there was a Microsoft employee named Julie Walker. On the fledgling Prodigy, America Online and CompuServe services, MSTies were forming small discussion groups as well.

Inevitably, word of minor internal disputes leaked out to fans and were reported on internet discussion boards. It was with this situation that BBI began to discover the power of the internet to spread and amplify rumors: By the time the rumors got back to them, it was being reported that Jim and Joel were practically at each other's throats, a massive exaggeration.

As fall approached, BBI again agreed to do Turkey Day marathon bumpers: This time, in each bumper, Dr. F. cruelly force-fed Frank a whole turkey, which had been decorated to represent the movie being presented. The bumpers were funny, but it was perhaps impossible to live up to the inspired bumpers of a year earlier. Also, the novelty of a Thanksgiving Day marathon was perhaps wearing off. Whatever the reason, ratings for Turkey Day dropped substantially.

Next, Comedy Central's "This is MST3K" hit the airwaves, and it marked a turning point for relations between the network and the show's fans. In the internet discussion forums, fans gave the special a mixed review. There were many good clips and some insightful comments by industry executives, critics and fans. Shales, ever the MST3K partisan in those days, said "It's the one show on television I always look forward to, it's the one show on television I always hate to see end, and I never go away unhappy from the show." (Shales would come to regret his enthusiasm.)

Viewers took to the internet to complain about CC spokesman Penn Jillette, who hosted the special, but the most common comment was that the people making the special did not seem to understand what they were reporting on.

SEASON FOUR: COMEDY CENTRAL, 1992-1993

Episode 401- SPACE TRAVELERS
First shown: 6/6/92

Movie: (1969) In a re-edited version of the movie "Marooned," various obstacles hamper attempts to rescue three NASA astronauts trapped aboard a crippled space capsule.

Opening: The Great Crowdini attempts an astounding escape.
Invention exchange: J&tB demonstrate The Dollaroid, while the Mads show off their "facial" tissue
Host segment 1: J&tB present a list of space race advancements
Host segment 2: Reenacting the movie so Crow can do his killer Peck
Host segment 3: J&tB wonder: If one of them had to sacrifice themselves...
End: Magic fun, letters
Stinger: Hackman, demonstrating that he's good in anything

Comments:

- And so we begin the second of four 24-episode seasons BBI pumped out. You can really feel how settled in and relaxed they are. As they said in the ACEG, they were luxuriating in that rarity of rarities in the TV world, job security. We start off with a very good but not spectacular episode. The riffing is comfortable and steady, and we haven't had a star-studded, very watchable movie like this since the KTMA days. None of the segments are clunkers, either, so it was a great way to start the season.

- This episode was included in Shout! Factory's "Mystery Science Theater 3000: Vol. XXXII."
- The stretch between the end of season 3 and the beginning of season 4 was 133 days.
- "Marooned," the movie Film Ventures International chopped up to create "Space Travelers," is the only MST3K movie that actually won an Oscar, sort of. It won for special visual effects, and was also nominated for cinematography and sound.
- In episode 201- ROCKETSHIP X-M, where Joel asks "Why didn't you just show us 'Marooned'?" and Dr. F replies "We couldn't get it!" Guess they could get it after all.
- The opening bit is a little complicated. You're supposed to notice that Crow accidentally drops the all-important key and nobody thinks to retrieve it for him before he is blown to kingdom come. But you could easily miss it.
- Joel's invention really doesn't make sense, but they got a good bit out of it anyway.
- In the ACEG, they tell a story about meeting Dennis Miller, whose chief comment to them was that he wished they hadn't riffed "Marooned." He likes it. It was an early instance of the response they would get a lot when they riffed "This Island Earth."
- The riffing in this one starts a little slowly, largely because the movie itself starts a little slowly. It seems insane now, but I was alive then and I can tell you: The workings of NASA fascinated most Americans, and just watching them work was captivating enough for a lot of people. I'm sure the filmmakers thought nothing of beginning their movie with 10 minutes or so of random NASA footage. But there's not a lot you can say about it.
- For a moment, J&tB do the ethereal "eeeee" singing bit — a reference to the movie "2001: A Space Odyssey" — that they used to such good effect in episode 205- ROCKET ATTACK USA.

- Then-current reference: Somebody mentions the president, and Servo says he'll "vomit on some Japanese people." Also: Baby Jessica. Jessica, by the way, is married with kids now.
- Crow's Gregory Peck is truly killer. Joel also attempts a Peck impression and pales by comparison.
- Servo, on the other hand, does a very good Burt Reynolds laugh.
- This episode has not one, not two, but three Firesign Theatre references!
- Host segment 2 is another "broken sketch sketch" — they try to put on a sketch and the whole thing goes to hell — that was a MST3K staple throughout the years. Not all of them were that funny but this one is pretty good.
- Callback: Crow recalls that he "called dibs" on the ability to say who lives and who dies, back in season 3. Also, "That was number 9!" (SIDEHACKERS)
- The wonderful "aaaaaaaahhh!" closing bit by the Mads became a great way to say goodbye to MSTie pals.
- CreditsWatch: Additional Contributing Writer: Bridget Jones. Host segments directed by: Jim, but, unlike most of last season, they will take turns as the season goes on. Trace and Frank are no longer "villians" but Dr. F's last name is still misspelled "Forrestor." Frank is, beginning with this episode, "TV's Frank." The new season means a new set of interns, most notably this episode marks the arrival of Patrick Brantseg. Also there was Nathan Devery, Brendan Glynn, Suzette Jamison and Steven Sande. Bryan Beaulieu and Bill W. are gone from the special thanks credit. Added have been Mark Gilbertson, all MSTies coast-to-coast and the authors of the 1st Amendment. This episode also marks the arrival of Bradley J. Keely, as assistant editor. For the entire season, they had the services of Rob "the engineer" Burkhardt in engineering. Clayton James comes in for a two-show stint in hair and makeup.
- Fave riff: "Oh they're dead. How's the rabbit?" Honorable mention: "We're all gonna die!"

Episode 402- THE GIANT GILA MONSTER
First shown: 6/13/92

Movie: (1959) A 30-foot killer lizard is loose in the woods near a small town and its gang of hot-roddin' teens.

Opening: Joel has made Crow and Tom the Thing with Two Heads
Invention exchange: J&tB show off their sitcom radio, the Mads demonstrate their renaissance festival punching bags
Host segment 1: Crow and Tom disrupt Joel's soda shop sketch
Host segment 2: J&tB discuss the funny drunk
Host segment 3: "Servo on Cinema" looks at Ray Kellogg's "Leg Up" directorial style, but Crow and Joel horn in
End: J&tB have formed the rock group Hee-La, Joel reads some letters (including one from TV's Frank!)
Stinger: Old guy chokes on sodie pop

Comments:

- It's hard to go wrong with this episode. It's got it all: weird movie, great riffing and some great host segments. I love it. It's also pretty good as a starter episode.
- This episode replaced episode 212- GODZILLA VS. MEGALON when Rhino re-released "Volume 10.2" because of its rights issues.
- This episode became infamous in the 1995-1996 period on Comedy Central, as a number of other episodes dropped out of the rotation due to movie rights issues. The movie in this episode is (or was) in PD (public domain), which meant that CC could play it as often as it liked, and it played it a lot, so much so that some online MSTies began to grumble about it.
- You've got to assume there were multiple puppeteers in the trench for that bit with the decapitated bots. Must have gotten a little crowded.

- That's Mike, of course, as the radio announcer
- We get more trashing of the Renaissance Fest, last bashed in episode 303- POD PEOPLE. "Bite me, Frodo."
- You can see Dr. F's mic cord during the invention exchange
- Servo does his great coughing car sound, sort of an impression of Mel Blanc as Jack Benny's car.
- Mildly naughty riff: "Old rubber? No! No!"
- Tom and Joel spit in the sheriff's hat! Ew!
- Another "broken sketch" sketch: this time it's the bots who sabotage Joel's sketch.
- Gypsy must be in a goth period. She's got black lipstick.
- This is the episode that would give us the "I sing whenever I sing whenever I singgg" bit they'll do in many future episodes whenever somebody was banging or pounding on something.
- Tom notices the reel change. I do that all the time.
- Joel does a little impression of comedian Kevin Meaney, who sadly passed in 2016.
- Joel asks: "Was the 'Richard Speck' a popular haircut back then?" Yes, Joel. Sadly, it was.
- There's a nice little TV in-joke during Tom's "Servo on Cinema" sketch when Tom turns to face a non-existent second camera during his introduction and has to be corrected by Joel.
- Nice film editing by Cambot!
- Joel (sort of) sneaks in the name of beloved cult band "They Might Be Giants"
- Callbacks: J&tB sing the "WILD REBELS" theme song. Also: "Glenn is 50 feet tall." (WAR OF THE COLOSSAL BEAST)
- For those who wondered why Pearl called Crow "Art" many seasons later, it's because of the illustration that accompanied one of the letters Joel reads in this episode. Apparently the young letter writer had just seen episode 203- JUNGLE GODDESS, in which Joel imitates the way Jackie Gleason would introduce his cast and the end of the show. For those who remember it, he would always

save longtime pal Art Carney for last, shouting "Art Carney!" over the already-applauding crowd. Joel, in a takeoff of that, shouted "Art Crow!" The little letter writer, not understanding the reference, just assumed Crow's name was Art.

- Watch and listen to Crow during the closing segment. Note how he says not a word, and when spoken to only sort of hums, exactly the way somebody WOULD do if they had a giant rolled-up tongue in their mouth and was waiting for the cue to unfurl it. I love it.
- CreditsWatch: Host segments directed by Jim. The name John Carney appears at the end of the list of writers; he would not appear again. Bridget Jones was added to the writers list for the rest of the season. Dr. F's last name is still misspelled Forrestor.
- Fave riff: "Not the coda! No!" Honorable mention: "Things make sense when yer all liquored up!"

Movie stuff:

1) The sound in this movie is uniformly terrible. One of the problems with a PD movie is that nobody takes care of it.
2) Part of the plot of this movie involves our hero eavesdropping on a party line, a long-dead technology almost everywhere. I wonder if, in the era of smart phones. young people even understand what's going on in those scenes.
3) Our hero also has one of those Hooterville/Mayberry put-the-thing-to-your-ear-and-talk-into-the-thing-on-the-wall phones. Did people really still have those in the '50s?
4) Not that I expect much from this movie, but I feel I must note that in the scene where the old drunkie guy is racing the train, there's footage of at least three, maybe four different trains that are all supposed to be the same train.

Episode 403- CITY LIMITS
First shown: 6/20/92

Movie: (1984) In a bleak future, teen biker gangs and a sinister corporation battle for control of an abandoned city.

Opening: Crow and Tom get Joel to say "ping-pong balls" and Joel soon wishes he hadn't
Invention exchange: J&tB present Mr. meat & potato head, while the Mads demonstrate pop star Tupperware, featuring Morrissey
Host segment 1: Crow sings: "Oh, Kim Cattrall!"
Host segment 2: J&tB list some of the Fantastic 85
Host segment 3: J&tB keep listing superheroes
End: J&tB try to play the City Limits trivia game, Joel reads letters, the Mads have had enough of Morrissey
Stinger: Tiny radio-controlled death from on high

Comments:

- I'm not a big fan of this one. It has its moments (every MST3K episode does) but J&tB seem to be fending this one off, rather than tearing it up. The host segments are just sort of so-so.
- This episode was included in Shout! Factory's MST3K: Volume XXXVI.
- It is, probably, with this episode that the "Turn down your lights (where applicable)" message at the beginning of each episode, was replaced by a title card featuring a still from the movie and a gruff voice (usually that of editor Tim Scott) saying "Mystery Science Theater 3000, show [show number here]; reel one."
- The ping-pong ball bit comes from the old "Captain Kangaroo" show. Unfortunately, like so many daily kids shows of that era, most of "Captain Kangaroo" was not recorded and very little of it survives. But a running gag on the show was that the puppet characters would try to trick the Captain into saying the words "ping-pong balls," at which point a veritable cloudburst of the little guys

would pour down from the heavens onto the Captain. You had to be there … and you had to be 6.

- Speaking of music: Score composer Mitchell Froom has produced recordings for such acts as Los Lobos, Del Fuegos, Crowded House, Elvis Costello, Richard Thompson and his then-wife (1995-98) Suzanne Vega. He was also one of the founders of The Latin Playboys. He also composed the theme for "Pee-Wee's Playhouse."
- Early on, there is a very clever solution to the appearance of some brief nudity when Joel inexplicably feels the urge to stand up and open an umbrella in the theater.
- Kim Cattrall tells the story that one evening she had just checked into a hotel and she turned on the TV and by pure chance host segment 1 was running on Comedy Central. At first she thought the hotel had cooked it up to welcome her. She says she was completely baffled as to why a golden puppet was repeatedly singing her name.
- There's a mention of "Far Side Gallery," a book I also owned. That shot does look like the cover, a little.
- Somewhat obscure riff: "I'm still here, Happer, you crap hound!" (From one of my favorite movies, "Local Hero.")
- More obscure riff: "But all I have is an alcove!" (From another of my favorite movies, "A Thousand Clowns.")
- A rare moment: Tom does something they almost never do—he quietly explains a riff (after quoting Lady Macbeth). Wonder why they felt that riff, among all the others, needed explaining.
- Several times the movie shows flashbacks of moments we've never seen. I assume this was stuff cut by either Film Ventures International or BBI.
- Dated reference: a mention of the shortlived-and-now-forgotten James Earl Jones series "Gabriel's Fire."
- Watch the handoff from Joel to Kevin following after segment 3. You can see Kevin moving around.

- There's another reference to Apple's System 7, along with observation "we gotta get Windows for this thing." In 1992 that was actually techie jargon.
- Tom still has ping pong balls in his head in a couple of segments.
- Great throwaway line by Crow: "Daddy needs a new pair o' hydraulic talons!"
- CreditsWatch: Host segments directed by Jim. Production person Ellen "Ellie" McDonough joins the show. She'll be there through season six. This is one of three episodes this season where Andrea DuCane did hair and makeup. Clayton James did most of them. Occasional prop assistant Barb Oswald, who did work back in season three as well, gets a new title this week: "Toolmaster Jr." Brendan Glynn finishes up a three-episode stint as intern. Additional writer: John Carney. Dr. F's name is still misspelled "Forrestor."
- Fave riff: "I'm getting beaten up by the cast of 'Pirates of Penzance!'" Honorable mention: "Okay, let's stop for a moment and look at our scripts. Oh, I guess it DOES say Boy George comes riding in lobbing molotov cocktails."
- Callbacks: "I sing whenever I sing" (GIANT GILA MONSTER), "help me!" (ROCKET ATTACK USA) "Hi, I'm Max Keller." (MASTER NINJA 1) "...after the ROBOT HOLOCAUST," "My own FLESH I don't love better!" (SIDEHACKERS), "I'm a Grimalt warrior!" (VIKING WOMEN), "I feel like a happy king!" (MR. B NATURAL), "...not allowed..." (THE CRAWLING HAND) and "McCloud!" (POD PEOPLE).
- Mike is just hilarious as Morrissey.

Movie stuff:

1) The opening of the movie says that it takes place "15 years from now." The movie was made in 1985, so "15 years from now" was 2000. Thankfully the world in 2000 looked very little like the one this movie predicts. (By the way, it's been more than 15 years

since this episode debuted, and it is 15 years [and counting] from "15 years from now.")

2) I do love how all the characters get gussied up to beat the band before making their big assault.

3) During her appearance at the second convention, Kim's recollections about making this movie included always filming at night in a dangerous part of L.A., and suffering with the ever-present stench from a nearby dogfood factory.

4) One of the minor characters in this movie (the guy J&tB keep calling "Michelle Shocked") is played by a fellow named Dean Devlin. He also appeared in the movies "My Bodyguard" and "The Wild Life" before going on to become a big Hollywood producer, bringing us such mindless, noisy blockbusters as "Independence Day" and "Godzilla." In 1997, Premiere magazine ranked Devlin and "ID4" director Roland Emmerich No. 44 on its list of the 100 Most Influential People in the Hollywood Industry. Really.

5) The plot's confusing and most of the action is a little hard to see. Part of the problem is I don't get why I am supposed to root for the biker kids. An apparently hopeful and rebuilding government has contracted with Kim Cattrall and Robbie Benson to restore basic services. That's evil why, again?

Episode 404- TEENAGERS FROM OUTER SPACE
First shown: 6/27/92

Movie: (1959) Aliens have a plan to use Earth as a farm for their giant lobster livestock. One of the crew rebels and flees to a small town, with another alien on his trail.

Opening: Joel uses behavior modification to prevent a recurrence of the "NBC Mystery Movie" gag
Invention exchange: J&tB demonstrate the scratch 'n' sniff report card, while the Mads show off their resusci-Annie ventriloquist doll

Host segment 1: J&tB present "Reel to real"
Host segment 2: J&TB recreate a pre-movie no-littering message
Host segment 3: A really boss-looking space ship visits, but the pilot is a disappointment.
End: Duct tape fashion statements, letters, Dr. F. dines with a friend
Stinger: "When we return to our planet, the high court may well sentence you to TORTURE!!"

Comments:

- How I love this episode. Maybe it's the easy-to-follow (albeit punishingly stupid) plot. Maybe it's the goofy host segments, most of which are not so much funny as wry. Maybe it's the charmingly naïve idea that somebody thought people would believe that giant lobsters walk upright. Whatever it is, this one's a lot of fun.
- This episode was included in Rhino's "The Mystery Science Theater 3000 Collection, Vol. 6."
- Body (or, rather, skeleton) count: 6, not counting Sparky and the lobster and the big mess at the end. And for you Dave Barry fans, Sparky and the Lobster WBAGNFARB.
- "Lisa Smithback," mentioned in the invention exchange, has to be a real name, probably a schoolmate of one of the Brains. Wonder if she's out there somewhere?
- I love the little Jeff Dunham-esque gestures Trace does around the dummy as he does the ventriloquist bit.
- Callbacks: Crow's desire for "hamburger sammich" is from episode 203- JUNGLE GODDESS. Later he retreads the "Welcome to Death Valley Days, the driver..." bit, and "How fortunate! This will seemplify everything!" from THE PHANTOM CREEPS.
- The word TORCHAA! became an immediate MSTie buzzword following this episode.
- I'm a little baffled by the "ironic" tone Joel and the bots adopt during the "Reel to Real" sketch? They read all their lines like

266 • MSTiepedia

a presenter at an awards ceremony who is given a bit to do and resents having to do it. Did they decide the material was too lame to be played straight? But wait a minute! Maybe they're parodying comedians who tell jokes ironically! That's TWO levels of irony! We're through the looking glass here, people!

- Host segment precognition: In the illustrations, we see Betty in a bathing suit, and Grandpa sleeping on the couch, but we haven't seen either in the movie yet.

- The repeated bit with the muffled voice coming from the car trunk almost gets a little unpleasant after a while. Tom just portrays it as so horribly desperate.

- As Derek and Betty enter the college, there are several riffs about the smell of school. Perhaps these riffs were the genesis of this episode's "scratch and sniff report card" invention exchange.

- Several characters have songs stuck in their heads. Grandpa's is the theme song for the TV show "New Zoo Revue." The ill-fated professor's secretary's is AC-DC's "You Shook Me All Night Long." The Doctor has two: first it's Nick Gilder's "Hot Child in the City," then Foreigner's "Hot Blooded." The nurse has several, including Apollonia 6's "Sex Shooter," "Aqualung" by Jethro Tull, The Beatles' "Lucy in the Sky with Diamonds" and the "Feel Like I'm Fixin' to Die Rag" by Country Joe and the Fish.

- So the point of segment two is to set up a few throwaway lines in segment three? (i.e. "goomy bears?")

- Naughty riff: "What until you see my tongues."

- During host segment three, Joel professes his faith. Or is he being ironic again?

- Gotta admit: the spaceship in segment three really is boss.

- The third segment is great. Joel seems incredibly relaxed. And anytime anybody tries to tell you he was always "sleepy," just show them this segment. He's wide awake, baby.

- Tom Servo has legs?
- The final bit in Deep 13 is a riot. "Help me!" "No, literally! I have a man up in space!"
- CreditsWatch: Mary Jo joined the writing staff with this episode. And, for the first time in at least three seasons, the host segments were directed by somebody other than Jim Mallon—this week, Kevin. Resusci-Anne provided by Nancy Mason. Dr. F's name is still misspelled "Forrestor."
- Fave riff: "There's a piece of green something between your–" Honorable mention: "I'm David Eisenhower! That makes you... Julie Nixon!!"

Movie stuff:

1) Derek says he saw the Commander stop Thor from killing him. He did not. He was 40 yards away and running like hell.
2) Continuity screwup: Thor pistol whips the nurse, there's a short cutaway, and in the next shot Thor and the nurse have magically switched seats in the car!
3) There is a LOT of juicy gossip about the making of this movie: Reportedly, Tom Graff, who played reporter Joe Rogers and wrote, directed, edited and co-produced the film, charmed producers Bryan and Ursula Pearson (who played "Thor" and "Hilda," respectively) into paying $5,000 of the movie's $14,000 shoestring budget. After they heard Graff got $25,000 from Warner Brothers for the distribution rights, they sued, but all they got was their $5,000 back.
4) The flying saucer was reportedly abandoned on property near the estate of Gloria Swanson, who used it for publicity. Graeff and David Love ("Derek") were reportedly lovers. The two met when Graff cast Love in a short film Graff made a few years earlier. Love vanished after the film and his whereabouts are unknown. Graeff never made another movie. In 1962, he bought a huge

ad in the L.A. Times proclaiming himself the second Christ. In 1968, he bought another ad, this time in Variety, announcing the upcoming production of a film called "Orf," to be directed by Carl Reiner (it wasn't true, and Reiner immediately threatened to sue). Graeff committed suicide in 1970. The Pearsons eventually divorced. Ursula ran a travel company in L.A. and died in 2006. Bryan, a struggling actor, was only able get a few acting roles and retired from acting in the late '60s. Last we heard, he was working in real estate in Hawaii.

5) This is yet another MST3k movie featuring Bronson Canyon in some of the exterior shots. Through the use of selected locations and very tight framing, Graeff was pretty successful in making the streets of Hollywood look like a small town.

Episode 405- BEING FROM ANOTHER PLANET
First shown: 7/4/92

Movie: (1982) Re-edit of a movie called "Time Walker." A mummy found in King Tut's tomb is x-rayed by a university team. This awakens the mummy, and it goes on a killing spree.

Opening: J&tB are playing movie slogan 20 questions
Invention exchange: The Mads present their "Tragic Moments" figurines, while J&tB demonstrate their Jack Palance impersonation kit
Host segment 1:J&tB's discussion of mummies leads to a discussion of Bill Mumy
Host segment 2: Crow and Tom are playing haunted house with Joel
Host segment 3: Joel's rainy-day funsketch and the HFVS funtime holoclowns fail to cheer up Tom & Crow
End: The TV's Frank shopping network has a great deal, Joel reads a letter, Dr. F invents the "die-master"
Stinger: The heartbreak of extraterrestrial psoriasis

- A middling-to-good episode for me. The movie itself is a bit easier to follow than, say, "City Limits," but waiting for the mummy to actually DO something starts to get tiresome. The "oh Joel it's scary in the basement" bit doesn't wear well for me, but the riffing is generally pretty crisp and funny. The movie compensates with some unintentionally hilarious moments, notably the impromptu costume parade through campus (wtf?). Lots of memorable host segment stuff, too.
- Here are the slogans from the "20 questions" sketch that I was able to track down (and note that some of these are not exactly accurate, but most are close approximations):

"Fueled by imagination" – "Radio Flyer" (1992)

"Be afraid. Be very afraid." – "The Fly" (1986)

"The most exciting undersea odyssey ever filmed." – "The Neptune Factor" (1973)

"100% pure adrenaline." – "Point Break" (1991).

"It's not only his nose that grows!" – "The Erotic Adventures of Pinocchio" (1971)

"This time, it's personal." – "Jaws: The Revenge" (1987)

"Dudley Moore juggles two women in an attempt to save his sanity" – "Micki & Maude" (1984)

"A sassy brassy musical humdinger." – "Funny Lady" (1975)

The ones I can't track down:

"A new high in adventure when they go thrill-deep in danger."

"A bikini-clad romp through summer's fun."

"A shocking expose of souls in bondage."

- Watch for the boom shadow on Frank's face as Dr. F says "Clayton Stonewall Forrester." They keep going.
- Joel says "we've came up with..." They keep going.
- This episode is included in Shout! Factory's Mystery Science Theater 3000 Collection: Vol. XXXV.

- Dark and obscure riff: "Hey it's Pete Duel" (Duel, Ben Murphy's co-star in the western series "Alias Smith and Jones" killed himself on New Year's Eve, 1971.)
- Callbacks: "Trumpy! You can do magic things!" (POD PEOPLE). Also: "Laurence, would you put that down please!" (CATALINA CAPER).
- Joel mentions Billy Mumy's early performance in the movie "Dear Bridget" and then mentions another movie, the title of which Joel can't remember, where he played "a super-genius mathematician." Sorry, Joel, but you're thinking of the same movie, "Dear Bridget." By the way, the "Twilight Zone" episode Joel mentions (where he wishes people into the cornfield) is entitled "It's a Good Life." Mumy was also in a couple of other TZ eps.
- Joel and Tom are already in the theater after the first segment, still discussing Butch Patrick, when Crow joins them.
- Then-current reference: "Hey, Jim Fixx!" Also, mentions of Intellivision and the Michelangelo virus (completely forgot that one).
- At one point they call the massive pipes in the basement "Coppolla's espresso machine." When I think of somebody who would be rich and powerful enough to have such a massive device, director Francis Ford Coppolla is not the first person I think of. Bill Gates? Aaron Spelling? Sure. But not Francis.
- Joel makes a reference to the '60s TV show "The Mod Squad." Amusingly, he makes virtually the same riff in the first Cinematic Titanic episode, and then follows it with a plaintive "Oh, I'm old!" What a difference 15 years makes.
- Crow once again requests to be carried out of the theater. Joel once again declines.
- During the haunted house sketch, Joel got spaghetti in the jell-o. Bleh. (And my OCD rears its ugly head.)
- Also during the sketch, there is another mention of a "Mrs. Reedy," previously mentioned in during the "POSTURE PALS" short.

- Tom explains a riff again: After singing "Michael Goldstein! Michael Goldstein! What a beautiful name!" he adds: "Funny Girl!"
- I think Crow attempts a Dr. Hibberd (from "The Simpsons") impression but he sounds more like Kingfish of "Amos and Andy."
- "Sarah …" "Jockman!" Somebody's an Allan Sherman fan.
- This episode begins our two-part encounter with the impossibly creepy holo-clowns. That's Mike and Paul, of course, and this is Paul's first on-screen appearance.
- Gypsy's still wearing black "lipstick" and it doesn't look very well applied.
- I love all the Ludlum titles, like "The Mingmang Pa-ting-ting."
- Nick Gilder's "Hot Child in the City" is referenced for the second week in a row.
- At one point, during a shot of Shari Belafonte, Joel says "Oh my God! I'll never be in another film!" Not true, Joel. Shari has done several movies since "Time Walker" (and many many TV shows and TV movies).
- Tom is entitled to his opinion, of course, but so am I, and no way is this movie worse than most of the movies he named. His rant is a funny trip down memory lane, though.
- The final segment brings back the notion of the "button that brings down the SOL," which we heard about a couple of times in season two.
- Firesign Theatre reference: "…and the snake knives, Mrs. Presky!"
- Fave riff: "Sizzler! Heeheeheehee!" Honorable mentions: "Caution: snow angels in progress." "And if you do find something, stay there."

Episode 406- ATTACK OF THE GIANT LEECHES (with short: 'UNDERSEA KINGDOM'–Episode 1)
First shown: 7/18/92

Short: (1936) In part one ("Beneath the Ocean Floor") of a serial, a submarine expedition to Atlantis discovers a hostile kingdom.

Movie: (1959) Folks begin vanishing near a Florida swamp, and a game warden discovers the culprits are mutant leeches.

Opening: Joel manages to shut off the holo-clowns
Invention exchange: The Mads introduce Patches the leech, while J&tB present the insty-adolescence kit
Host segment 1: J&tB discuss taking over the world and what you'd wear to do it
Host segment 2: J&tB chat about dreams over coffee
Host segment 3: J&tB sing: "A Danger to Myself And Others"
End: J&tB try to understand the leeches, Joel reads a letter; meanwhile in Deep 13, Patches has been on Frank too long
Stinger: Billy gets into it.

Comments:

- Plenty of fun here, in an episode that is deservedly a fan favorite. Most of the host segments are great and the riffing is terrific. A great all-around episode.
- This episode was included in Rhino's "The Mystery Science Theater 3000 Collection, Vol. 6."
- Part two of the holo-clowns bit is classic MST3K: "Get on your orange and yellow knees and kiss my clown feet that I haven't killed you!!!" That bit may be a true litmus test of MSTiedom. If you don't think it's hilarious, you really shouldn't bother with this show.
- Joel says he started up the holoclowns "about three weeks ago." Actually it was two weeks since the previous episode aired.
- Dr. F is reading "Putting the One-Minute Manager to Work" (the edition he's reading is now out of print but a new edition was pub-

lished in 2006), while Frank is reading "Working with Difficult People." Again, that edition is rare since an updated edition came out in 2006.

- That's Kevin, of course, as the giant leech. That bit gave us another great moment in the poopie tape: "Is it my sucking you?" By the way, doctors have in fact found useful medical applications for leeches.
- Yay! The first short of season 4 and the first in 10 episodes.
- "Undersea Kingdom," made in 1936, is the oldest thing (movie or short) MST3K ever riffed on.
- Then-still-somewhat-current reference: Mayor Dinkins. Remember him?
- Tom Servo attempts a complicated joke that sort of misfires and Joel responds: "That's a Swiss army joke."
- For the third episode running, the song "Hot Child in the City" is referenced.
- This movie has a pretty much classic Corman cast, including Bruno VeSota, Michael Emmet, Russ Sturlin and Gene Roth. Surprisingly, no Merritt Stone.
- Servo's coffee head is a nice touch, and the best part is that nobody even really mentions it. It's just kinda there and nobody thinks much of it.
- Joel pours some cream for Gypsy and she interrupts him to say "when" and that seems to amuse Joel.

- Joel quietly hums a line of the upcoming song in the theater.
- Lots of characters are humming internal songs in this episode.
- "A Danger to Mahself and Others" is one of the truly great MST3K original songs. Joel and Mike share the writing credit, by the way. My only complaint is that they taped a pipe to Tom's lower lip and we can hear it bonking loudly against his torso during the song. Very distracting.
- Tom Servo's head practically FLIES off as they leave the theater for the last time. They cover beautifully.

- CreditsWatch: Host segments directed by Jim. Dr. F's last name is still misspelled "Forrestor."
- Fave riff from the short: "This looks like a fine place to set down my pasty white bottom." Honorable mention: "How come they all turned when he said 'Dad'?
- Fave riff from the feature: "…or someone might stab you in your sleep…" Honorable mention: "Looks like the cave of Dr. Calamari."

Movie stuff:

1) Our cuckolded store keeper Dave clearly has a double-barreled shotgun. Now I'm no firearms expert, but I believe such a weapon, assuming it is fully loaded, has the capability of firing, at the most, twice before the user has to reload, correct? And in fact, we do see Dave reload, placing a shell in each barrel. But that's after we've heard him fire at least four shots. And after he reloads, he fires another four shots before backing Liz and her paramour into the lake. Now it's possible he reloaded off-camera, but if I was Liz's boyfriend, I wouldn't shrink in fear of that obviously empty gun.
2) Sexy Liz is played by Yvette Vickers. She met a sad end: her decomposed body was found in her Hollywood home. The 82 year old may have been dead for perhaps as long as a year and nobody had checked on her.
3) The exterior swamp shots were done at the Arboretum in Arcadia, Calif., where shots for TV's "Fantasy Island" were done years later.
4) Some of the cast were almost electrocuted on the set when a water tank full of actors collapsed.

Episode 407- THE KILLER SHREWS (with short: 'JUNIOR RODEO DAREDEVILS')
First shown: 7/25/92

Short: (1949) Cowpoke and old-timer Billy Slater straightens out some wayward kids by making them put on a junior rodeo.

Movie: (1959) A hunky skipper makes a delivery to a small island, where heavy-drinking scientists are conducting genetic experiments.

Opening: Joel gives out presents to the bots
Invention exchange: The Mads prepare to destroy Earth, but are stopped by Jim Henson's Edgar Winter Babies
Host segment 1: Joel vapor-locks while trying to do Will Rogers
Host segment 2: While presenting the Killer Shrews board game, the bots snap
Host segment 3: J&tB concoct the Killer Shrew drink
End: The shrewbots attack scientist Joel, letter, Frank isn't feeling good
Stinger: Festus swipes Roscoe's drink.

Comments:

- This is one of those episodes where the movie is SO stupid and the print is SO bad that it takes a lot of really good riffing to overcome it — and that, for the most part, is what you get. You can tell the writing team struggled with the movie's tediousness -- it comes out in one segment -- but overall I think they did a pretty good job. The host segments are lots of fun too. I'm not sure I'd recommend this one for a newbie, because the movie's just so hard to see and hear, but the episode is plenty funny.
- This episode is featured on Shout's "Mystery Science Theater 3000 Collection, Volume 7" and became notorious after fans noticed that the movie had been cut a little bit and that there were some mastering issues, causing Rhino to send corrected disks free to anybody who complained.

- People always talk about the way Joel was a "dad" to the bots in a way that Mike never tried to be. The opening sketch is pretty much a pristine example of that dynamic. Who hasn't been in poor Crow's place at one time or another?
- This ep has another use of the "aaaaaaahh!" farewell by the mads, first used (I think) in episode 321- SANTA CLAUS CONQUERS THE MARTIANS.
- Servo is still wearing his hat in the theater during the short, but it's gone by the time the movie starts.
- The whole "Jim Henson's [fill in the blank] babies" concept, which was clearly a phrase that was being batted around the BBI writing room for the past several weeks, reaches its peak with this episode: it was used three times, including the invention exchange.
- The riffs get very dark during the short — a taste of the way it's going to be in plenty of shorts to come.
- Crow DID get some use out of those slacks: He is wearing them in segment 1.
- Segment 1 is an corollary to the "sabotaged sketch" — the "Joel vapor locks" sketch. Mike had a tendency to vapor-lock too.
- You have to be a certain age to get the "He's the guy who taught LBJ how to hold dogs" riff. For those too young, President Lyndon Johnson loved his beagles, but caused a kerfuffle among animal lovers when he was photographed lifting them by the ears. He insisted there was nothing wrong with doing so, but dog lovers howled.
- Some entirely understandable tears are shed during segment 2, as the bots seem to express the feelings of writers about the dull, actionless movie.
- Has anybody noticed that this movie has, in a general sort of way, the same plot as "Jurassic Park"?
- Two "Dune" references in this one: "It's the Gom Jabbar" and "Tell me about your home world, Usul."

- Segment two is a great example of what movie sign can be good for — giving the sketch an ending it otherwise doesn't have.
- J&tB decide Hispanic Mario is Manuel from "Fawlty Towers." It allows them to do foreigner jokes that they otherwise probably couldn't have gotten away with.
- I remember after this episode aired that a few people actually tried to follow the recipe for a killer shrew. Anybody who did probably ended up in a diabetic coma. This sketch also has a nice little visit to Deep 13, something that doesn't happen that often in mid-movie.
- The sound is so bad in this movie that there are about a dozen riffs where they are essentially asking what the hell some character just said. Way more than usual.
- The killer shrew costumes, far from "not cutting it," are a riot.
- Joel says "we will be-ack" and "MST3 viewers." They keep going.
- Ipecacs reappear; they first reared their ugly head in episode 315-TEENAGE CAVEMAN.
- CreditsWatch: Additional contributing writer: Steve Hollenhorst. Host segments directed by Jim. Dr. F's last name is still misspelled "Forrestor."
- Fave riff from the short: "And the crowd goes wild — yay." Honorable mention: "Oh no. This is wrong. I signed up for debaaaaate…"
- Fave riff from the movie: "Imagine in how much detail, senor?" Honorable mentions: "I've been going through the script and I think I'm in this scene." "The…end…"

Episode 408- HERCULES UNCHAINED
First shown: 8/1/92

Movie: (1959) Traveling with his young companion Ulysses, Herc's mission to stop a war is sidetracked by hypnotic Queen Onfale, while his wife Iole pines for him.

Opening: It's wash and wax day for the bots
Invention exchange: The Mads have created decorator roaches (and Steve Reeves visits!), while J&tB present the Steve-o-meter
Host segment 1: Gypsy demonstrates that she is the Hellenistic ideal
Host segment 2: J&tB consume the water of forgetfulness, among other waters
Host segment 3: Tom and Crow want to know what are Hercules and the nice lady are doing
End: J&tB ponder the meaning of the Hercules movies; while in Deep 13, Steve is no help
Stinger: The queen REALLY misses Herc

Comments:

- This is the first of several sword-and-sandal outings for MST3K. I think they're perfect for the show: colorful, action-filled, mildly sexy and really really weird. I don't think this is their best one, but it's a lot of fun. The riffing is great, and the host segments are slyly funny.
- This episode was included in Shout's "The Mystery Science Theater 3000 Collection, Vol. 7."
- The opening segment ends as Joel leaps over the desk at Crow. It's actually a more difficult move than you may think: For those who don't know, directly behind the desk is the puppeteer "trench"– essentially an approximately two-foot drop. In order for Joel (and later Mike) to stand right up next to the desk, there was a narrow wooden plank laid across the trench that they stood on. So, to make that move, Joel had to launch himself forward, carefully plant one foot on the plank (and not misstep and go crashing into the trench), and spring over the desk. A fellow could hurt himself, he could.
- That's Mike as Steve, of course. I love that "Nuh-uh." By this time it was really becoming a delight anytime Mike popped up with a new character.

- A little personal story related to the Steve-o-meter sketch: In a previous incarnation I used to write, for the Philadelphia Inquirer (and the now-defunct Knight-Ridder news syndicate), that little write-up next to the TV grid that tells you what's worth watching on TV that night. In one column, I said something nice about a performance by Steve Allen's wife, Jayne Meadows. A few weeks later I was stunned to receive a hand-written letter from Ms. Meadows herself, thanking me for my kind words. I wrote back thanking HER for being so nice, and in the letter I mentioned MST3K, briefly explained the premise of the Steve-O-meter and ended my letter with something to the effect of "now I know something else Steve thought of, marrying a class act." A week or so later I was even MORE stunned to receive ANOTHER letter, informing me that Steve thought the Steve-O-meter bit sounded funny and asking where they could get their hands on a tape of that show. I duped off a copy and sent it to them, and later got a short note saying Steve thought the sketch was very funny.
- Somewhat obscure reference: "He's everywhere! He's everywhere!" From the legendary Chickenman radio series back in the '60s. God, I loved that show.
- I can't hear exactly what Servo says under his breath when Oedipus is mentioned, but it's something about his mom…
- Note the mention of Rondo Hatton, who we'll later meet in "The Brute Man"
- Every once in a while in the theater, you can really tell that Joel/Mike and the bots are in a large echoey room. Listen when Joel yells "I haven't showered since Zeus was a pup!" The acoustics are not good.
- Great job by Jim in segment 1. He really belts out that song.
- The riff "Look! I'm hungry." "Listen! It's cold" brought back a memory: my daughter, about 8 at the time, thought that was one of the funniest things she'd ever heard. I remember her just rolling on the couch with laughter for about five minutes after she heard it.

- Vaguely naughty riffs: "You mean nymph loads!" "Ow! My eye!" "It's twue! It's twue!" The Herc movies brought out the naughty.
- Then-current references: Distant entertainment memories "Curly Sue" and "Remington Steele."
- As segment 3 opens, Joel is reading, highlighting and apparently really enjoying the novel "Tek Wars" by William Shatner. But he is — quite rightly — embarrassed by it.
- Segment 3 seems like it's not in the right place. Tom says that by this point in the movie Herc is living with the nice lady. But actually by the time the segment comes up Herc has already left the nice lady. Seems like they could have moved Segment 1 to the third spot, Segment 2 to the first spot and Segment 3 to the second spot and it would have flowed with the movie a bit better.
- Tom says: "Oh for the clarity of Mighty Jack." It's a funny line, but really this movie has a much more easily-discernible plot than "Mighty Jack" which I had to watch about five times before I began to make any sort of sense of.
- Joel invokes the memory of short-lived '60s TV show "Garrison's Guerrillas," which I think most boys loved because it had that cool Jeep-mounted machine gun. Who didn't want to ride around in that when you were about 9?
- Callbacks: "He hit big Jake!" ("Sidehackers") and the "He learned too late" speech from "It Conquered the World." "Hikeeeba!" (Women of the Prehistoric Planet).
- Firesign Theatre reference: "He's no fun, he fell right over."
- The final segment is great, but I do wish they could have led into it a bit more smoothly. Gypsy's question –"Why these kind of movies?"– sort of comes out of nowhere. But the rest of sketch is hilarious: Gypsy tries to contribute, but doesn't quite have the mental dexterity. Crow has clearly paged through Campbell's "Hero With a Thousand Faces" but, like an under-educated guy at a snooty cocktail party, can't quite pull his thoughts together. Tom, ever the realist, cuts to the chase. Wonderful writing like "…which trans-

lates into big sweaty guys pushin' girls around..." is one of the reasons why I love MST3K so much.

- CreditsWatch: Additional contributing writer: Don Jurek. And, at last, the last name of Dr. F is corrected to "Forrester."
- Fave riff: "You win the crazy award!" Also: Centurion: "Great Queen!" Joel: "Thanks!"

Movie stuff:

1) Herc is surprised to encounter Oedipus (whom Ulysses says is "a good man") blind and banished, but nobody really thinks to ask why. The whole thing is kind of glossed over...
2) I've never been a fan of "detour" movies and that's really what this is: The main plot – Hercules returns to his hometown of Thebes only to find it in the midst of a power struggle between Oedipus' two sons – is sidetracked for most of the movie as Herc lumbers down one plot cul-de-sac after another. When he finally gets where he wanted to get, the big battle scene is actually pretty cool. Plus ya got lots of scantily clad nymphs...
3) This movie was originally released in Italy as ""Ercole e la regina di Lidia"
4) The whole little plot cul-de-sac at the beginning of the movie with Anteus the giant just seems like filler. It really has no relevance to the rest of the movie. And Herc is kind of a jerk during it.
5) Primo Carnera, who played Anteus the giant, was a household name in the 1930s. He was the world heavyweight boxing champion in 1933-34, during which he was also the heavyweight wrestling champion.
6) The guy tests if Ulysses is actually deaf by hurling a spear into the deck right next to him. I hate to break it to the movie, but any deaf person would feel the vibration of that. Not really a good test.

282 • MSTIEPEDIA

Episode 409- INDESTRUCTIBLE MAN (with short: 'UNDERSEA KINGDOM'–Episode 2)
First shown: 8/1/92

Short: (1936) In part two ("The Undersea City") of a serial, our heroes are menaced by Atlantean soldiers.

Movie: (1956) A vicious criminal is executed, but then resurrected by scientists. Discovering that he is now invincible, he vows vengeance on those who testified against him.

Opening: Something's different about the bots (and Magic Voice), but Joel can't quite figure it out
Invention exchange: The Mads' have an invention, but they can't show it to us; J&tB show off their cereal novels
Host segment 1: Tragedy strikes the Undersea Kingdom parade goes awry
Host segment 2: Joel asks: "What would you do if you were indestructible?"
Host segment 3: Joel tries the Lon Chaney "eye thing," Tom and Crow are no help
End: J&tB sign the "no cop/doughnut joke" pledge, while the Mads deal with cops in Deep 13
Stinger: Indestructible man struggles with a manhole cover

Comments:

• We're getting into the meat of season four, and this is another of those great, seemingly effortless episodes. Terrible but watchable movie, great riffing, funny segments. Another winner.
• This episode was included in Shout's "The Mystery Science Theater 3000 Collection, Vol. 11."

- I assume Trace was running Tom and Kevin was running Crow in the opening segment. I don't think that was the only time that has ever happened.
- A little biting literary commentary as Tom refers to the "controversial-yet-all-but-forgotten" novel "American Psycho."
- This episode contains a notorious goof by the Brains: Dr. F says that the movie features "Casey Adams of 'Catalina Caper' fame." In fact, Adams (whose real name was Max Showalter) does not appear in "Catalina Caper." The Brains are confusing him with "Catalina Caper" star Del Moore, whom Adams somewhat looks and sounds like ... but not that much, really. Throughout the movie, when J&tB are supposedly doing impressions of Casey Adams, they're really imitating Moore's campy portrayal in "Catalina Caper." They don't really much sound like Adams at all.
- How could they make such a dumb mistake? Not to sound too much like an old "I walked uphill in the snow to school" fogey, but it's important to remember that this episode was done before the World Wide Web — and the ability to just pop on to the IMDB and get your cast information straight — existed. My sense is that Best Brains' entire movie research department, at that time, consisted of a dog-eared copy of the Leonard Maltin Movie Guide — which would have given them the correct name of the "Catalina Caper" actor, had they bothered to consult it.
- This is the only episode I'm aware of in which an actor appears in both the short and the main feature. It's Lon Chaney Jr., the star of the main feature, who also appears in the short and actually has a few lines.
- The Rodney King incident was fresh in the writers' minds. There are several references to it.
- Several times during the short, when a character refers to the "strange prisoners" or "strange captives" J&tB respond with "... weeeeird prisoners..." and "...weeeeird captives...". For those wondering what that's about, it's reference to the early Marx

Brothers movie "Animal Crackers." In it, Groucho briefly parodies the trance-like intonations used in the monologues that are the gimmick in Eugene O'Neill's play "Strange Interlude" (which was playing down the street when "Animal Crackers" was a Broadway musical). Aren't you sorry you asked?

- Whoa! A somewhat startling reference to future Vice President Dick Cheney. I forgot he was SecDef when this episode was made.
- In segment 1, Crow's little commercial for pepper sounds like a lot like the ones Garrison Keillor used to do on his St. Paul-based radio show "A Prairie Home Companion." I wonder if it's an homage or just a coincidence.
- There's also something incredibly silly about "Pollixfen, for your den-fen-tures…." That's about three levels away from an actual joke, but it's still funny.
- Props, so to speak. to Jef Maynard and the rest of the props team for the parade in segment 1. Very cool.
- As segment 1 ends, Crow says "I'm just going to step into this doorway," a reference to newsman Les Nessman in the famous "Turkey Drop" episode of "WKRP in Cincinnati."
- J&tB get mighty cranky during the incredibly static car conversation. Maybe I'm just hardened off to boring movie scenes, but it doesn't seem that bad to me.
- They still make Old Smuggler. From one who knows.
- The cop-donut thing is funny, but by my count there were only three of them in this episode. Doesn't seem like Joel overdid it to me…
- Another overtly religious remark from Joel: "…only millions of Christians…"
- The Brains treat Joe Flynn's appearance in this movie a little strangely. The recognition of him comes when they make a joke that he's a Joe Flynn lookalike. Later they seem to get that it IS Joe Flynn, croaking "McHale!" several times and they even make a great "Inspector Henderson and Captain Binghampton" joke. I

wonder if that first riff was a leftover from an early pass through the movie.

- Lon must have loved this role—there were hardly any lines to learn.
- Try to not blink as long as the witness lady goes without blinking. It's tough!
- Fans of Joel got about as close as they're likely ever going to get to their hero in segment 3. You can count the pores!
- Callbacks: "Hikeeba!" (WOMEN OF THE PREHISTORIC PLANET). "Want some?" (DADDY-O). The routine Tom and Crow fall into at the end of segment 3 is from "SIDEHACK-ERS." That they are still going on about it two seasons later is amazing.
- Obscure ref: "I'm Dickens, He's Fenster" – the name of a very short-lived '60s TV series. Also, Tom refers to "that Crazy Glue demonstration," a reference to an all-but-forgotten TV commercial in which an actor playing a construction worker Crazy Glues his hardhat to the bottom of a girder and then hangs from it.
- Gypsy's a notary?
- Mike and Kevin are great as the cops in the final segment. By the way, that scene also provided a wonderful poopie moment, with Mike and Frank cracking each other up.
- CreditsWatch: Andrea Ducane does the makeup for the second of three shows this season (Clayton James was the main makeup guy at this point). Suzette Jamison finishes up her internship. Additional contributing writer: David Sussman.
- Fave riffs from the short: "This looks like a set the Monkees would end up on." Honorable mention: "It's Jim Henson's Birth of a Nation Babies."
- Fave riffs from the movie: (As Irish cop) "Alright, gather round everybody, lots to see, show's just startin'." Honorable mention: Detective in movie: "You wanted me?" Joel: "For years!!"

286 • MSTIEPEDIA

Short stuff:

1) This installment of "Undersea Kingdom" is largely people running and riding around. It doesn't really advance the plot very much...

Movie stuff:

1) This movie offers extensive footage of the Angels Flight trolley, a popular (and, in 2001, deadly) L.A. tourist attraction.

Episode 410- HERCULES AGAINST THE MOON MEN
First shown: 8/22/92

Movie: (1964) Evil Queen Samar is in cahoots with a gang of monstrous moon men. Herc is determined to stop them.

Opening: Crow and Tom run away from home (briefly)
Invention exchange: The Mads unveil DEEP HURTING!; J&tB demonstrate their super freak-out kit
Host segment 1: Tom & Crow present the amazing BOOBY trap illusion
Host segment 2: Newly muscular Crow and Tom consider tough guy names
Host segment 3: Song: "Ode to Pants!"
End: J&tB discuss the switch from Steve Reeves to Alan Steele, Joel reads a letter, Crow gets disciplined, Tom reads another letter; In Deep 13, Dr. F is baffled by the outcome of the experiment, while Frank is wistful
Stinger: Old guy gets skewered

Comments:

- This is, for me, the funniest of the sword-and-sandal movie episodes, and an all-around great episode. As I said with the last one, these Herc movies are just perfect for MST3K, very watchable and very riffable. Strong riffing, great segments, just lots of fun.
- This episode was included in Rhino's "The Mystery Science Theater 3000 Collection, Vol. 7."
- "Deeeeeeep hurting!" (and, to a lesser extent, "saaaaaannndstoooorrrmmm") became an immediate catchphrase. By the way, it's a reference to a commercial for a nostrum called "Mentholatum Deep Heating Rub." You can see it on Youtube.
- Ya gotta love "Wishbone Ash" Frank's freakout. Traaaaiiills!
- Obscure riff: "The Mighty Favog!" That was a character invented for The Muppets' very brief and now largely forgotten stint on Saturday Night Live during its first season.
- Love the "pizza-pizza" stuff. A reference to popular commercials for the Little Caesars pizza restaurant chain.
- I always enjoy the bit where some character in the movie has a long speech with odd little pauses and Tom tries to get a word in edgewise, as he does here when the old guy talks.
- During segment one, the walls of the amazing BOOBY trap illusion swing rather freely ... Not really very threatening. This is also a "meta" bit, essentially a joke about a joke.
- Callbacks: "Hikeeba." (WOMEN OF THE PREHISTORIC PLANET). "Trumpy, you're angry!" (POD PEOPLE). o/` "Hey, it's the UNDERSEA KINGDOM..." o/` "I'm a Grimault warrior!" (VIKING WOMEN). "You told me a fabricated story..." (THE UNEARTHLY). "It was after the apocalypse. They had to get to the power station..." (ROBOT HOLOCAUST).
- Mildly naughty moment: "Guys, I am so homesick right now..." Poor horny Joel.

- The first time I saw this I was floored when they referenced "Marvel the Mustang." What horse do!
- Although Tom's body rejected his muscle-man arms in segment 2, Joel has put his old arms back by the time he reenters the theater. He quietly thanks Joel.
- During the brawl on screen, J&tB do a terrific version of the "Star Trek" fight music. Harmony and everything.
- Segment three features one of my favorite MST3K songs: "Pants!" Even Frank gets into it! (This segment also gave us a couple of great poopie moments.)
- When the sandstorm scene finally arrives, it definitely is punishing. In earlier seasons, it's the sort of thing that might have gotten the movie rejected. What can you riff on when essentially nothing is happening in the movie for several minutes? But the geniuses at MST3K found a way, and it's a great example of turning a liability into an asset. Instead of ruining the episode, the sandstorm is one of the highlights.
- Joel actually uses the term "riffing" several times, something he didn't do a lot.
- In the discussion of the movie at the end of the episode, J&tB speak of the movie as if it was a direct sequel to the movie they watched a couple of episodes back, but really the two aren't related at all.
- CreditsWatch: Host segments directed by Jim. Barb Oswald was "Toolmaster Jr." one last time. "Pants" was written and arranged by Mike and Frank. Beginning with this episode and for the next seven episodes, the credits misspell "Ammendment" in "the authors of the 1st Ammendment."
- Fave riff: "Meet Sammy SPEAR and his orchestra!" Honorable mention: "Don't make me laugh, Woodsy Owl!"

Movie stuff:

1) While the title and the dubbing refer to our hero as Hercules, in the original Italian he is Maciste (aka "My cheesesteak"). The strongman character has a long history: he originated in the 1914 Italian movie "Cabiria" and was resurrected when sword-and-sandal epics suddenly became very popular in the late 1950s.
2) Because American audiences were unfamiliar with Maciste, the title character's name was usually changed to Atlas, Colossus (as in "Colossus and the Headhunters," although nobody calls him that in that movie), Goliath, Hercules or Samson.

Episode 411- THE MAGIC SWORD
First shown: 8/29/92

Movie: (1962) A knight tries to save a damsel from an evil sorcerer with the help of his magical foster mother.

Opening: Joel fancies himself a caricature artist
Invention exchange: J&tB demonstrate their Big Gulp berets; The Mads have created designer bio-hazard absorbent throw pillows and Frank demonstrates
Host segment 1: J&tB present their commercial for Basil Rathbones for dogs
Host segment 2: Joel, Gypsy and Crow, in medieval costumes, present a pageant on life in the middle ages, but Tom ruins things
Host segment 3: Crow sings: "Estelle"
End: J&tB discuss words you can't say on TV, Joel reads a letter, TV's Frank's not looking good
Stinger: Estelle's two-headed assistant

Comments:

- I agree with Joel (in the theater), Tom (in a host segment) and Paul (in the ACEG): this movie is not that bad for a Bert I. Gordon movie, which makes the whole affair more watchable. The riffing is decent and the host segments are fun. This one may not be great, but it's very good.
- This episode was included in Shout! Factory's "Mystery Science Theater 3000 Collection: Vol XXVI."
- RiffTrax has re-riffed this movie.
- In the opening bit, Trace and Kevin must have been crouching in front of the SOL set. Probably uncomfortable.
- Nice cartoon sound effect as the needle is removed from Frank's neck.
- I love the phrase "criminally-priced spring water." It hasn't gone away.
- One thing I'll say for about this episode, it answers at last the question of who Merritt Stone is ... he's the guy who plays "King Grady."
- Callbacks: "Hey, it's the UNDERSEA KINGDOM..." "I say it's foggy!" (THE CRAWLING EYE), "Ya got me!" (CATALINA CAPER), "I'm so sleepy I can barely keep awake!" (The Hercmeister) "Hikeeba" (WOMEN OF THE PREHISTORIC PLANET) and "...Happy king..." (MR B NATURAL).
- Joel mentions a "Jane Fonda video." It's been decades since she's made one, so a lot of people may not remember that Fonda was once the queen of exercise and fitness videos.
- Joel does another Biblical riff: "Why do you seek the living among the dead?"
- As they head out of the theater toward segment 1, they start talking about the host segment they're about to do. I like when they do that. Adds continuity.
- Great reference: "They're packed with bits of Nigel Bruce!"

Note the LOTR reference before LOTR references were common-place.
- Crow's song is easily a highlight, though I confess I like Tom's list of people better looking than Estelle even better. (However, hate to break it to Tom, but Jesus Jones is not a person.)
- Alas, Crow's love was not to be. Estelle died in 1984.
- Joel again mentions Ashwaubenon High, his alma mater.
- While reading the letter, Joel actually says "keep circulating the tapes." I think it's the only time he ever did that on the show.
- Poor Frank at the end — and, hey, didn't something very similar happen to Dr. Erhardt?
- CreditsWatch: Host segments directed by Jim. Crist Ballas did the hair and makeup, the only episode he worked this season. "Ode on Estelle" was written and arranged by Mike and Paul. "Ammend-ment" is misspelled.
- Fave riff: "Just came to freak you out, baby..." Honorable mention: "Ga-nish!"

Movie stuff:

1) That's Maili Nurma, aka Vampira, as the enchantress, one of two roles in the movie.

Episode 412- HERCULES AND THE CAPTIVE WOMEN
First shown: 9/12/92

Movie: (1961) Hercules goes to Atlantis to save his son, but evil Queen Antinea stands in his way.

Opening: Gypsy wants to join Joel, Tom and Crow in the theater and Joel agrees, though Tom and Crow are dubious
Invention exchange: Frank demonstrates The lawn baby, J&tB show off the womb-mate

Host segment 1: Joel wonders: is there such a thing as "good-natured" brawling

Host segment 2: Crow presents his rather dubious "history" of Hercules

Host segment 3: The bots' have created a Hercules action figure, and it's pretty lame

End: Laying the Hercules movies to rest, Joel reads letter, Frank is being chased by mower

Stinger: "Hercules! Help me!"

Comments:

- This is one of the lesser sword-and-sandal outings. Confusing movie, hit and miss riffing, pretty good segments. Of course, this one includes the classic line: "Today is dedicated to Uranus," and is the landmark episode in which Gypsy watches a short portion of the movie along with Joel, Tom and Crow. All in all, fun, but a lesser effort.
- This episode was included in Shout! Factory's "Mystery Science Theater 3000 Collection: Vol XXIX."
- Joel's confidence in Gypsy is admirable, but let's note for the record that, sadly, Crow and Tom's instincts were correct. Gypsy is not down with the street.
- Joel says "Zatharatu." I've always heard it was "Zarathustra."
- Despite all the hoopla to the contrary, this is NOT the last Hercules movie.
- As Tom sagely notes: "This would really be exciting if I knew what was goin' on." All the excitement about Gypsy in the theater takes place when the movie is setting up the plot, with the result that I never did really figure out what the heck is going on in this movie.
- I suspect a hunk of the movie was cut right around the first commercial. Before the commercial, there are portents of danger and Herc is tossin' thrones around. After the break, Herc wakes up on a ship and everybody is smirking silently at him. The heck?

- Gypsy's riff: "They're steam-cleaning the horses!" delights Joel, Tom and Crow. Eh, not bad. But of her few riffs, I actually like "Oh, they've got a fun friend!" better.
- By my count, Gypsy lasts 5 and a half minutes. Sheesh, Gypsy, these sword-and-sandal things are among the more watchable movies MST did! What a lightweight!
- Gypsy exits left. A few other characters have exited or entered this way. Where does that exit lead? And how do they eat and breathe?
- Firesign Theatre reference: "...The Golden Hind."
- Crow goes a bit overboard with the "I have my rights! It was Callahan!" bit. (For those who don't know, it's a reference to the movie "Dirty Harry.") He does it five times by my count, practically every time the little guy in the movie has a line.
- Callback: "Hurry, Diana!" (UNDERSEA KINGDOM), Frank sings "I sing whenever I sing..." (GIANT GILA MONSTER), "Rock Candy Baby" (DADDY-O), "...I've heard them talk about so much lately..." (GAMERA).
- That's Frank as the voice of the action figure when he says "I'm so sleepy..." but the final comment is by Mike. Wonder why they didn't just have one of them do all the comments? By the way, the action figure's arm falls off in the middle of the sketch. Joel conceals pretty well and they keep going.
- CreditsWatch: Nathan Devery finished up his internship with this episode. "Ammendment" is still misspelled.
- Fave riff: "Dear lord, the canary exploded!" Honorable mention: Tom: "You guys are supposed to be nice to me! Today is dedicated to my..." Joel: "We know!" Also: "Well, whatever tugs at your bobber, little fella."

Movie stuff:

1) All these movies have men in miniskirts, but this one has to have the miniest minis I've seen yet (not that there's anything wrong with it).

294 • MSTiepedia

2) I never noticed before that, a couple of times, they do a needle drop on that musical sting that I think was originally composed for "This Island Earth," and that I've heard in a lot of Universal movies.

Episode 413- MANHUNT IN SPACE (with short: 'GENERAL HOSPITAL'–Segment 1)
First shown: 9/19/92

Short: (1963) A few scenes from the early days of the famed soap opera "General Hospital." Jesse plans a party while Dr. Hardy gives a worried patient a diagnosis.

Movie: (1954) Edited-together episodes of the TV series "Rocky Jones, Space Ranger." Our hero and his sidekick Winky rescue stranded Vena and confront space pirates working for evil Queen Cleolanta.

Opening: Crow isn't happy that the movie is going to be in black and white, leading to the discovery that Tom Servo is color blind!
Invention exchange: The Mads have invented beanbag pants, while J&tB demonstrate recycled paper clothing
Host segment 1: The bots are playing soap opera, but Joel won't play
Host segment 2: J&tB discuss the overuse of modifiers, such as "space"
Host segment 3: J&tB get a visit from Winkie on the Hexfield
End: Crow is Joel's guitar and Tom is the amp, Joel reads a letter, the Mads are stuck in their bean bag chairs
Stinger: Space traitor Ken tosses a chair

Comments:

• Of the two Rocky Jones episodes, I prefer "Crash of the Moons," but this one is a good time too. The previous time I watched this

I was really, really sick. The consequence was that the black-and-white movie and all that monotonous rocketship taking off and landing practically put me to sleep (the meds might have contributed to this). This time through I was fully functional (more or less) and I liked it a lot more. The movie is pretty strange but the cast really commits to the premise, which makes the riffing easier and more fun. The host segments are mostly pretty good (although the "space modifier" segment wears out its welcome) and generally I didn't have any trouble staying awake and laughing a lot.

- This episode was included in Shout! Factory's "Mystery Science Theater 3000 Collection: Vol XIV."
- A little backstage info: Kevin has acknowledged that he actually does have red-green color blindness, which I guess is where the idea for the bit came from.
- I love how, in the short, the doc tells his patient that his treatment for her apparently minor condition is TWO WEEKS in the hospital. How times have changed.
- When John "Dr. Hardy" Beradino appears, Crow says "Wow, he was old even then!" Beradino was in his mid-40s when that scene was shot. Wonder if Trace would still make that joke? I know I wouldn't!
- Showbiz info: The syndicated television series "Rocky Jones, Space Ranger," lasted only one season, because it lost a considerable amount of money. It was the first space opera to be shot on film, (which is why it survives so well today) and had huge overhead costs (sets, special effects, large cast) compared to other shows of the early 1950s (I know, hard to believe THOSE were bank-breaking special effects, but...). The show was popular and had no lack of advertising sponsors, but it became evident during its first season that it would probably never break even.
- Tom Servo thinks a shot of a planet looks like the MST3K logo — Joel hushes him.

- All the rocket ship footage seemed to push some "Thunderbirds" buttons for the cast: they mention it a couple of times and Crow says "Scott Tracy!" at one point.
- During segment one, Crow mentions "mogo-on-the-g-go-go" a W.C. Fields reference.
- Nice reminder that Cambot is there at the end of segment 1. We sometimes forget but they seldom did.
- Callbacks: "I told you to find adventure not bring it home with you!" (City Limits); Hikeeba (Women of the Prehistoric Planet); "I'm a Grimault warrior!" (Viking Women); "Chief? McCloud!" (Pod People); The Gamera song.
- Then-current reference: "What's your position?" "Leaning towards Perot."
- Last time, I thought Tom said, "What is this, Radio Oz?" Turns out it's Radio AAHS.
- Did they really say 'space' that much? I can't remember them doing it even once.
- In segment three, Crow has an acid-flashback to episode 310-FUGITIVE ALIEN, which Joel notes was "like, 20 experiments ago." It was 26 episodes ago, to be exact.
- Mike is great as Winkie and Frank sure does a great little old lady voice.
- Shoes for industry! (Another Firesign Theatre reference.)
- Um, Joel can call Earth? (I know, I know…)
- CreditsWatch: Curtis Anderson and Kelly Ann Nathe started their internships. Jim directed the host segments once again, but this was his last time in season four. Kevin, Joel and Trace would trade off for the rest of the season."Ammendment" is still spelled wrong.
- Fave riff from the short: "Here comes Nurse Feratu." Honorable mention: "Nothing an expensive operation can't complicate."
- Fave riff from the feature: "What are you doing in Alan Brady's office?" Honorable mention: "I've got something that'll put you through the floor, boys."

Movie stuff:

1) Winkie says "the ship won't land on its tail" and then it does. Several times. Hmm. But I always enjoyed the notion of a rocket ship landing back on its tail, like a car backing into a parking space. I recently read an article about scientists that are actually trying to do this in reality with real rockets, and are, understandably, having a difficult time.
2) Scotty "Winkie" Beckett wrote that song he sings.

Episode 414- TORMENTED
First shown: 9/26/92

Movie: (1960) A betrothed jazz pianist believes he's escaped his troublesome mistress when he fails to save her from a fall. But then he's visited by a blackmailer ... and her ghost.

Opening: The bots are living in a ventilation duct
Invention exchange: J&tB demonstrate the Aunt Catherine wheel, while the Mads show off the drinking jacket
Host segment 1: Joel is stuck in ventilation duct, Crow and Tom are no help
Host segment 2: Joel asks the bots which pop singers they'd like to throw from a lighthouse
Host segment 3: Crow and Tom pretend to be bodyless ghosts, but Joel has the last laugh
End: J&tB are depressed so they think happy thoughts and sing a happy song, and so does Frank
Stinger: "Tom Stewart killed me!"
- A lot of people say this may be Bert I.'s best, and it may be true. It's definitely possible to get caught up in this one, as strange as it is. The riffing is good and the host segments are what we've come to expect from season four. Definitely a fun episode.

298 • MSTiepedia

- This episode was included in Shout's "The Mystery Science Theater 3000 Collection, Vol. 11."
- Cambot is leaning WAY over the desk to shoot Joel in the opening.
- That's definitely Mike as "The Aunt Catherine Wheel" and "Uncle Carl," and it sounds like the same voice as "Grammy Fisher" and "Aunt Ethel" but who is it? Trace, maybe?
- I have a special fondness for the "drinking jacket" invention — I created my own and wore it in the costume contest at the second convention.
- Sadly, the "Spalding, old man!" joke is not so funny now.
- I'm no expert on men's calves but certain people have expressed agreement with Crow's assessment.
- This episode's overused joke: "Sessions presents..." Once or twice, okay, but they really beat it to death.
- After segment 2, Joel is so excited he playfully tosses Tom as they reenter the theater (Kevin is apparently laying on his back waiting to catch him).
- Crow goofs: The snack bar chef is NOT Merritt Stone. That's Gene Roth. But Stone IS in the movie: he's the clergyman who marries Tom and his bride.
- Callback: "Charles Moffett..." (Ring of Terror)
- Joel suggests this is more depressing than hanging in a bar talking to Neil Young. Why is talking to Neil Young depressing? He seems like a pretty cheerful guy.
- One highlight of the episode is the hilarious "happy thoughts song," including Frank's verse at the end. Great stuff. Note that the Prince roach from episode 408- HERCULES UNCHAINED is on the floor near Frank.
- I've always enjoyed the phrase "K'nerping for moisture."
- During the song, Tom Servo's head falls off. They keep going.
- CreditsWatch: Host segments directed by Kevin. Tim Scott replaces Brian Wright as audio guy. Andrea DuCane did hair and

makeup (the third of three times this season). And it is with this episode that we say farewell to Alexandra Carr, who was with the show since the KTMA days and did just about every job, including writer and performer. Her departure caused a lot of title shifts, but we'll deal with that in the next episode. Also, "ammendment" is still spelled wrong.
- Fave riff: "Honey, I'm ho-o-o-o-oh, yeah, you're dead." Honorable mention: "C'mon, we're going bowling."

Movie stuff:

1) They're sending the invitations only a week before the wedding?
2) "This is one dark mama-jama of a movie," Joel says toward the end, and, wow, is it ever. It's also kinda dull for the first half, although the weirdness overwhelms the blandness in the second half. The script makes some bold narrative choices: nobody can sympathize with the awful, grasping, brassy Vi, and Tom didn't actively kill her. Yet he is still subjected to blackmail and a nightmarish haunting. It seems like Tom's biggest mistake (not counting killing the hipster) was not immediately reporting Vi's accidental death.

Episode 415- THE BEATNIKS (with short: 'GENERAL HOSPI-TAL'–Segment 2)
First shown: 11/25/92

Short: (1963) A scene from the soap opera "General Hospital." Nurse Jesse throws the most tense and awkward party ever.

Movie: (1960) Hoodlum and wannabe singer Tony gets his big break, but can't shake his psycho pseudo-beatnik buddies.

Opening: An uncharacteristically mean Joel dominates the bots in a game of rock-paper-scissors

Invention exchange: The Mads have donned troll doll costumes, Joel demonstrates pocket pool

Host segment 1: Joel, Crow and Tom present: Either you are or aren't a beatnik

Host segment 2: The bots' slumber party gets a call from Tony Travis!

Host segment 3: Tom Servo stars in a dramatization of the life of a '50s rock star

End: Crow is in Moon mode, Joel reads a letter, while the Mads are a hot property

Stinger: Moon gets hysterical

Comments:

- There's so much to love about this episode. The movie is both watchable and eminently stupid, a perfect combination for MST3K. The riffing is solid, and you would expect no less at this stage of season 4. Even the segments are uniformly good. A great episode for newbies and just all-around fun.
- This episode was included in Shout's "The Mystery Science Theater 3000 Collection, Vol. XVII."
- This episode debuted on the Turkey Day 1992 marathon, and was the first new episode to air in two months.
- As noted, Joel is uncharacteristically mean in the opening! Anybody who says Joel was always a father figure to the bots should watch this sketch. (Although he reminds me a bit of MY father.) Thankfully, GYPSY CRUSHES JOEL! and we have a happy ending.
- That's Mary Jo as Magic Voice, for the first time.
- Naughty line: "You got a snooker down there!"

- During the short, J&tB do probably their best "commercial" for the Booze Council, featuring the classic line: "Booze takes a dull party and makes it better!"
- Callbacks: "Rock candy baby you're mine, yeah!" (Daddy-O). "Brought to you by Ken-L Ration" and "I have a hiatus hernia" (General Hospital).
- Odd moment in the movie: Does Harry really have to ask permission to use the pay phone in Iris' mom's diner?
- "I killed that fat barkeep!!" became an immediate MSTie catchphrase.
- Firesign Theatre reference: As segment 2 begins, Tom is singing the "Porgie Tirebiter" theme song.
- That's Mike, of course, as the voice of Tony Travis. "If you're a bill collector or if you're with the military..."
- In segment 3, Crow's wig falls off. They keep going.
- The letter they read at the end is from a kid who got in trouble for calling his mom a "dickweed." J&tB state that it is NOT a swear word and they're right ... but I think you still shouldn't call your mom a dickweed (even if she's being one).
- CreditsWatch: Host segments directed by Joel (the first of four eps this season). But the big news is the departure of Alex Carr, causing everybody to move up a rung: Jann Johnson becomes production manager (Alex's old title) and Ellen (Ellie) McDonough becomes production coordinator (Jann's old title). Alex's name comes off and Ellen's name is added to the "post production coordination" credit along with Jann. Ellie comes off the list under "production assistant." Clayton James did hair and makeup for all the rest of the episodes this season. Amazingly, considering all the changes that were made, "Ammendment" is still spelled wrong.
- Fave riff from short: "This is Pete from props. Don't eat the cake!" Honorable mention: "There's a layer of squirrel in here!"

302 • MSTIEPEDIA

- Fave riff from the movie: "Dish of ice cream! Don't tempt me!" Honorable mention: o/` "...a tight leather mask..." o/`, "Accessory After The Fact Theater will return after this."

Movie stuff:

1) You can hear director/scriptwriter Paul Frees (the voice of Boris Badenov) introducing Eddie when he makes his first TV appearance and also as the voice of the police detective in the hospital. Frees also did voices for Inspector Fenwick on "The Dudley Do-Right Show" and the magpies on "The Heckle and Jeckle Show" among many many other voice jobs he had.
2) One great thing about this episode is that all Eddie's songs have these giant gaps after each line of lyrics, allowing J&tB to insert a riff after practically every one.
3) One of the weirdest things about this movie is the casting of the hatchet-faced Joyce Terry (aka "Donald Sutherland in drag") as Helen. Her beauty is supposed to tempt Eddie away from the dim-witted, co-dependent Iris, but it's hard to understand what Eddie could possibly see in her. (The answer: She and Frees were married in real life.)

Episode 416- FIRE MAIDENS OF OUTER SPACE
First shown: 11/26/92

Movie: (1956) Astronauts travel to a moon of Jupiter and discover a civilization populated almost entirely by women. Soon they're battling a monster that has been terrorizing the settlement.

Opening: During a posture check, Timmy the dark Crow appears — and attacks Cambot!
Invention exchange: The Mads have the big checkbook, while Joel demonstrates cheese sneaker

Host segment 1: Tom wants to discuss double entendres, but Timmy acts out
Host segment 2: Joel tries to explain the twin-screw controller, but Timmy interferes
Host segment 3: Joel defeats Timmy in a battle to the death
End: Joel, Crow and Tom discuss the lessons they've learned, Joel reads a letter, and Timmy's in Deep 13
Stinger: It's a secret passage miracle

Comments:

- What a great, great episode, featuring the truly inspired "dark Timmy" host segments. The Brains rarely gave us a complete story within the 15 minutes or so that the host segments run, and this is one of the funniest and most creative attempts. Witty and captivating all the way through. The riffing is, again, just what you would expect at this point in season four, when this team was firing on all cylinders. As for the movie, well ... you know, in the theme song when they talk about "cheesy movies"? This is about as cheesy as it gets.
- I would really love to see this one on a future DVD collection, but I hear it's a licensing nightmare.
- This was the second of two new episodes shown on Thanksgiving Day, 1992.
- Of course, for the one or two people who don't know, Timmy is the Crow they use in the theater, painted black to make a nicer silhouette. But are they using two black Crows in the theater when Timmy sneaks in? I can't really see a difference in the silhouettes.
- Callbacks: Joel's posture check during the opening is a callback to the "Posture Pals" short (shown in episode 320- THE UNEARTHLY). Crow is right, that is the same footage from "King Dinosaur." Joel says "tenperature" in segment 2, a callback to "Fugitive Alien." "I'm

feeling REALLY good!" (Gamera vs Guiron). "Lawrence would you get back there..." (Catalina Caper).

- "I prayed for a friend and he came" is from a Frankenstein movie.
- I love Frank's zoned out expression when they first cut to Deep 13.
- I guess with the holiday season approaching, "It's a Wonderful Life" was on their minds — not only do they make references to it during the movie, but Frank and Dr. F approximate a scene from it during the giant checkbook bit.
- Dr. F is evil, so he pronounces "WimbleDON" incorrectly.
- Frank has a hilarious bit of business during the invention exchange: He needs to sign a giant check, so of course he needs a pen. He pats his pockets looking for a pen but can't find one, then steps off camera and returns with a GIANT pen the same size as the giant check book. Funny stuff.
- I wonder who art directed the costumes and set pieces in the blackout scenes after Timmy commandeers the twin-screw controller. The images are wonderfully surrealistic and also vaguely reminiscent of the Daffy Duck cartoon "Duck Amuck."
- Tom still has the rotisserie in his head when comes back into the theater. Joel helps him out.
- That's Jef Maynard running Timmy (he's in the credits). In those days he tended to be their go-to guy when they needed somebody else in the puppet trench; later it was Pat Brantseg.
- Servo applauds several times in the theater. How does he do that with inoperable arms? (I know, I know.)
- Timmy enters the theater between segments two and three. When they come back from commercial he can't be seen, but then he slowly reappears and then starts to creep over to attack Tom. This is one of only about a dozen times someone or something other than Joel, Mike, Tom and Crow enters the theater.
- As Tom is attacked, Joel says "You didn't tell us Tommy was in here..." He meant "Timmy." They keep going.
- After Tom is attacked, Joel runs off left. A rare move.

- Then-current reference: The then-controversial, now mostly forgotten book "Final Exit."
- The fan letter read at the end of this episode was written by a woman who now uses the stage name Christmas Sagan, and is a member of the rock group Freezepop. Joel invited her to appear on the Thanksgiving marathon in 2015. She appeared again, and performed a cover of the MST3k theme song, during the live Kickstarter telethon in December of that year.
- CreditsWatch: Host segments directed by Trace (the first of three eps in this season). Jim directed most of the first half of the season but in the second half directing duties are being spread around. "Ammendment" is still spelled wrong.
- Fave riff: "Thank you, that's all." Honorable mention: "Yeah, it's Nancy Kulp night."

Movie stuff:

1) When they first encounter the girl being molested by the monster, the astronauts are at least 50 yards away and the girl is standing right next to the monster, but one of them calmly levels his revolver and shoots in their direction. He misses both of them, but either he thinks he's a REEEEALLY good shot or he's incredibly reckless. Or he's in a cheesy movie. Sheesh.

Episode 417- CRASH OF MOONS (with short: 'GENERAL HOSPITAL'–Segment 3)
First shown: 11/28/92

Short: (1963) From the soap opera "General Hospital," Cynthia and Phil have it out.

Movie: (1954) Edited-together episodes of the TV series "Rocky Jones, Space Ranger." Our hero tries to save the inhabitants of two worlds that are about to collide, but evil Queen Cleolanta stands in his way.

Opening: Crow is selling true grit
Invention exchange: The Mads present Sugary Deep 13 toothpaste; J&tB demonstrate the rock & wreck guitar
Host segment 1: Crow and Tom serenade Gypsy with "The Gypsy Moons"
Host segment 2: J&tB present a commercial for John Banner-grams
Host segment 3: J&tB read through Crow's latest screenplay: a space opera
End: Joel reads a letter, John Banner visits on the Hexfield; then the SOL sends Deep 13 a Banner-gram
Stinger: "Boopie!"

Comments:

- A lot of folks love this one and it definitely has a lot going for it besides the aggressive geniality of John Banner. This is the most bearable of the three GH segments and its also the most fun of the Rocky Jones outings, so it's basically watchable all the way through. Combine that with pretty decent host segments and some strong riffing and you've got a winner.
- This episode is included in Shout! Factory's "Mystery Science Theater 3000 Collection: Vol. XVIII."
- The 1992 Turkey Day marathon was over, but this was the third new episode in four days. MSTies had a wonderful weekend.
- I remember seeing ads when I was a kid trying to get me to sell Grit. But I've never seen it on news stands or anything. It's still around. Maybe it's a Midwestern thing.
- Dr. F's invention is extra evil this week. Conversely, Joel's doesn't look that well-put-together.

- Nice to see they called an unofficial moratorium on "Oh, is the great [name here] going to direct?" riff. Funny back in season two, but...
- I love Crow's riff: "Orbit? What does that mean?" a reference to the painful explanation of what an orbit is in a previous Rocky Jones episode.
- Callback: "Yew and yor dawtah aw doomt!" (Robot Holocaust) "But you don't love Ken." (An almost instant callback to the "General Hospital" short minutes earlier.) "Not since Fire Maidens of Outer Space..."
- Firesign Theatre reference: "He's not your son, Fred."
- Satellite News' Erhardt, dressed as Bavaro, introduced this episode in the 1993 Turkey Day bumpers.
- I like Tom Servo's beak moving as he reads over Joel's shoulder. And Mike is so klandinkto as John Banner! (Hi, Bavaro.)
- Joel says "Gimme that pinkle, Weekie!" They keep going.
- CreditsWatch: Host segments directed by Kevin. Sarah E. Wisner joins the staff as production assistant, Ellie McDonough's old role before her recent promotion. Patrick Brantseg joins the staff as prop assistant, after interning for the first half of the season. This was intern Kelly Ann Nathe's last episode. "Ammendment" is still spelled wrong.
- Fave riff from the short: "Would you folks break it up? Your party's depressing everyone in the building." Honorable mention: "How can you not love a skull like this?"
- Fave riff: "Horowitz is visibly shaken..." Honorable mention: "... would get beat up in the third grade."

Movie stuff:

1) The space station doesn't have any ability to propel itself? Not even some little thruster rockets? Seems like a design flaw. Or a plot contrivance.

308 • MSTIEPEDIA

2) Occasionally you pick up a new vocabulary word from these movies. I'd never heard of a "suzerain" before, but it's a thing.
3) Is it just me or is Cleolanta kinda hot? Headstrong and evil, sure, but still, rrowr.

Episode 418- ATTACK OF THE THE EYE CREATURES
First shown: 12/5/92

Movie: (1965) Multi-eyed aliens try to frame a pair of smoochin' teens.

Opening: Crow and Tom quickly go through their "best friends" stage
Invention exchange: Tom is mocking Crow; The Mads demonstrate the router Ouija board, J&tB show off the funny gag fax
Host segment 1: Tom wants learn how to make out
Host segment 2: J&tB present their tribute to Earrrrrrl Holliman
Host segment 3: J&tB are the Rip Taylor Trio!
End: The case against the film-makers (they just didn't care!); Larry Buchanan visits Deep 13
Stinger: Greasy drifter in sweater dress

• I enjoyed this a lot. The biggest drawback is that the movie is sort of a comedy in parts — a failed comedy to be sure, but the film is intentionally trying to be funny and, as we saw with "Catalina Caper" and a few others, that's always a bit rougher to riff on. Still, the team slogs through pretty well, just as you'd expect at this point in season four. It's a good example of what they were capable of by this point. In season two, this movie might have gotten the better of them. In season four, this is a movie they could successfully take on. The host segments help somewhat; even the Earl Holliman sketch — a "wtf" bit if there ever was one — somehow comes off.
• This episode has not been released on commercial DVD.

- This ep was number 10 on the summer 1995 countdown Comedy Central did.
- Doesn't it seem like this episode ought to have a short?
- Crow's arm (which was apparently taped to Tom) comes off during the opening. They keep going, and it's still taped to Tom's back in the next segment.
- Wonder if the presence of somebody (or some THING) named Ethan Allen in the credits sparked the idea for the Mads' invention?
- I can't find anything definitive, but I think Homer Formby IS dead. But I found an interesting tidbit: when he hit it big with his furniture refinishing products, he bought an entire island in the Florida Keys. He later sold it.
- "Dern smoochers!" and other variations became an immediate catchphrase.
- Wow, it turns out that MST3K invented rickrolling! Tom breaks into a chorus of "Never Gonna Give You Up," at one point.
- Joel kinda has to lean over the puppet trench to smooch Servo, but he covers well.
- Literary reference: Joel invokes Ignatius Riley from John Kennedy Toole's Pulitzer Prize-winning novel "Confederacy of Dunces." I PRESUME everybody in this audience has read it. If you haven't, go and do so before Lady Fortuna spins the wheel of your destiny downward.
- This one was never released on DVD but I have one saved from TV. My copy is from the late summer of 1995. Amusing commercial: the one for this new thing you can get for your computer called America Online. "My kid gets help with his homework!"
- The Earl Holliman sketch is silly and pointless, but I do like the line "...who would have been William Shatner had there not already been one." How true that is.
- Callback: "...sing whenever I sing whenever I..." (GIANT GILA MONSTER)

- Note that the giant handkerchief is monogrammed "KM." Hmmm…
- Mike scores again as "Larry Buchanan."
- CreditsWatch: Host segments directed by Joel. Additional music written and performed by Mike and Kevin — I assume they're referring to the Rip Taylor music. And good news: the "Ammendment" mistake has been corrected.
- Fave riff: "And don't be alarmed if it suddenly becomes 2 in the afternoon." Honorable mention: "She's a female. They have less plumage."

Movie stuff:

1) This movie, believe it or not, is (with some minor changes) a scene-for-scene, line-for-line remake of a movie called "Invasion of the Saucer Men." As you might guess, that movie also stinks. Larry Buchanan did a number of these remakes for AIP.
2) For those who don't know, the double THE in the movie title occurred when the movie was re-released. It was originally titled just "The Eye Creatures." Somebody decided to jazz up the title and slapped ATTACK OF THE on the title card, not noticing that there was already a THE. They just didn't care (which also became a catchphrase).

Episode 419- THE REBEL SET (with short: "JOHNNY AT THE FAIR")
First shown: 12/12/92

Short: (1947) Young Johnny wanders around the 1947 Canadian National Exhibition after his negligent parents lose track of him.

Movie: (1959) A coffeehouse owner wants to knock off an armored car, and gets three losers to help him.

Opening: Joel has something really scary to read to the bots at bedtime
Invention exchange: The Mads demonstrate their "quick primp kit," while J&tB present their paint-by-number Mark Rothko
Host segment 1: Crow tries record album acting lessons with Scott Baio
Host segment 2: J&tB discuss what to do during a four-hour layover in Chicago
Host segment 3: J&tB have a writing workshop, with Merritt Stone in mind
End: Tom "Hercule" Servo tries to ferret out the mystery of Merritt Stone (and his head explodes. In Deep 13, Frank is equally confused
Stinger: "I am bugged!"

- This is the beginning of a stretch of good to really excellent episodes, with everybody on the staff firing on all cylinders. The riffing of the short is classic, and it carries over into the movie. The movie itself is pretty static and dull in the first half, but finally gets going once the robbery starts, giving them plenty to riff on. The segments aren't all classics, but there are no real clunkers either.
- This was included in Shout's "The Mystery Science Theater 3000 Collection, Vol. 12."
- Clearly the Brains' don't like "Life's Little Instruction Book," (which I had never heard of when I initially saw this show). Two decades later, it is still available.
- The quick primp kit is a favorite invention exchange of mine, especially Frank's Fonzie-esque "ayyyy!"
- What a great short and despite Joel's admonition, they get plenty dark ... you know, the way we like it.
- I love the little record player they use in segment 1; and that's Mike's voice, of course, as Scott Baio.
- What would YOU do with a four-hour layover in Chicago? (Although if it's a plane layover, it would take you two hours to get

into town from O'Hare and two to get back, so…) Me, I think I'd take the architecture boat tour of the Chicago River and note how the structures of so many of the buildings tend to draw my eyes upward … oh, okay, I'd go Navy Pier and get hammered. By the way, I believe what Tom refers to as the Continental Bank building is now the Bank of America building, unless it's been sold again.

- I was glad they kept the "Get Smart" jokes to a minimum, though that's fairly typical. They don't like to beat one reference to death … usually.
- Obscure reference: "Bizarre" with John Byner.
- The "chasing Ed Platt dressed as a priest" scene features every hymn and church song the guys could think of, as well as plenty of religious terminology (example: "I. am. in. a. state. of. GRACE!")
- CreditsWatch: Host segments directed by Trace.
- Fave riff from the short: "Jiminy, thinks Johnny, if only I could get a ride in one of those." Honorable mention: "Johnny feels dark hands pressing him onward. The voices in his head start to get meaner."
- Fave riff from the movie: "And be sure you have your tickets ready. They're really strict about that." Honorable mention: "It's Officer Not Appearing In This Film!"

Short stuff:

1) I've exchanged emails with Charles Pachter, who at the age of 4 played little Johnny. He has only vague memories of the whole thing. He is now is a fairly prominent Toronto artist. Those were his real parents playing his parents, by the way.

Movie stuff:

1) Alright, let's settle this once and for all. Tom's right, he's not Merritt Stone. In fact, Merritt Stone is not IN this movie. He's Gene Roth. Merritt Stone played the spider-eaten dad at the very beginning

of "Earth Vs. The Spider," the clergyman in "Tormented," and the King Grady in "The Magic Sword."

Episode 420- THE HUMAN DUPLICATORS
First shown: 12/26/92

Movie: (1965) An alien takes over scientist's human duplicating machine, hoping to infiltrate the government. But a top agent is on the case.

Opening: The bots have suggestions for ways they could be improved.
Invention exchange: The Mads have the a case of the sillies, Joel demonstrates the beanie chopper, the Mads have invented the William Conrad fridge alert
Host segment 1: Joel has assigned the bots a craft project: to make spaceships made from household items
Host segment 2: Tom Servo duplicates himself–many times over!
Host segment 3: A grumpy Hugh Beaumont revisits on the Hexfield
End: Crow and Tom come out as robots, meanwhile, in Deep 13, William Conrad shows up
Stinger: Duplicates cracking up as they choke each other
- I said last episode that this was the beginning of a stretch of good to very good episodes. but I forgot about this speed bump on the road to those goodies. The movie is strange but dull and talky, and the riffing, while okay, isn't up to the level we've had in the last couple shows, and will have going forward. There's some pretty good host segments, though.
- This episode was included on Shout's MST3K: Volume XXXVII.
- I'm sure "the sillies" bit is an approximation of many moments on the set. I wonder how much of the laughter we see is genuine.
- In a "Simpsons" episode called "Grampa vs. Sexual Inadequacy," which came out two years after this episode, Homer says he ... "...

could have been the inventor of a hilarious refrigerator alarm." Can that be anything but a reference to this invention exchange?"

- Callbacks: "Calling Scott Tracy..." (one of the SuperMarionation movies they did at KTMA), "I'm a grimaldi warrior!" (VIKING WOMEN), o/` S-A-N-T-A...o/` (SANTA CLAUS CONQUERS THE MARTIANS"), "Knew your father, I did!" (MR. B NATURAL), "To think like the hu-man!" (ROBOT MONSTER), "And a good friend" (ROCKETSHIP XM).
- Firesign Theatre reference: "Everything You Know is Wrong!"
- The movie makes the same comment at the same time one of the riffers does, and Crow calls it "riffback." I'm sure that came from writing room experiences. It's one of those little things that helps the show feel improvised.
- Trace built that SOL model shown in segment one; it spent a lot of time sitting in a corner of the studio. To my knowledge he has not, as of this date, put lighter fluid on it and burned it in the driveway.
- I love segment 2. It may be one of my top ten segments. How did they control them all? However they did it, they really created a sense of each one moving independently.
- Then-current reference: Madonna's once-scandalous nudie book "Sex," now languishing in remainder bins everywhere.
- Hugh: "...resembling a human." Joel: "See David Geffen." Ouch!
- Segment 3 is Mike's second visit as Hugh; and of course that's Kevin as William Conrad.
- CreditsWatch: Host segments directed by Kevin.
- Fave riff: "The boys did what? They duplicated Lumpy?" Honorable mention: "Phil Harris and Bubbles Rothermere back there, for those of you playing along at home."

Movie stuff:

1) The woman playing the Gale seems to be channeling Adelaide from "Guys and Dolls," and it's very distracting. " I expect her to break into "Take Back Your Mink" any minute.

Episode 421- MONSTER A-GO-GO (with short: 'CIRCUS ON ICE')
First shown: 1/9/93

Short: (1954) A look at the 40th annual carnival of the Toronto Skating Club.

Movie: (1965) Authorities launch a search for an irradiated astronaut they believe has returned to Earth as a giant mutant.

Opening: The bots have opened a micro-cheesery.
Invention exchange: After making a wager on an action figure invention exchange, the Mads present Johnny Longtorso, and the bots present three non-violent action figures
Host segment 1: Gypsy "doesn't get" Crow (or is it Tom?)
Host segment 2: Joel and Servo play keep-away from Crow
Host segment 3: Examining "The Pina Colada Song"
End: Joel knights Happy King Servo and Sir Giggles von Laffsalot Crow
Stinger: Monster on the go-go

Comments:

- This is a deservedly infamous episode featuring a deservedly infamous short and movie. There's plenty for them to work with here and they knock it out of the park. The riffing is top-notch and the segments are all terrific. Just a really strong episode — if you can take the movie.
- This episode was included in Shout's "The Mystery Science Theater 3000 Collection, Vol. 8."
- The wonderful movie "Local Hero" is streaming. If you haven't seen it, do. One of the best movies ever.

- A hook falls off the peg board with a loud clang during the Mads' invention exchange. They keep going. And there's also a lovely crunch as Dr. F. steps toward the camera, right onto the blister packs on the floor.
- You can see Frank ALMOST crack up while singing the Johnny Longtorso theme song, as he actually does on the poopie reel.
- Frank does a nice little bit with the pitchpipe: he blows into several random pipes, making the whole thing pointless.
- Trace is hilarious as he introduces the movie, giving us Dr. F at perhaps his most maniacal. It's an all-time favorite Trace moment for me.
- Terrific riffing in the short, and Joel doesn't even try to keep them from getting too dark. The highlight is the great "pink girls" song.
- Segment 1 is rightly famous. If you wanted to introduce the personalities of all three robots to newbie, this would do it very well in just a few minutes.
- Joel opens a can of "pop" (or as normal people call it, soda) in the theater! What a rebel!
- The workings of Tom's hoverskirt are never explained in detail, but in segment two we see a new use demonstrated: sports!
- Then-topical riff: The now-forgotten Matthias Rust.
- J&tB do a little of the Richard Kiel voice they did a LOT in the last episode.
- Both a callback and a call-forward in closing segment: Joel crowns Tom a "happy king," recalling the MR. B. NATURAL short and Crow is holding the stick with the tiny Crow on it, which we will see again.
- Creditswatch: Host segments directed by Joel.
- Fave riff from the short: "Vomit sprays out in a beautiful Technicolor dream." Honorable mention: "Now a clown will deliver her eulogy."
- Fave riff from the movie: Narrator: "There is one terrifying word in the world of nuclear physics." Tom: "Oops." Honorable mention: "He made her bark!"

MSTIEPEDIA • 317

Movie stuff:

1) How could such a horrible movie have happened? "You know, four movies went into the making of this film," Joel says at one point. He's not far off. Bill Rebane made some of the movie, but ran out of money before it was completed. Meanwhile Herschell Gordon Lewis was looking for a co-feature for his recently completed movie "Moonshine Mountain," and he needed it quickly. So he bought Rebane's unfinished film, added some new scenes and hey-presto ... a movie with no continuity and no sense.
2) When the movie ends up in what looks very much like Chicago's Lower Wacker Drive, they begin to rattle off some great Chicago references, including McCormick Place and the Arie Crown Theater.

Episode 422- THE DAY THE EARTH FROZE (with short: 'HERE COMES THE CIRCUS')
First shown: 1/16/93

Short: (1946) We visit the circus, featuring legendary clown Emmett Kelly.

Movie: (1959) Nordic fantasy tale about a wicked witch's schemes to get, and later regain, a magic mill.

Opening: J&tB try to pose for a family photo
Invention exchange: J&tB have invented Snack-tion; The Mads show off their "unhappy meals"
Host segment 1: The bots have some ideas for clown acts but Joel is no help
Host segment 2: So, what's a sampo?
Host segment 3: Gypsy's presents her one-woman show: "Gypsy Rose...Me!"

End: The bots are imprisoned wind, Joel reads a letter, Frank is also wind and still mad
Stinger: "What's going to happen to us now?!"

- I just love this episode. Fun, goofy, watchable movie, great riffing, great host segments, one of this series' crowning achievements and the beginning of what became known as the "Russo-Finnish trilogy," a memorable trio of terrific episodes.
- This episode was included in Shout's "Mystery Science Theater 3000 Collection: The 25th Anniversary Edition" aka Vol. XXVIII."
- As you might have guessed, this episode had a big effect on me. For a long time it was my all-time favorite. Up until this point, on the Prodigy MST3K boards I had just been "Chris in Phila." The night this was shown (or maybe the next day, I forget), I officially announced that I was taking the handle Sampo, and I've had it ever since.
- The unhappy meals are truly an evil invention. I love Dr. F's Charles Nelson Reilly laugh as he describes them.
- The acrobat is said to be both Dag Hammarskjöld and Albert Speer. Both references are pretty out of the blue…
- Largely forgotten reference: "Hey, it's Skylab!"
- The "Scandinavian sketch" is obviously drawn from their personal experiences. What I find amusing is how much those Minnesota accents sound like the accents of folks in the Northeastern corner of Pennsylvania, where I now live. There's probably a linguistic explanation.
- Local riff: "Mini golf at Crosslake." It's still around.
- I was very amused by Servo's grumbling about "Half & Half." This sounds like a disgruntled husband speaking from a real-life experience.
- Another obscure reference: Crow's silly voiced: "I thought it was a costume ball!" is a reference to a movie called "Start the Revolution Without Me."

- In the '94 Turkey Day, in his introduction, Adam West mistakenly says that this is episode number 424.
- Callback: "I sing whenever I sing…" (Giant Gila Monster)
- Naughty riff: "HE's got delusions of grandeur."
- There are not one but two Ross Perot references in this episode. I guess it counts as "then-topical" but I would hope most people would remember who he was.
- Of course, one highlight is the classic "failure" song. Joel even gets up to dance!
- Jim gives a real tour de force in "Gypsy Rose ME!"
- Tom gently joshes Garrison Keillor's "Prairie Home Companion" during the long, tedious harp attack.
- Creditwatch: Host segments directed by Trace. "Gypsy Rose Me" was written and arranged by Mike, with lyrics by Mary Jo.
- Fave riff from the short: "You know, don't laugh, but, in a way, this is this town's Passion Play." Honorable mention: "A rogue elephant snaps its tether and kills a coolie."
- Fave riff from the movie: "Great wedding. You get half a buzz on and you're sent home with a torch." Honorable mention: "I'm relative humidity. It's not so much the heat as it is me."

Short stuff:

1) The announcer says "pamalino horses." The hell?
2) The circus in the short is never named, but it's the Clyde Beatty Circus.
3) In the short, during the part toward the end when the lady is dancing with the elephants, you can easily see that one of the elephants has rolled in some poop. Gross.

Movie stuff

1) This movie (originally titled "Sampo" but cheesily renamed to trick American audiences into think it was sci-fi) was based on the Kalevala, the national epic of Finland. (As an aside, J.R.R. Tolkien was heavily influenced by the Kalevala, and his "Silmarillion" was originally begun as an attempt to create a sort of British Kalevala.)
2) As I noted in 1993 when I introduced this episode on national TV during Turkey Day, the movie DOES explain what a sampo is. J&tB are just in mid-riff when the explanation comes.

Episode 423- BRIDE OF THE MONSTER (with short: 'HIRED!'– Part 1)
First shown: 1/23/93

Short: (1941) A Chevrolet sales manager wonders why his team is having trouble selling their product door-to-door.

Movie: (1956) A mad scientist's efforts to create a race of supermen attract the attention of a reporter and the police.

Opening: Joel gets to see what Crow is dreaming … and soon regrets it
Invention exchange: The tough love seat, microwave Faith Popcorn
Host segment 1: "Hired!" the musical
Host segment 2: Joel, Tom and Crow's discussion rambles from the lame octopus to food monsters
Host segment 3: Willy the Waffle returns to defend advertising
End: Cambot re-edits the ending of the movie, letter, the Mads are playing Bela and Tor
Stinger: Bela has looked better

Comments:

- I try not to overuse the already-overused word "classic" but this is one. It's got a wacky short, an Ed Wood movie (probably his most competent, which isn't saying much) and we've all seen all that backstory in the "Ed Wood" film. The host segments are good to fair, but they're certainly not awful, and the riffing is top-notch.
- This episode was included in Shout's "Mystery Science Theater 3000 Collection: Vol. XIX."
- This show first aired three days after the beginning of the Clinton administration. It was certainly made before then, but probably after Bubba's election, which allows Crow to talk about "The Bush Administration" in the past tense early in the short.
- Joel's horrified, slightly nauseated take to the camera at the end of the opening is great.
- Then-topical: Faith Popcorn (though she would probably disagree that she isn't still topical; she's still around).
- "Hired, the Musical" is a lot of fun. I especially like Joel's pained takes to the camera when Gypsy sings.
- Segment 2 is what the kids today call "random." I have a feeling it's a slightly stylized version of a actual conversation among the Brains.
- In this movie, Bela does his classic "sleep" bit, complete with the hand gesture. And yet the cast have been referencing it for at least two seasons. I wonder if they were they just making a reference to a movie they assumed we'd seen?
- Crow references two elements of the classic driver's ed Smith System: "Hands at 10 and 2" and "watch your space cushion." This is how I learned to drive too.
- Tom Servo does a lovely Flash Bazbo impression.
- The random segment 2 is followed by the complete non-sequitur of segment 3. What does advertising have to do with anything?

322 • MSTIEPEDIA

- As is often the case, you can often spot where BBI has made cuts for time: usually at the spots where the commercials have been inserted.
- Callbacks: Tom says: "Weird! That's what it is. Weird." (Ring of Terror); "Hi, Bavaro." (Crash of Moons); Willy says "Knew your father I did!" (Mr B Natural); I'm a Grimault warrior!" (Viking Women)
- It's pronounced REK-yah-veek! As in: "One day in Iceland can Reykjavik."
- I wonder how many other military bases were showing eps on their TV stations?
- CreditsWatch: Host segments directed by Kevin. Camera: John Finley. "Hired! Song" written and arranged by Mike and Kevin. "This episode dedicated to the spirit of William A. Murphy. Thanks, Dad."
- Fave line from short: "You've killed again, haven't you, son?" Honorable mention: "...And I don't have a car ... HEY!"
- Fave riff from feature: "Nobody's kissin' the bird today..." Honorable mention: "Tor go to DeVry."

Short stuff:

1) I wonder at what point were door-to-door car salesmen discontinued. I never knew they existed before this short.
2) If you look carefully you'll notice that one of the houses the salesman visits is the house where Gilbert the spring lover lived in "A Case of Spring Fever."

Movie stuff:

1) The scene where the captain goes to see the file lady has a continuity mistake. She has a pencil behind her ear when shot from behind, and doesn't have one when she's shot from the front. I

remember pointing it out to my daughter, who was about six at the time, and I remember she found it hilarious and asked me to rerun it over and over.

Episode 424- 'MANOS' THE HANDS OF FATE (with short: 'Hired!'–Part 2)
First shown: 1/30/93

Short: (1941) In the conclusion of a two-part short, our sales manager hero gets advice from his handkerchief-wearin' dad.

Movie: (1966) A hapless family, on a car trip in rural Texas, takes refuge at the home of a deadly cult.

Opening: Joel has programed the bots to agree with everything he says
Invention exchange: The Mads present the chocolate bunny guillotine; J&tB show off the cartuner
Host segment 1: J&tB's car trip sketch is ruined by Manos footage, Frank apologizes
Host segment 2: J&tB discuss the physical attributes that would make them a monster
Host segment 3: Joel dons a Manos cape, Dr. F. apologizes
End: The bots reenact the lady wrestling scene, Torgo's pizza arrives
Stinger: "Why don't you guys leave us alone?"

Comments:

- Whatever else they study, every Civil War buff has an opinion about Gettysburg. Whatever else they grow, every gardener has an opinion about tomatoes. No matter which team they root for, every baseball fan has an opinion about the Yankees. And no matter what other episodes they love, every MSTie has an opinion about "'Manos' The Hands of Fate." So much has been written about this awful, awful movie, and this justly famous episode, that it's hard to make a fresh observation, but here are a few thoughts.

- This episode was issued by Shout as a single, and also as part of the "Essentials" set.
- This is one of two or three episodes that I practically have memorized. I can pretty much do all the riffs right along with J&tB.
- Paul once noted that many MST3K movies are "made by oily guys who elect to direct the camera largely on themselves." He was talking about a different movie, but this movie is a perfect example.
- The opening bit is great, and I suspect every fan of Joel has felt a little like the programmed bots at one time or another. You see this butt? Kick this butt.
- There's a funny clank as chocolate bunny guillotine falls. I'm guessing it's the weight that held the blade up, falling to the floor somewhere off camera.
- The last issuance of The Cartuner isn't really that strange: It sounds pretty much like something Gary Larson would have actually done (if he wasn't afraid of getting sued by the Bil Keane empire).
- I had the opportunity, a few years ago, to exchange emails with Hal Warren's daughter, who told me that her brother wore the Master costume on several Halloweens and that the painting of the Master adorned a wall of her home for many years.
- Joel's looks of disgust and horror in segment two are great.
- As I was watching segment 3, my wife wandered through and said, "You should have worn THAT to the costume party at one of the conventions. I could have made that." I had to break it to her that about 20 guys were wearing versions of the Master cape.
- Joel mentions Mentos, commercials for which were being seen regularly on MST3K.
- Then topical: "The Tasters Choice saga." Remember when people cared about that nonsense? Also, I'm betting fewer and fewer people remember who Marilyn Quayle is.

- That's Mike, of course, in the first of several appearances as Torgo. Let me just get your complementary crazy bread…
- Creditswatch: Host segments directed by Joel. This was intern Curtis Anderson's last show.
- Callback: "Torgo, you're the laziest man on Mars." (SANTA CLAUS CONQUERS THE MARTIANS). "He tampered in God's domain" (BRIDE OF THE MONSTER).
- Fave riff from the short: "Gah! Flying elves are back!" Honorable mention: "Seein' as how we're salesmen and all."
- Fave riff from the movie: "And now the Manos Women's Guild will re-enact the Battle of Pearl Harbor." Honorable mention: "Yeah, here I go! Vroom!"

Short stuff:

1) If you look carefully you'll notice that one of the houses the salesman visits is the house where Gilbert the spring lover lived in "A Case of Spring Fever."

Movie stuff:

1) A sequel called "Manos Returns," featuring cast members from the original movie, was released in 2018.
2) Work to restore the movie and create a high-definition version was completed in 2012.
3) The RiffTrax crew used that restored print to bravely re-riff it for a live show and it was surprisingly good.
4) A fascinating article in Playboy investigated the bitter legal battle for the rights to the movie.
5) The movie was shot with a camera that could only shoot a small amount of film at a time, making long, continuous takes impossible. Hence the "dissolving to the same scene" Crow observes early on.

6) The long pointless driving scene was supposed to have credits supered on it, but Hal forgot.

And now begins the strange tale of a young woman we'll call Audrey.

Beginning in the spring of 1992, she began posting in the Usenet newsgroups, especially alt.tv.mst3k, which had the most traffic. Mostly, her posts were fan musings, at least to start. She posted schedules of when episodes were to air. She devised an FAQ. But over the weeks and months, her comments began to get, well, a bit pushy. As the holiday season approached she posted that she was planning to throw a holiday party, and said that BBI staffers were going to attend.

Nobody at BBI had agreed to anything of the sort.

Jim let the date of the party pass and, in the first week of '93, this message was posted:

To all our friends on Internet:
Recently there has appeared notice about a holiday party called "A Patrick Swayze X-Mas" posted by [Audrey]. We want you to know that we have not sanctioned this event in any way and that no one from the cast of Mystery Science Theater 3000 or the staff of Best Brains will be attending. We apologize to anyone who was planning to attend this event based on the belief that we would be in attendance.
You can be sure that we'd let you know through the Information Club of any live appearance or special events that Best Brains would be undertaking.
Jim Mallon Producer

The letter was actually posted by Julie Walker, from her Microsoft account. She stated that she was posting it for Jim.

[Audrey] responded that she was disappointed that BBI did not initiate a "dialog" with her, with the hope of negotiating an appearance by someone from the show. BBI responded with silence.

This sort of thing was rare, but it did happen.

CHAPTER 7

Episode 501- WARRIOR OF THE LOST WORLD
First shown: 7/24/93

Movie: (1983) A nameless hero and his talking motorcycle fight an evil dictator in a post-apocalyptic world.

Opening: Servo attempts a formal welcome but Crow rattles him
Invention exchange: The Mads demonstrate the Square Master, J&tB show Bittersweet Hearts
Host segment 1: Joel retrofits the bots to be slot cars, but Tom still needs some work
Host segment 2: J&tB put on a sketch: The warrior tries to get a driving permit
Host segment 3: J&tB discuss things you could do after the apocalypse
End: J&tB get a phone call from Megaweapon, Joel reads a letter, the Mads enjoy an active lifestyle
Stinger: The Paper Chase Guy checkin' out Persis

Comments:

- This episode has its moments, I'll give you that. The movie is all over the place, from the whiny, chipmunk-cheeked hero and his air-headed onboard computer, to the squeaky spiders, to guerrilla leader Jimmy Carter/Ronnie Cox, to hapless Persis Khambata, to perhaps Donald Pleasance's creepiest performance (and that's saying something), to the "Road Warrior" rejects, to the raw star power that IS Megaweapon. The riffing is solid for the most part, and the host segments are decent. It doesn't quite add up to a classic for me, but, yes, it has its moments.

- This episode is in included in Shout!Factory's "Mystery Science Theater 3000 Collection: Vol. XVI."
- The stretch between the end of season 4 and the beginning of season 5 was 168 days, the sixth-longest amount of time MSTies had to wait between episodes.
- That said, longtime fans will recall that, although this is episode 501, it is NOT the first episode shown in season 5. That honor went to episode 502- HERCULES, which aired a week before this one. Why? They've never said, I don't think, but my guess is that the Comedy Central suits decided the Hercules movie was a more marketable opener. In any case, as we've done in the past, we go by episode number.
- I wonder who Dickie Schnable is (and where he is).
- Joel's bittersweet hearts invention has since come true. You can now buy little chalky hearts that say all sorts of weird things. And I think that the odd, pointless little comments of the onboard computer were the inspiration for that sketch.
- Joel makes what I've always thought was an astute observation: that the afterlife would be a little like Ellis Island. I'd never thought about it like that…
- Callback: "Ator? Tong?" (CAVE DWELLERS) "Old Time bus driver Billy Slater…" (JUNIOR RODEO DAREDEVILS); Crow mentions "HANGAR 18" (wow, an oldie); "He hit Big Jake" (SIDE-HACKERS).
- I wonder how are they controlling the robots during the slot car host segment.
- Everyone loves that bit during the movie when Joel and Tom Servo get into a little dual-riff that is, I guess, a parody of a Robitussin commercial -- one I don't remember ever seeing. Maybe that's why I don't find it as hilarious as everybody else seemed to.
- It's nice to see Tom Servo forthrightly admit that they never bothered to write an ending to bit in segment 2. Having movie sign

330 • MSTiepedia

just kind of pop up is a little like when Monty Python "drops the cow."

- I believe this episode contains the very first reference to then-newly elected President Bill Clinton.
- Persis Khambatta's character gets called Natasha and Nastasia, depending on who is addressing, or referring to, her.
- Then-topical: The "woo-woo-woo" thing audiences of the Arsenio Hall Show did.
- Probably my (and many people's) favorite moment of the episode is toward the end when the camera does that long pan of all the revolutionaries celebrating and Tom Servo has a celebrity name for every single one. Amazing and hilarious.
- That's Mike, it hardly needs saying, providing the voice of Megaweapon. The rapport all the actors have with one another at this point in the show is really remarkable.
- CreditsWatch: The writers list is now: Trace Beaulieu, Paul Chaplin, Frank Conniff, Joel Hodgson, Bridget Jones, Kevin Murphy and Mary Jo. (Mike is still head writer). Contributing writers: Colleen Henjum and Jim. Host segments were directed by Trace. New credit: utility infielder, Patrick Brantseg (which I think means Patrick started actually getting paid for what he was already doing). Hair and make-up: Andrea J. DuCane (she will do it for all but five episodes this season). New interns: Stephanie Hynes, Peter Keffer, Michael J. Sheehan and E. Jane Shortt.
- Fave riff: "Heeeeyyyeee, it's the crazy Guggenheim museum!" Honorable mention: "They love it when he signals a left turn!"

Episode 502- HERCULES
First shown: 7/17/93

Movie: (1957) Hercules helps Jason, the true king, wrest the throne away from pretender Pelias and his son Iphitus, while wooing the lovely Iole.

Opening: J&tB "wing it" with the intro
Invention exchange: The Mads demonstrate the cellular desk, J&tB demonstrate Instant Karma
Host segment 1: Tom has updated the constellations for the '90s; Crow disapproves
Host segment 2: Crow and Tom want to know about Hamilton Joe Frank and Reynolds
Host segment 3: Crow valiantly performs a solo version if the 'Match Game'
End: The bots discuss Amazons, then some visit on the Hexfield; Frank is now at the desk
Stinger: "It's like something out of a bad dream!"

Comments:

- Pardon if it seems like I'm channeling Leonard Maltin, but I'd give this one two-and-a-half stars. The host segments are fair at best, and the movie is so cut up that it's almost impossible to follow. It has its moments, but the episode is a bit frustrating.
- This episode was included in Shout!Factory's "Mystery Science Theater 3000: Vol. XXXII."
- It's clear that the Brains chose to make most of their cuts at the commercial breaks, but the result is that half the time the characters are in the midst of one plot development before the commercial, and by the time we get back they're somewhere else entirely. Important plot information was apparently cut as well. Why does the floor make a sound when Jason crosses it? We're never told, but it seems an important point to everyone in the movie. How does Herc go from retrieving a discus to fighting a lion? No idea. How do Herc and his pals escape the Amazons? One minute they're being fed sleeping potions and watching dancers, after the commercial break they're back on the ship. You almost have to treat each of the eight movie segments separately. The riffing is good,

332 • MSTiepedia

and they have plenty of weird stuff to work with, but I'm afraid this episode is less than the sum of its parts.

- This was a widescreen movie, but in this print we see about half of the screen at any moment. It's not even pan-and-scan. It just sits in the same spot no matter what's happening on the screen.
- Callbacks: "Where is the sampo??!" (DAY THE EARTH FROZE) "Hey, it's Commando Cody!"
- As noted in the previous writeup, despite being episode 502, this was the first episode shown in season 5. In the previous writeup, I offered a guess as to why.
- During the invention exchange, the third "instant karma" bag leaks. They keep going.
- Many of the riffs in this episode were used in that MST3K program for Windows 3.1 somebody created. For those who weren't computing then, it put shadowrama at the bottom of your screen and played one of only about 15 quick sound bites every so often. It got very old very fast and, worse, it turned out to be a very invasive program that was hard to remove.
- The first host segment is clever but creating modern constellations that make about as much sense as the old ones do is really not an original idea. That said, they put a great spin on it.
- Arcane reference: something is said to resemble a Jim Dine sculpture.
- Tom Servo channels every naughty third-grader with: "Claude Balls, ladies and gentlemen..."
- Note the completely unremarked-upon box of Capt'n Ron cereal sitting on the desk in the second segment.
- If you're wondering, they were a trio, composed of Dan Hamilton, Joe Frank Carollo and Tommy Reynolds.
- The Match Game bit, while funny, is another one of those "huh?" sketches.
- One of the cleverest bits comes right at the end, as they sit through the closing credits and Tom explains what happened to the char-

acters after the story. Pretty funny stuff, but I wondered why they sat through the credits when large chunks of the film were edited. Maybe it was some contractual thing.

- Mary Jo makes her first physical appearance on the show, and Bridget makes her first appearance since season three, as the Minnesota amazons.
- Creditswatch: Host segments directed by Kevin. Hair and makeup by Clayton James (one of only two times this season).
- Fave riff: "Stay away from their powerful hind legs!" Honorable mention: "It's the Andrea Dworkin memorial cemetery!" "Do you have a reservation

for Hercules? It might be under Heracles…"

Episode 503- SWAMP DIAMONDS (with short: 'WHAT TO DO ON A DATE')
First shown: 7/31/93

Short: (1951) Young Nick hopes to ask schoolmate Kay for a date, but can't think of a venue.

Movie: (1956) Four women (including one undercover cop) break out of prison, with a plan to recover a cache of stolen diamonds.

Opening: Crow and Tom are obsessed with the 'Spock in love' episode of "Star Trek."
Invention exchange: The Mads present the U-view, J&tB demonstrate the Andrew Lloyd Webber grill
Host segment 1: Tom has decided that he wants to date Gypsy
Host segment 2: Tom calls Gypsy to ask for a date
Host segment 3: Tom and Gypsy go out on a date, briefly
End: Tom thought the date went well, Gypsy dumps him, Joel reads a letter that upsets Tom, Frank is still watching himself
Stinger: "Sssssssshut up!"

334 • MSTIEPEDIA

Comments:

- This is one of those episodes where the short pretty much overwhelms the movie that follows it. The short is just so precious and silly, and the movie is so tense and gritty, the result is that, despite some very good riffing) the tail wags the dog.
- This episode appeared on Shout's "Mystery Science Theater 3000 Collection, Vol. 10.2.
- Callback: Shut up, Iris! (THE BEATNIKS); "To be like the Cor-Man…" (ROBOT MONSTER)
- Watch carefully during the "U-View" bit: Both Frank and Dr. F reach about six feet to take things from each other. A great blink-and-you-missed-it, unremarked-upon sight gag.
- We spend that entire invention exchange looking at the back of an old-style CRT TV, dating the whole sketch.
- The ST:TOS episode Joel calls "the Elias Sandoval episode" (aka the "Spock in Love" episode) was in fact called "This Side of Paradise." I'm not going back, Jim!
- Mike "Touch" Connors was born Kreker Ohanian. So "Touch" doesn't sound so bad after all.
- Naughty riff: "Beverly can handle a Johnson, can't she?"
- The "Baywatch" bit during the "U-View" invention exchange is kind of an expansion of a throw-away gag Tom Servo did in the previous episode: "Don't get drunk and swim under the dock." Doodly-doo-dly-doodly… "I'm drunk and swimming under the dock!"
- The guitar Joel is playing in segment 1 is a copy of a Stratocaster, probably a Yamaha, I've been told. The song he was singing was Neil Young's "Old Man."
- Gypsy seems a little grumpy in this one. She's usually more easy-going.
- Then-current reference: "The Gun in Betty Lou's Handbag" (1992).
- When BBI cleared out of the studio after the show was cancelled, they held an auction designed, mostly, to sell off office furniture

and the like. But Barb says there was a bit of confusion that day, and among the things offered for bid were boxes of unlabled video tapes, most of which had unedited rough footage of host segments (sometimes three or four or five takes of the same segment; you can see them trying different line readings) and a few aborted theater sequences where they got started and then stopped for some reason. One of the tapes included some stuff from this episode. BBI was a little embarrassed that these tapes made it into circulation. A lot of it was recovered, but some stuff has been copied and shared a bit.

- CreditsWatch: Host segments directed by Joel. And he's not in the credits, but that's Mike doing the "Baywatch" voices, of course.
- Fave riff from the short: "Kay has worked on the kill floor. She knows where to deliver the blow." Honorable mention: "The sensuous pagan ritual begins."
- Fave riff from the movie: "Let's just stand here and jut some more." Honorable mention: "As we left the clam flowage that day..."

Movie stuff:

1) I was bothered, the first time I saw the "cutting off the legs of the pants" scene. I thought: "They're in a mosquito/tick-infested swamp and they want to expose MORE skin?? Are they crazy??" Then I saw them in shorts and I forgot about all that...
2) Let's keep in mind: a snake was shot and killed – on camera – in the making of this movie.

Episode 504- SECRET AGENT SUPER DRAGON
First shown: 8/7/93

Movie: (1966) A report of drugged chewing gum in Michigan sends a suave super agent to Amsterdam to investigate a sinister crime organization.

Opening: Crow and Tom build a robot, who soon becomes annoying

Invention exchange: Frank demonstrates virtual comedy until Dr. F. programs in a few hecklers, J&tB demonstrate micro-golf

Host segment 1: Joel, Crow and Tom are a jazz trio playing the "Secret Agent Super Dragon" theme

Host segment 2: J&tB read through Crow's latest screenplay: "The Spy Who Hugged Me"

Host segment 3: J&tB discuss spy movie post-kill puns

End: Dr. F.'s holds a super-villain conference call

Stinger: Jumping the Super Dragon, with xylophone accompaniment

Comments:

- I don't watch this one often, but when I do, it always surprises me all over again. It's really a solid episode. The host segments are clever and the riffing is very good. My biggest gripe is the awful awful condition of the print.
- This episode is on Rhino's "Mystery Science Theater 3000, Vol. 12."
- Minsky the robot is an actual vintage toy, and that is what it really says. But Minsky wasn't the name of the toy. The Brains named it that, in homage to artificial intelligence genius Marvin Minsky.
- Tom invokes "WKRP in Cincinnati" with the mention of "Chychy Rodragweez."
- Callbacks: "I killed that fat barkeep." (The Beatniks). "Any talent to declare?" (Warrior of the Lost World). A mention of Ward E (Stranded in Space), "...but there was no monster" (Monster A-Go-Go).
- Joel wears his glasses in segment 2, which tells me he's actually reading his lines off that script.
- Then current: "Herb from Burger King." Also: "I ate the last Frusen Gladje."

MSTiepedia • 337

- Naughty riff: "We'll be covering you from behind." Crow: "You've been in prison too long."
- Frank is great in the ending segment, humming: " ...I sing whenever I sing..." and doing the exact minimum required to assist Dr. F. "Eagerly."
- Creditswatch: Host segments directed by Trace. Clayton James does hair and makeup for the last time in season 5.
- Fave riff: "Emo, avec lute." Honorable mention: "Remind your engineers to use coasters on me."

Movie stuff:

1) Why did the bad guys choose a college town in Michigan to test their drug, when it's fairly clear all their operations are in Europe? I don't think the movie ever says, though that explanation might have been cut.

Episode 505- MAGIC VOYAGE OF SINBAD
First shown: 8/14/93

Movie: (1952) A sea-going adventurer sets sail to find the bluebird of happiness, which he believes will help his down-on-its-luck hometown.

Opening: J&tB are presenters and nominees at the SOL-tie awards
Invention exchange: The Mads present chin-derwear, while J&tB show off the rat pack chess set
Host segment 1: J&tB have a meeting of the Junior Jester Club
Host segment 2: J&tB are the bearded town council debating the Sinbad problem
Host segment 3: Crow's lifelong quest thingy goes awry
End: The bots are amazed by Joel's channel cat puppet, letter, Frank meets Mr. Fistie

338 • MSTIEPEDIA

Stinger: Laughing horse

- Oh my, oh my, oh my, what a wonderful episode. An all-time fave. Everything works, everything clicks. Great invention exchanges, great host segments, great riffing and a well-shot, expensive – albeit weird – movie. Despite my personal attachment to "The Day the Earth Froze," I have to say this is the best of the Russo-Finnish movie episodes.
- This episode was included in Shout! Factory's "Mystery Science Theater 3000 Collection: Vol XX."
- You gotta assume the opening is perhaps a reflection on their "always a nominee, never a winner" TV award history.
- Both inventions, chin-derwear and the Rat Pack chess set, are not just clever, they are downright witty.
- That's Mike, of course, attempting Frank Sinatra. He doesn't sound much like ol' Blue Eyes, but he has the intonation down pretty good. In any case, it's interesting to note, as we approach the switch in hosts, that Mike is seen and heard more and more.
- Comedy Central used this episode for a contest: viewers were asked to write in and guess what the riff would be after Morgana (or whatever her name was) said "You seem troubled." The correct answer was: "Have some Prozac." The winner was a very nice lady who lived in New Jersey named Susan Schneider, who was a semi-regular on, I forget, either the Prodigy or AOL. computer services. The prize was one of those god-awful giant-screen rear-projection TVs that were unaccountably popular at the time, along with five grand in cash, which was pretty sweet, even if the ridiculous TV took up half her rec room). To celebrate her win, she threw a party and invited some of the folks she knew on line for the weekend – a decision she came to regret, but that's a story for another day. I'm sure that behemoth she won is moldering in a landfill somewhere.
- Crow the jester is carrying the little mini Crow that was last seen in the possession of Sir Giggles Von Laughs-a-lot.

MSTIEPEDIA • 339

- Again, the writing in the Junior Jester Club sketch is off-handedly brilliant.
- J&tB are still wearing jester hats when they enter the theater after the first segment. Also, Crow has no net for a lot of the riffing.
- Arty reference: "I can't tell if that's a Magritte or a hole in the wall." Did Magritte do many giant frescos?
- Odd riff: "...and a tetherball." What's that about?
- As if the segments up to this point haven't been great, the second sketch is a riot, maybe one of their best. It even has an ending. I, too, wanna be Labor MP from Brixton.
- Callback: "Tom Stewart killed me!" (Tormented), "Please give my best wishes to everybody!" (Minsky the robot in the previous episode) "A sampo?" (Day the Earth Froze), "Hikeeba!" (Women of the Prehistoric Planet).
- There is some theater business in this one: First Joel and Crow drift off under the spell of the magic bird, then off goes Crow on his lifelong quest thingy. I love how Crow flies in from above upon his return. I guess Jef Maynard or somebody was up on a ladder next to the riffing chairs.
- Obscure reference: the infant of Prague.
- Gypsy seems a little hungry in the final segment.
- Firesign Theatre reference: "Those eyes! Weird!"
- There are not one but two uses of Mary Jo's "wha happa?" in this episode.
- And just to finish things off, an instant classic: Mr. Fistie.
- CreditsWatch: Andrea J. DuCane is back for a 14-episode run doing hair and makeup. Host segments directed by Kevin.
- Fave riff: "And stock up on socks! You know, you're never gonna have this chance again!" Honorable mention: "Is this really the best away team he could have chosen?"

Movie stuff:

1) He's not Sinbad, and director Aleksandr Ptushko never intended him to be. But when this Soviet-financed film was released to American audiences, the lead character was given the name "Sinbad" in hopes of fooling American moms and dads, who, the American importers knew, would never allow their kids to see a movie made by commies.
2) I noticed a similarity between the creepy laughing horse in this movie and the creepy laughing reindeer in "Santa Claus."
3) The movie was already really strange, but in the last 15 minutes it really gets goofy.

Episode 506- EEGAH
First shown: 8/28/93

Movie: (1962) A teen girl, her weird-faced boyfriend and her scientist dad discover a cave man living in the desert.

Opening: Crow has been frozen to nearly absolute zero
Invention exchange: Rebuilt Crow is just like new; J&tB presents the Pork-orina, while the Dr. F replaces Frank's blood with antifreeze
Host segment 1: J&tB consider subtle forms of hell
Host segment 2: The bots alter Joel's face to look like Arch Hall Jr.
Host segment 3: J&tB discuss why '60s sitcoms are run by single dads
End: Washing the movie off the bots, Joel reads a letter, Frank gets a fluid change
Stinger: "Fake it." "That's what I've BEEN doing. Now I'm getting sick!"

MSTiepedia • 341

Comments:

- We're in a very good stretch of episodes here. This is another winner, following close on the heels of the previous one. Great host segments, great inventions, great riffing. Shtemlo!
- This was one of the first episodes released on DVD by Rhino, in April of '00.
- If you're wondering what the "porkorina" instrument really is, it is a bass harmonica, aka a bass harp.
- Then-current reference: While doing his Cryptkeeper impression, Crow mentions the now-forgotten cable series "Dream On."
- Callbacks: "Glen was 50 feet tall!" (WAR OF THE COLOSSAL BEAST), "The Torgo school of fondling," "To live like the hu-man" (ROBOT MONSTER) "Durn smoochers!" (ATTACK OF THE THE EYE CREATURES) "He tampered in God's domain" (BRIDE OF THE MONSTER), "GIANT GILA MONSTER."
- Segment one, is another pithy, brilliant sketch, one that assumes a certain level of sophistication on the part of its viewers. It's classic MST3K.
- I hate to tell Joel, but maybe the reason he didn't see anything in the papers about Charley Weaver dying is that Charley's real name was Cliff Arquette.
- After having referenced "Last of the Mohicans" with the classic "Stay alive! Whatever may occur! I will find you!" line in the previous episode, they go ahead and do it again ... and then they do it again!
- The second segment, while not as witty, is a great example of the sort of Looney Tunes silliness they often did well.
- Crow is once again netless following the second segment, as he was in the previous episode.
- This is an episode that launched so many catchphrases, from "Stop saying 'whee!' Nobody says 'whee!'" to "My tires are filled with water!" to "Watch out for snakes!" to "Shtemlo!"

342 • MSTIEPEDIA

- Joel again invokes Gregg Toland, the cinematographer for "Citizen Kane," because a shot shows a ceiling.
- Arty reference: Keith Haring.
- CreditsWatch: Contributing writer Colleen Henjum becomes Colleen Henjum-Williams. Host segments directed by Joel.
- Fave riff: "Sit down, pie face, it's a long list." Honorable mention: "That little satchel will be the death of him." "Poor shovel. Didn't ask to be in this movie."

Movie stuff:

1) There is very little that needs to be said about this travesty of a movie, since it's been thoroughly examined many times, but it's worth saying again, as so many have before, that the scenes in the cave, with Roxy's dad cheerfully suggesting she give in to Eegah's romantic advances – particularly the horrifying shaving scene – are the very dictionary definition of the term "icky."

507- I ACCUSE MY PARENTS (with short: 'THE TRUCK FARMER')
First shown: 9/4/93

Short: (1954) A look at the then-new techniques that enabled farmers to rush fresh produce to market.

Movie: (1944) Ruined by – but in astonishing denial about – his boozy, carousing parents, a neglected essay-contest-winning young man gets involved with gangsters.

Opening: Tom Servo is naked!
Invention exchange: The Mads present cake 'n' shake, and Frank bakes the exotic dancer right into the recipe; J&tB demonstrate the junk drawer organizer
Host segment 1: Joel analyzes the bots' art therapy projects

Host segment 2: J&tB reenact the night club scene from the movie
Host segment 3: J&tB analyze troubled Jimmy from the movie
End: The bots try to reenact the cafe scene from movie to scam a hamburger, Joel reads a letter, the Mads are digging out Rodney
Stinger: "What? What's so funny?"

Comments:

- Another in a string of wonderful episodes. The movie is a little bland, but the riffing is great.
- I begin to suspect that, for any given episode, you can tell whether the movie held the riffers' interest and sparked a lot of discussions and ideas or whether their minds were wandering, based on how much the host segments have to do with the movie. You can tell they were really following the movie this time. Just about all the segments are related to the movie.
- Personal golden memory: I watched this on a big screen (with Joel sitting next to me) and the audience was simply roaring with laughter all the way through.
- Early versions of the Rhino packaging of this episode had a small goof. It lists the episode number as 424. It got fixed in later printings.
- Great line: "How many times have you gone rootin' through your junk drawer muttering to yourself 'Where'd I put that gun?'" Toward the end of the movie, our hero roots through a drawer of a table of his parents' house, looking for a gun. The riffers noticed.
- Now, duck news! Here's Hugh McQuacken! They do the "quacking" gag five times, and it gets funnier each time. For those who didn't get it (and I remember that every time this show aired, a number of people would post questions online asking, "Why were they quacking?"), look at the wall of the hallway outside the heroine's apartment door.
- The short would be incredibly depressing if not for the riffing. As it is, it's still a LITTLE depressing.

Movie stuff:

1) Sam Newfield did NOT direct the movie in episode 203- JUNGLE GODDESS, as Joel says when his credit appears. But Crow has every reason to express dismay nonetheless. Because he DID direct the movies in episodes 103- THE MAD MONSTER, 208- LOST CONTINENT and 520- RADAR SECRET SERVICE. He also directed the infamous "Terror of the Tiny Town," the all-little-people Western. Again, this was the era when you couldn't just look stuff up online, though a rough early version to the fledgling, Usenet-based IMDB existed.

2) What could have led them to have made that mistake? I'll bet it has something to do with the phrase "hamburger sammich with French-fried potatoes," which is used in this movie AND in "Jungle Goddess."

- In the previous episode, Crow was shattered. This week Tom gets painted. They really started doing stuff to the bots in this period.
- Then somewhat current reference: Joe Bolster, a standup comedian who worked in the same era as the BBI writers.
- Host segment 1 is, um, quirky, and only vaguely movie-related. Peggy Cass is an odd element.
- Segment 2 is a riot, especially Joel's takes to the camera. I think it works so well because it comes IMMEDIATELY after the actual movie sequence. Nice to see Gypsy was willing to go along. Also, listen for another "wha happa!"
- I love the PA announcements J&tB do during the second song. Cheese fries are up!
- Another VERY movie-focused sketch in segment 3, and very funny.
- Obscure reference: the religious TV show "Insight." I remember watching that a little. It used to run on Sunday mornings, but to me they always felt like defanged "Twilight Zone" episodes.

- Some people wondered why Anne Blythe's name is written on the tank. I suspect they're just trying for World War II authenticity.
- I remember that somebody in the AOL MSTie forum – or it might have been on RATMM – had an idea for a MSTie cookbook. My submission was a hamburger sammich with French-fried potato garnish, complete with handgun on the side and a required trip to church every Sunday.
- That's Brad Keeley as Rodney in his first on-camera role.
- CreditsWatch: Host segments directed by Trace.
- Fave riff from the short: "Texans!" Honorable mention: "A pre-teen is put to work; her beauty will soon fade."
- Fave riff: "How do ya like my swingin' church, son?" Honorable mention: o/` I knew I'd go from rags to riches... o/`

Episode 508- OPERATION DOUBLE 007
First shown: 9/11/93

Movie: (1967) A famed plastic surgeon/hypnotist/championship archer, whose brother is a "top agent," is recruited to stop a villain and his scheme involving radioactive rugs.

Opening: Tom is enjoying Joel's home movies; Crow is scared
Invention exchange: The Mads show off Frank's Lederhosen-hosen, Crow has invented Sara, the bobbin' buzzard
Host segment 1: Joel's is an evil supervillian! "I know."
Host segment 2: J&tB parallel the lives of Sean and Neil
Host segment 3: While Joel tries to hypnotize Tom, Torgo returns in Deep 13
End: Dr. F. uses his magnetizer, much to J&tB's dismay
Stinger: Mr. "Thunderball" pushes the button

346 • MSTiepedia

Comments:

- This is episode is fun, and funny, but I don't love it quite as much as the previous couple of shows. The host segments are hit and miss, for one thing. But an even bigger problem for me is that I never understood the bad guy's plan. Or is it plans?
- This episode appears in "Mystery Science Theater 3000 Collection: Vol XXV" as "Operation Kid Brother." They had to use the alternate title to get the rights.
- Frank really commits to the lederhosen bit. You have to wonder how they felt doing some of those bits, without any audience to tell them if it was hilarious or dreadful. In the absence of feedback, they just committed.
- The Bobbin' Buzzard is a lovely prop. Kudos to Jef Maynard or whoever was responsible.
- This movie may very well have the greatest theme song of any MSTed movie.
- Callbacks: "Hooray for Santy Claus!" (SANTA CLAUS CONQUERS THE MARTIANS). Tom does the "That must be one of those [fill in noun here]s I've heard them talk...about...so... much...lately..." bit twice (GAMERA). "There WAS no Yashuko." (MONSTER-A-GO-GO). "To see your land!" (MAGIC VOYAGE OF SINBAD).
- Obscure reference: "Michael, I want all the episodes of 'Captain Nice' burned."
- If you think this was Neil's one and only film role, you're mistaken. He was also in "The Body Stealers" in the 1970s, then he "retired" for a while, but ten years later he returned to movies and worked intermittently until his passing in 2021.
- Literary riff: "She thinks she's in Dresden during the war."
- The Rodney King incident is still on the writers' minds.
- Joel makes a rare entrance through the "G" door in the first segment. This segment is a good example of what I call an "aren't they

adorable" sketch. What I mean by that is: The sketch only works because, at this point, all Joel has to do is look at the camera and arch an eyebrow and we laugh. If you showed this sketch to somebody with no knowledge of the show or its performers, they'd be probably be baffled as to what's funny about it. But fans who know and love the characters get it. I think it's hilarious.

- Kevin really tapped into his Catholic upbringing during the nun scene.
- Crow does his Phyllis Diller impression twice, using the same line: "I'm looking for Fang!" (Fang was an invention of Diller's from her standup days: a boorish husband she could mock.) The reason he does it is because the lady's wacky hat looks like something Diller might have worn when performing.
- Segment two reminds me of one of those long, over-written, complicated sketches from season two. But you can sense Mike's influence: it makes reference to a cheese factory.
- Mike returns, eight episodes later, as Torgo. With the lag time these episodes had, I'm guessing the Brains had only recently picked up on the rave reviews from fans about "Manos."
- Yet another "wha-happa?" "Wha happa" is to season 5 what "I thought you were Dale" was to season 8.
- Dr. F. is nice and evil in the closing segment. Oh, and nice job of building the magnetizer, which looks a LOT like the one in the movie. This was one of those prop-heavy episodes Jef Maynard talked about in the documentary about the show.
- CreditsWatch: Host segments directed by Kevin. Manager of Business Affairs Heide A. LeClerc becomes Heide A. LeClerc-Becker. Alpine horn provided by: Josef Diethelm. (Diethelm was the front man for a Twin Cities-based polka band.)
- Fave riff: "Do I have enough time to beat up the band?" Honorable mention: "Oh, who's the sign for?"

348 • MSTiepedia

Movie stuff

1) During the weird hijacking scene, Tom notes that the melody in the score sounds very similar to the classic kids' hymn "Jesus Loves Me." But what's interesting (to me, anyway) is that this mockery displeases Joel, who makes him stop singing it.

Episode 509- THE GIRL IN LOVERS LANE
First shown: 9/18/93

Movie: (1960) A whiny runaway is befriended by a world-weary drifter, but the duo's arrival in a small town spells trouble for a local waitress.

Opening: Tom and Crow are retrofitting themselves with bellybuttons; Joel approves
Invention exchange: The Mads present evil baseball promotions, Joel presents "Don Martins"
Host segment 1: J&tB sing "What a Pleasant Journey"
Host segment 2: The bots want to reenact the pool hall scene
Host segment 3: Crow is Crow Elam
End: Furious about the ending of the movie, the bots devise new endings, Joel reads letters, Frank devises endings too
Stinger: "Are you waiting for a bus?"

Comments:

• This is what I used to call a "little" episode. The movie has a very narrow scope. The host segments are fun but nothing spectacular. The riffing is decent but workmanlike. It's good, not great. But, like practically every episode, it has its moments.
• This episode is included on Shout's Mystery Science Theater 3000 Collection: Vol. XV.

- Once again they're doing stuff to the bots in the opening segment. This time it's belly buttons. I do love the way Joel thinks it over and decides to go for it.
- Something I never noticed before: In the opener, when they turn on the electric drill, the lights dim a little for a second. A great subtle little touch.
- The baseball promotion invention exchange is as dark as Frank predicts it will be, at least for any baseball fan. (I'm old enough to remember when my dad took me and my two brothers to "bat day" at Connie Mack Stadium in Philadelphia: every kid got an actual regulation wooden bat, and yet we behaved. I suspect there'd be mayhem in the stands if they did that today.
- Note that Joel's jumpsuit comes equipped with ONE kneepad.
- One of the best things about this episode is the songs. The song Tom makes up to go with the movie's theme during the credit sequence is just marvelous. Joel and Crow add a line or two, but of course it's dominated by Tom.
- This episode also features the "Camera three get off the tracks!! Arrgghhh!" sequence, which was later used in a promo for the show.
- The other great song: "What a pleasant journey." What can you say? One of the funniest songs of the series. The impression they're doing, by the way is sort of Woody Guthrie.
- The Mary Jo influence: Mentions of Appleton and Circle Pines.
- Callbacks: o/` "Leather coat..." o/` (THE BEATNIKS) "To live like the E-lam..." (ROBOT MONSTER) "You're stuck here!" (FUGITIVE ALIEN)
- Elam does look a little like Garrison Keillor, which they point out at least twice.
- There are several references to the "This Side of Paradise" Star Trek episode again.
- Crow notes that Jack Elam was a fine character actor, "and for all I know he still is." He was indeed still alive when this episode first aired ... not so much now, sadly. He passed in 2003.

350 • MSTIEPEDIA

- I lost count of the "Carrie, you're so very..." riffs, which did NOT get funnier with each iteration.
- Yes, the truck driver does look a little like Gene Kelly, if you squint. I counted SIX riffs in which they point that out.
- The bots are upset about the ending of the movie in the final sketch, and there is also some outrage expressed in the ACEG, but J&tB don't seem that upset in the theater when Carrie's brutal and completely undeserved murder actually occurs.
- CreditsWatch: Host segments directed by Joel. The music for "The Train Song" a.k.a. "What a Pleasant Journey" was by Mike; the lyrics are by Frank.
- Fave riff: "I always wanted to be nuzzled by a hobo." Honorable mention: "Did his head just turn into a big sucker?"

Episode 510- THE PAINTED HILLS (with short: 'BODY CARE & GROOMING')
First shown: 9/26/93

Short: (1947) College students are reminded that they need to bathe and wear clean clothes if they hope to get some.

Movie: (1951) In 1870s California, a loyal collie witnesses the murder of a gold prospector.

Opening: The bots are putting on their own version of "The Tonight Show" (circa 1993)
Invention exchange: Dr. F presents the cholester-do all, J&tB demonstrate back-talk
Host segment 1: Crow and Tom debate the messy woman in the short
Host segment 2: Reports on bearded guys include Crow's paper on Rutherford B. Hayes
Host segment 3: Crow is crushed into an ingot

End: J&tB discuss is Lassie is guilty of murder, Dr. F. tries to revive Frank

Stinger: Naughty girl goes into the shower

Comments:

- It was certainly a bold move, picking this movie, and westerns are always fun to riff, even westerns like this one, that do it doggy style. But I have to put this in the "good not great" category, something like the previous episode. The movie's just a little too good (I actually got caught up in the story), while the riffing and segments are hit and miss.
- This episode was included in Shout's Mystery Science Theater 3000: The Turkey Day Collection (aka Vol. XXXI).
- In the opening bit, I know Joel is just setting up Crow's last punchline, but you can't get sued for making fun of Congress. Kinda ruined the joke for me.
- A YouTube clip of the opening bit was often linked to as a way to disparage Leno during the great Leno/Coco wars. Leno hasn't changed much.
- The actual prop Frank is wearing around his neck during the invention exchange is kinda cool. "Eee-kay-gee, does it work great!"
- Then-current reference: short-lived TV show "Delta."
- The short seems to be aimed at college students. Did they really show this sort of thing in COLLEGE? Did college kids in the 1950s really need to be told to shower occasionally?
- That moment in the short where the movie moves backwards and Tom does the backward talking: seems like that's what sparked the "Back Talk" invention?
- Segment 1 is MST3K at its best, witty, wise and fun. Love the reference to "Scoop Jackson Democrats and Jacob Javitz Republicans." Those are pretty much gone.

- "Pile-On Pete" was an instant sensation in the message boards following this episode. As was the line "Snausages!"

Movie stuff:

1) This movie was a Lassie rarity. In most Lassie movies, Lassie is a female character that was generally played by male dogs. But in this case, the character of Shep, a female, is actually played by a female dog. It's a little like a canine version of "Victor/Victoria."
- Segment 2 goes on a little long, but there's some good stuff there. I like how you can hear Tom say "Rutherford B. Hays!" as Cambot is halfway down through the movie sign door.
- Callback: "Smoochers on mah property!" (EYE CREATURES) "Sampo!" (DAY THE EARTH FROZE).
- Segment 3: well, they're doin' stuff to the bots again. Funny puppet, though.
- As they enter the theater, Crow says "Thank you for extruding me" like a little kid thanking his grandma for an itchy sweater he'll never wear.
- The ending bit in Deep 13 is great: I love the food popping out of Frank's mouth as Dr. F gives him CPR.
- A rarity: the stinger is from the short, rather than the movie.
- CreditsWatch: Host segments directed by Trace.
- Fave riff from short: "And look at that sidewalk!" Honorable mention: "Those ... nose!"
- Fave riff from the movie: "First thing I'm gonna do is buy me a montage!" Honorable mention: "Oh for the want of a Frisbee!"

Episode 511- GUNSLINGER
First shown: 10/9/93

Movie: The widow of a murdered sheriff attempts to clean up the crime in her small town with help from the man whose been hired to kill her.

Opening: Tom goes "Ka-Boom!"
Invention exchange: The Mads show off the scanner planner, J&tB demonstrate new whiffle items
Host segment 1: J&tB imagine their funerals
Host segment 2: The Gypsy Express
Host segment 3: Tom demonstrates quantum linear super-positioning
End: The '70s: A pretty foul decade, Joel reads a deep-fried letter, Dr. F. scans Frank!
Stinger: "What about our clothes?"

Comments:

- Well, here we go, the penultimate Joel episode in the legacy era, the last before big changes occur. I generally like this one. Corman always brings out the best in them, and while it isn't a slam dunk, it's pretty consistently entertaining. Good not great.
- This episode was released by Shout as a single.
- Did Gypsy mean to throw the dice onto the floor behind the desk? They keep going.
- Jim blows a line in the opening bit. They keep going.
- The opening bit is downright hilarious, a brilliant melding of attitude and great prop building.
- I love how Frank does the classic Harpo Marx "gookie" when being "scanned."
- Dr. F. says this is their first western. Doesn't "The Painted Hills" count?
- Callback: "I'm a Grimault warrior!" (Viking Women)
- Segment 1 is great. It's kind of a funeral for the Joel years (at least it feels that way to me) and it's got great writing. However, is it my imagination or is everybody a little short with each other in this sketch? I may be imagining things.

354 • MSTiepedia

- Segment two: meh. It goes on a little too long. Oh and: peanut butter and Dijonnaise?? Ew!
- This one has one of the season's funniest running gags: the riffs about the doors that open the wrong way. They just get funnier.
- Joel seems to lose patience with the movie about two thirds the way through. "Man, this movie is just sitting on my head and crushing it."
- I forgot this episode has a "I thought you were Dale"!
- Segment 3 is one of the best of season 5, witty and intelligent, but not too talky.
- We are entering the "Honey" period of this show – the epoch when everyone was calling each other "honey" constantly. There are at least four instances in this ep.
- I imagine they had a ton of letters to Joel laying around that they wouldn't be able to use any more. Deep frying them seems like a nice bit of closure.
- CreditsWatch: Host segments directed by Joel, his last one. Additional writer: Timothy Scott.
- Fave riff: "Oh, rut like crazed weasel. You?" Honorable mentions: "Most people are morally ambiguous, which explains our random dyin' patterns" and "Come out!"

Movie stuff:

1) Crow wasn't far off when he said Corman did "Swamp Diamonds" on Tuesday and this on Friday. The movie actually had a seven-day shooting schedule. Among the problems on the set: John Ireland and Beverly Garland were attacked by red ants during their romantic tree-sitting scene, Beverly twisted her ankle and it became so swollen that her boot had to be cut off. Allison Hayes broke her arm falling off a horse.

MSTIEPEDIA • 355

Episode 512- MITCHELL
First shown: 10/23/93

Movie: (1975) A slovenly cop is determined to bring a drug kingpin to justice.

Opening: Joel's unveils his toothpicky creation; the bots know what they have to do
Invention exchange: The Mads are being audited, so they've hired a temp by the name of Mike; J&tB present the Daktari stool
Host segment 1: Gypsy overhears the Mads plotting and thinks they're talking about Joel
Host segment 2: A worried Gypsy tries to think of a way to get Joel off the SOL; Crow and Tom are no help
Host segment 3: Mike learns of a hidden escape pod, and gives Gypsy control
End: Joel is ejected into the escape pod, leaving behind a plaque and a final word; Dr. F. is furious…until Mike presents his time card
Stinger: "Your lying through your teeth!" "Buzz off!" "No, you buzz off!" "I SAID BUZZ OFF, KID!"

Comments:

- It all starts so normally. Just another episode, right? Wrong. This is, of course, the most famous of the show's "transition" episodes, and I've seen it perhaps a dozen times now. What sticks out is how well the whole thing falls together. There's a lot going on here, but it's all accomplished in about 15 minutes. Tight scripting, tight performances, tight editing, it's a marvel of precision. It's sentimental, but it doesn't get mawkish. And it's very funny all the way through.
- This episode was put out as a single-disk release on November of 2001.

- You want a metaphor? How about Joel building an extremely fragile creation, certain in the knowledge that it will be destroyed? Now, that's a metaphor.
- Mike makes his first appearance as, well, Mike. Wow is he young.
- Recently I saw a movie starring a young Tab Hunter, and I'd never noticed before how much a young Mike and young Tab vaguely resemble each other. Maybe it's the square heads.
- The Daktari stool sat in the hallway of BBI for years. It was still there when I visited the set in 1999.
- Segment 1 features a parody of the scene in "2001: A Space Odyssey" in which computer Hal reads the lips of the astronauts. Interesting (to me anyway) that, "2001" is again parodied in another transition episode at the end of season seven.
- Segment 1 takes us as close to Dr. F and Frank as most of us will ever get. I remember some fans of Trace rather enjoyed it.
- Jim does a great job in segment 2. "Breathe through your nose"
- I love the moment when Mitchell says: "Shh.." and Joel finishes his line with: '...ugar?"
- Not mentioned in the references list is the "OPE" thing Gypsy is muttering. It's a reference to the movie "Dr. Strangelove."
- Then current reference: the forgotten movie "Cop and a Half."
- Hamdingers suddenly took over the MSTie consciousness after this episode, but it was funny how Gypsy and Mike (and, by extension, BBI) seemed very clear on what Hamdingers were … but nobody else seemed to be. It was hard to nail down just what they were, and descriptions seemed contradictory. Some said the Swift-Premium folks made them (I believe Kevin invoked Swift Premium during an online chat). Not true. Hamdingers were a short-lived meat product produced by the Patrick Cudahy Co. out of Cudahy, Wisconsin, in the mid '70s … The product was sliced ham patties, about the size of a hamburger patty, and it came in a round can. It was like Spam, but it came pre-sliced.

- I love that DOS command Mike has to type in to the "techtronic panel" (apparently this was the one and only time that the control panel in Deep 13 was called this).
- Callbacks: Several references to "Eegah"; reference to rock climbing.
- Toward the end of the movie, we get Joel's last bit of fatherly control during the bit where Tom and Crow get a bit dark and suggest Mitchell should turn the gun on himself.
- Naughty riff: "I'm huge."
- I love the classic, low-tech use of confetti to simulate static in the Hexfield. Very Joel.
- When fans on the internet weren't obsessing about Hamdingers, they were arguing about the correct pronunciation of "Lao" as in "Dr. Lao."
- Tom and Crow fall apart (literally!) during their PANIC, but I think this may be one time it was on purpose.
- I love Mike's expression as Dr. F and Frank laugh about his fate.
- CreditsWatch: Host segments directed by Kevin. Jim is listed as a contributing writer for every episode in season 5 except this one, where he is listed as an "additional writer."
- Fave riff: "We're going to control the ghetto, you and I, young man." Honorable mention: "BABY OIL??? NOOOO!!!!"

Movie stuff:

1) Want a connection from this movie to the Robert Blake murder case? Sure, we all do! Gary McLarty and Ronald (Duffy) Hambleton, both of whom testified against Blake when he was accused of killing his wife, had small roles in this movie. McLarty played one of Mistretta's henchmen and Hambleton played mob boss Edmondo Bocca, who gets dropped by Mitchell just short of the green. Both testified that Blake told them of his plans to kill his wife. But, unfortunately for the prosecution, both of these guys

had somewhat checkered pasts. Blake's defense team successfully undermined the credibility of both witnesses, introducing evidence of mental illness, drug addiction, etc. In the end, their testimony may have actually helped Blake get off.

2) The presence of that Christmas tree in John Saxon's house – and pretty much no other references to it being Christmas time – is one of the many odd things about this movie.

3) Joel seems to lose it during the "Adam Rich" scene. Actually, the kid is played by a Todd Bass, in his second and last role in show business. By the way, the kid is supposed to be the son of Linda Evans' character, but the portion of the movie that establishes that was cut.

4) Toward the end of the movie, Mitchell inserts a portion of his handkerchief (there's a lesson, kids!: always remember to carry a handkerchief; you never know when you might want to blow up a drug dealer's car), then screws the gas cap back on over it, so that the rest of the handkerchief is hanging down. He then drives to the meeting place and when the deal goes south he, all in a split second, whips out a lighter, lunges forward and holds the lighter to the handkerchief, which INSTANTANEOUSLY lights up and blows up the car almost at once.

Now maybe, just maybe, the tank was very, very full and the handkerchief got nice and soaked with gasoline on the ride over. But the tank might also have been mostly empty, meaning the handkerchief could have been bone dry. That seems far more likely, doesn't it? Which would mean it would have taken maybe ten seconds for Mitchell to light it, plenty of time to stop Mitchell. What I'm saying is that it seems unlikely that the handkerchief would immediately burst into flames in a fraction of a second like it does here. The whole thing is about as implausible as a sultry callgirl falling in love with Mitchell.

- It was in this period, (late winter '92 to spring '03) with MST3K-focused communities established and growing, that fans began to feel that they should have a say in the way their favorite "cowtown puppet show" was being treated by the suits at CC. For example, Penn Jillette's growling voice-overs were heard constantly on the channel and they began to be a target for online gripes. The largest number complaints tended to happen when the voiceovers were heard during the show's closing credits. But the majority of fans seemed to grudgingly understand that these voiceovers were part of the TV business.

- But the chorus grew louder as the year went along, following several incidents where Penn voice-overs were played despite the fact that more than just the closing theme was playing.

  In one case, it was at the end of a rerun of episode 311- IT CONQUERED THE WORLD where Peter Graves' dry pronouncements about mankind were drowned out by Penn's comments. Even worse was when a Penn voice-over was played, in its entirety, during the closing of episode 307- DADDY-O -- which is actually an extended host segment.

- Fans were stunned that CC would be paying so little attention to the show that a voice-over would be run during an actual comedy bit, and the network was flooded with angry calls, letters and emails--and the network was excoriated in cyberspace. In July, mentioning a heartfelt letter written by long-time fan Jonathan "El Mystico" Whitney, Jillette made an on-air apology and voice-over announcements during the closing theme ceased. Online MSTies rejoiced, declaring victory. But the battles with CC were not over.

Acknowledgments

My heartfelt thanks go out…:

To my loving wife and daughter, who took my obsession in stride for decades.

To my understanding family and in-laws.

To my mother, (RIP) who sat with me and watched every single episode, in order, and laughed.

To anyone who worked or interned at Best Brains.

To anyone who spent time on the Prodigy MST3K message boards.

To anyone who spent time on the Usenet MST3K message boards.

To anyone who spent time on the Compuserve MST3K message boards.

To anyone who spent time on the AOL MST3K message boards and chat rooms.

To Brian, who has great skills and gives great advice.

To all the members of my riffing group, for whom I never had to explain a joke.

To anyone who created and maintained a MST3K-themed web site.

To anyone who ever owned an MST3K Info Club membership card.

To staffers at KTMA, Comedy Channel, Comedy Central, Sci-Fi (aka Syfy) Channel and Netflix, who championed the show even when it was not cool to do so, and everyone who donated to the Kickstarter campaign.

To the patient and long-suffering folks at Bear Manor.

and to all the right people, who got it.

Made in the USA
Middletown, DE
30 September 2023

39266206R00205